T0314054

Equality and the City

THE CITY IN THE TWENTY-FIRST CENTURY

Eugenie L. Birch and Susan M. Wachter, Series Editors

A complete list of books in the series is available from
the publisher.

EQUALITY AND THE CITY

Urban Innovations for All Citizens

Enrique Peñalosa Londoño

PENN

UNIVERSITY OF PENNSYLVANIA PRESS

PHILADELPHIA

Published by
University of Pennsylvania Press
Philadelphia, Pennsylvania 19104-4112
www.upenn.edu/pennpress

Printed in the United States of America on acid-free paper

10   9   8   7   6   5   4   3   2   1

Hardcover ISBN: 978-1-5128-2570-1
eBook ISBN: 978-1-5128-2571-8

A catalogue record for this book is available from the
Library of Congress

To Renata and Martín

To all the members of my mayoral teams who worked with passion
and generosity to make a more egalitarian and happier city.
My special gratitude to Andrés Camargo, a brave and honest man.

CONTENTS

Introduction

Almost a year had passed since the Covid-19 pandemic had forced lockdowns and other restrictions when Rosa asked an unusual favor of my friend Edgardo, a prestigious lawyer. Rosa worked as a maid in his home. To reduce the risk of contagion on public transport, Edgardo had been hiring a car to pick up Rosa at her home in Soacha, a municipality adjacent to Bogotá, and take her back in the afternoon. On this morning Edgardo was rather surprised when she said, "Mister Edgardo, I am very thankful to you for hiring a car for me, but I want to ask you the favor of letting me come by TransMilenio. By car it takes me more than two hours to get here, and it would take me less than an hour if I came in a TransMilenio bus."

TransMilenio, the bus-based transit system (BRT) we had created during my first mayoral term, had already been in operation for twenty years, but upper-income citizens, and particularly those older than forty, still assumed that travel by car was superior in every respect to public transport. It wasn't. TransMilenio not only made it possible for people to find jobs in places far from their homes but also achieved the amazing feat of making public transport faster than car travel.

In this way TransMilenio had also constructed equality—something our society needed even more than good transport. And not just any equality but a visible equality: to see expensive cars idling in traffic while buses pass swiftly alongside them amounts to democracy at work. Although BRTs improve mobility for public transport users and private cars as well, their image is that they take road space from private cars and give it to public transport. So they implement tangibly the democratic principle of giving priority to the common good over private interest—in this case, giving priority to public transport over private transport. Moreover, since cars are an unsurpassed status symbol in developing societies, TransMilenio's impact on the symbolism and idea of equality construction was even greater.

Like TransMilenio, many innovations that can help us make better cities demand equality struggles: in other words, they require that politicians take on the challenge of implementing equality. Throughout this book I will return to the importance of cities for our quality of life and economic competitiveness from the perspective of the equality challenge. I propose that a good city constructs and promotes equality and that urban policies can be evaluated in terms of how much they contribute to that objective.

Private property of land around growing cities enriches a few landowners and is an obstacle for cities to grow in the right places and with enough quality public spaces. This impediment will occur unless governments have the capacity to define private land uses and tax any gain derived from land speculation, which in developing cities is rarely the case. In a good city, people of all income levels meet as equals in public transport or public spaces.

Quality public pedestrian space is crucial for equality. Moreover, it is during leisure time that inequality is most keenly felt. Since low-income citizens can't do much in their leisure time beyond enjoying public pedestrian space, it is crucial for equity that it be high quality. In any developing country where more than half of households do not own a car and most of those who walk are lower-income citizens, making safe and accessible sidewalks constructs equality, particularly if illegal or legal parking bays are eliminated to do it. Physically protected bikeways are a symbol that a citizen on an old bicycle is as important as one in a new luxury car.

Classism is often disguised as environmentalism, such as when the construction of a sports field is blocked to "protect trees," when in fact its opponents are simply trying to impede low-income people from coming to play in their neighborhoods. Or when a mountain path along a city is opposed to "protect the trees," when in reality the aim is to block low-income citizens' access to the mountain through paths in high-income neighborhoods. Nothing is said, of course, by the same ones who sabotage the sports field or the mountain path when thousands of trees are felled to widen a motor-vehicle road.

In unequal developing societies, high-income people will go to any lengths to keep lower-income people from coming to their neighborhoods, the most extreme case being the construction of gated communities. If cities reflect the democratic principle that states public good prevails over private interest, urban golf courses should become parks and no waterfront should be private and exclusive.

In this book I will refer to such issues and many more to illustrate a perspective that can be helpful in making cities more propitious to equality and happiness. I'll draw on firsthand experiences in cities around the world that I have visited as a lecturer or consultant and, of course, on my experiences as the mayor of Bogotá between 1998 and 2000 and 2016 and 2019.

A Young Colombian with a Dream of Equality

When I was about ten, the older boys at school used to shout insults, or even have at me with their fists, because my father was the first director and the public face of a national agrarian land reform institute.[1] Part of his job was to expropriate[2] large tracts of idle land from absentee landlords and redistribute them to subsistence farmers. Like all upper-middle-class children in developing world cities, I attended a private school, and at my school in particular there was much discontent because many of my classmates' families owned large country estates—just the sort that my father's institute was expropriating. My father became the most visible enemy of the power elites of 1960s Colombia, which was still a largely rural country. More modern activities, such as industry or banking, were in their infancy, and wealth and political power still mostly stemmed from land ownership.

Thus, from a very early age, I was more or less bullied into thinking about the merits of agrarian land reform and, more broadly, about inequality. I learned that important changes meet great resistance and that some fights, such as those for equality, are worthwhile, regardless of costs or defeats. My concerns, almost obsessions, focused on how Colombia could overcome poverty and achieve equality.

In Colombia any lunch or dinner party can easily turn into a dance. With very few exceptions, and I'm one of them, Colombians are amazingly good dancers. I remember the first dance I was invited to when I was thirteen. I was dancing with a girl and started to talk to her about socialism. That, as well as the fact that I had two left feet, made her quickly excuse herself.

In the 1960s I had concluded, like many others, that communism was the best course to achieve economic development and equality. With communism all enterprises would be publicly owned and all workers would be public employees. Salaries would be kept low so that consumption would be minimal. Saving and investment would therefore increase and produce high rates of economic growth. Of course, I believed that communism would also solve inequality.

The Soviet Union had been crucial in the alliance to defeat Hitler. And in the postwar decades, well into the 1960s, communist countries appeared to be recovering at the same pace as capitalist ones. In 1970, when I was fifteen, my father went to work at the Interamerican Development Bank in Washington, DC, and my family moved there. In 1973 I entered Duke University on a soccer scholarship. I wouldn't have been admitted based on my high school grades. There, as a long-haired idealist, I majored in economics and history. I wanted to learn at Duke how to run a socialist economy efficiently in order to apply those lessons to Colombia.

My socialist ideal slowly crumbled at Duke. My professors helped me understand that socialism, my panacea, created such massive inefficiency that high investment rates bore little fruit in terms of economic growth. It didn't produce equality either, because its bureaucrats enjoyed all sorts of privileges that constituted their own form of inequality.

In the 1970s it became increasingly clear that communist countries were lagging behind capitalist ones, as illustrated by the comparison of East Germany to West Germany. Reluctantly I came to accept that private ownership and the market were the best ways to manage most of society's resources in order to achieve high economic growth. Unfortunately, that entailed an indefinite persistence of inequality, which was still unacceptable to me.

Then, suddenly, I discovered the city. While I was at university, my father was appointed secretary general of the United Nations Habitat I Conference, held in Vancouver in 1976. A whole new world opened up to me as a result of my father's experience there. At the time, Latin American cities' population was growing at an astonishing rate—Bogotá at 4.3 percent a year, which meant that it doubled in seventeen years. My father often sent me documents and occasionally even let me draft his speeches. I was fascinated to discover the importance of cities in the creation of equality and the possibilities of making them different and better.

Gradually, I became more interested in cities than in socialism. I believed economic development would arrive in Colombia anyway, sooner or later: it might take fifty years, more or less, but it would come. However, if cities were not designed well, the damage would be irreparable. For example, if ten hectares (about twenty-five acres) could be set aside for a park, then millions of people would enjoy it for hundreds of years. But if those ten hectares were covered with buildings, it would be almost impossible to demolish them to make a park there later.

The cities I had in mind were Colombian—Bogotá in particular. I was born in Washington, DC, and had lived in the United States for the last three years of high school and my four years at university. Although I enjoyed my experience enormously, I never considered spending my life there.[3] At the time, I was not interested in what had to be done to be elected to public office in Colombia, but deep down I had a feeling that I would want to run for office. And the fact I was born in the United States and had that nationality could be an electoral disadvantage. During a trip to Colombia halfway through my studies at Duke, I went with my father to see the American ambassador and told him I wanted to surrender my nationality. He was astounded. "Just look out of that window, take a look at that queue two blocks long of people waiting to get a visa! They would give an arm and a leg to have what you want to give up. Why don't you go home, think a bit, and if you want to, come back in a few days' time." So I went home, I thought about it, and a week later returned to the embassy and formally renounced my US nationality.

After graduation I didn't want to embark on a professional career. I wanted to travel around the world for a while. For many summer holidays as a student, I had worked on construction sites, and after graduation I had to do so again: I asked a great professor of mine to add his recommendation to my folder that the university provided to potential employees, and he wrote a positive one but commented that my ideology was rather far to the left. It would have been a good recommendation if I had wanted to apply to a graduate program—perhaps he thought that's what I was doing—but it didn't appeal to the recruitment officers of various companies that interviewed me.[4]

With the savings from ten months of construction work, I set out with a friend, intending to follow the Silk Road from Turkey to Iran and Afghanistan and through to China. The first stop was London, where we had our initial taste of the wonders of the great cities of Europe, and when we arrived in Paris, I was dazzled—ecstatic about the city's beauty. I simply *had* to live there for a while! And so I did and never reached Afghanistan. In Paris I enrolled in graduate studies, which took me more than two years to complete. Four nights a week I worked as a doorman and receptionist at the hotel Céramic on Avenue de Wagram. I always wanted to be as independent as possible and to ask my father for as little help as I could. I lived an austere student life, for a while sharing a room so small that when the two narrow cots were unfolded, there was no room to walk around them. There was no shower, just a little basin, and the toilet was in the corridor, shared with another fifteen similar rooms. The other residents on that floor were natives of Guadeloupe and Martinique, huddled four to a room. Those were days when I window-shopped the pastries in the bakery downstairs and my mouth watered, but my budget rarely allowed me to buy one as they cost five francs. At that time, before salmon farming had been invented, *charcuteries* would display huge smoked salmons, which I perceived as the last word in luxury. Of course I could never actually try one. I was able to sit in a café a couple of times a month, not for lunch but to savor a cup of coffee, and I had to be careful about money even when I did that.

It was only many years later, however, that I realized I had been poor in Paris because while I was living there, I missed nothing. I had Paris! It was totally different from the beautiful but antiseptic Duke University campus, from the Washington suburb where I had lived while in high school, or from the Bogotá of my childhood, which lacked so much. Paris was a fresh delight every day. It generated happiness and equality: I shared the sidewalks, public transport, and parks with people from all walks of life, as well as the beauty of the architecture, the river, the museums, and free cultural activities. I experienced what I had intuitively believed since I'd become disillusioned with socialism: the city could be more effective than communism in building equality and more powerful than economic development in building happiness.

Happiness and Equality

Happiness is difficult to define and impossible to measure, yet it is the only thing that truly matters. In recent decades a whole new science of happiness or "subjective well-being" has developed that is too extensive to summarize here, but as I understand it, it finds that happiness is closely related to the realization of human potential. An obstacle to achieving happiness, I would add, is feeling inferior or excluded. What I focus on in this book is the inequality that causes unhappiness and the ways to resolve it.

Capitalism might seem to defy equality because it, by definition, produces and relies on inequality. Some enterprises succeed, others fail; some people earn more, others less. Yet the nations of the world adopted private ownership and the market economy not because it would be good for the rich but because it is what best serves all citizens, even the poorest ones. With a market economy regulated and moderated through redistributive interventions by the state, more and better goods and services are produced, and society prospers. There is less poverty and more opportunity. In other words, private ownership and the market economy were adopted because they satisfy that essential democratic principle of the prevalence of public good.

However, there is nothing sacred about private ownership. It's merely a means of managing society's resources. It was adopted because the majorities were convinced that it produced desirable results and then constitutions and laws were drawn to protect it. Congress could do away with private property in a few weeks. Its existence depends on the state's protection of it and therefore on majority support.

A consensus about the advantages of the market economy does not mean we must abandon the objective of equality. The Gini index, which economists use to measure a society's income inequality, is now commonly discussed even in mainstream political debates. In fact, it is not possible to interrupt the social advance toward equality.

Politicians and others worry about the concentration of income in the developing world and even in advanced countries, but it is obvious that Marx's prediction that the proletariat or the salaried class would have progressively lower incomes has not come to pass; indeed, many people earn very high salaries. Marx's complementary prediction, that just a few capitalists would monopolize almost all capital and income, has not come to pass either—although the enormous enrichment of a few is indeed one of the problems of our time.

Societies should find ways to move toward greater income equality, such as instituting more progressive taxing (while taking care, of course, and particularly in developing countries, not to discourage private investment). However, what I want to emphasize is that regardless of (desirable) reductions in income inequality, it's impossible to have income equality in a market economy.

Although it does not receive much attention from economists, I believe that if income inequality is important, so too is inequality of consumption. A business magnate may earn several billion dollars a year, but he will certainly spend less than 1 percent of that for his personal consumption, usually much less than that. The great entrepreneurs don't want to consume all they earn, nor *could* they. If we were to measure consumption distribution, we would find much less inequality than exists in income distribution. For practical purposes, businesspeople are administrators of society's resources, similar to governments, though certainly with greater autonomy. And I do not refer here to philanthropic uses of their wealth. Their for-profit investments advance society's productivity and wealth. Inequality of income is not irrelevant, but it can be viewed in a different light, if a businessperson who earns a billion dollars annually only spends 0,1% of it and reinvests 99,9%. More so, if she or he goes to the neighborhood café, walks in the neighborhood's sidewalks, jogs in the park, rides a bicycle and uses public transport.

Max Weber wrote that the essence of capitalism is the Protestant ethic because it promotes austerity and saving. In the post–World War II United States, the great entrepreneurs often had simple lifestyles, and the children of high-income earners would spend their free time working in hamburger joints or ice cream parlors. To be sure, there are still immensely rich people such as Bill Gates and Warren Buffett whose way of life does not differ much from that of others, and they even give up much of their time and fortunes to altruistic causes. But there are growing numbers of people who revel in conspicuous consumption and extravagant lifestyles. That weakens the legitimacy of capitalism and the market economy. A few years ago Bogotá residents told a funny story. A thief robs someone on the street and runs away, and everyone on the street first shouts, "Catch him! Catch him!" But if the police somehow manage to catch the thief, the crowd will start to chant, "Let him go, let the poor fellow go." Bogotá citizens found this amusing, or ironic, because similar scenes took place in real life. The man on the street imagined that the thief was possibly stealing because he was poor and needy, and the state, because of great inequalities, corruption, or other reasons, had no moral authority or legitimacy to punish the criminal.

"Legitimacy" is a peculiar concept. It is not contingent on income per capita, child mortality or literacy rates, or any other development indicator. Instead, it's a subjective perception about society's ethics or fairness. It has to do with equality and the state's commitment to build it. It relates to the perception of integrity and shared principles, which the individual has in relation to those who wield political or economic power. Where there is legitimacy, individuals feel they are members of a community of equals. Where there is legitimacy, individuals play by the rules, report those who break them, and even demand punishment for them; individuals don't evade taxes or litter the street, and they walk their dog with a plastic bag in hand. Individuals join civic initiatives and government plans. Legitimacy is the mortar that binds the edifice of organized society.

Visible inequality and exclusion such as that caused by conspicuous and extravagant consumption—mansions reminiscent of the palaces of the nobility that sparked the French Revolution, enormous fuel-guzzling yachts, private beaches and exclusive clubs—gnaw at legitimacy. The state loses its moral authority. When there is no legitimacy, citizens evade the rules and populist leaders prosper. If they get power, they not only harm the market economy but also democracy.

The funds a wealthy person owns, contrary to what he may suppose, are not entirely for his free and unrestricted use. They are better conceptualized as society's resources, which he manages by virtue of the market economy that has been democratically adopted. If a wealthy person manages substantial resources of society, even if he is not the government, he has responsibilities to society. Those in government administer society's resources because they have been elected. In parallel, billionaires administer society's resources because of their talent to profit from the opportunities society provided them or because they received an inheritance. They cannot use their money in a way that the system's legitimacy is undermined.

Legitimacy requires that individuals feel equality is a fundamental objective of their society and that public good truly prevails over private interest. Anything that constructs equality strengthens legitimacy.

For example, in Sweden, there is not as much rejection of the market economy as elsewhere because Swedes believe that their state controls abuse and prioritizes the construction of equality. Nor is there as much resentment of billionaires because they know that they didn't become rich through government favoritism, as sometimes happens in the developing world. They recognize that their creativity enriches society and generates jobs. Furthermore, their consumption is not conspicuous. The very wealthy live like everyone else: Swedes meet them on the street or on a bicycle, in a café or a supermarket.

If we were to expropriate the richest one hundred citizens of a country, income distribution and the Gini coefficient would automatically improve, but no one's life would improve. We wouldn't see more employment, higher salaries, or less poverty. Indeed, socially, there would be no benefits of any kind. On the contrary, since businesses are managed less efficiently by government than by private owners, progress would be slowed.

The concern for inequality and the concentration of income has recently acquired renewed importance. Numerous books on the subject have been published, the most renowned of which is probably Thomas Piketty's *Capital in the Twenty-First Century*. At the same time the world has witnessed a number of antiestablishment political expressions that depart from the traditional poor-versus-rich discourse of the left. Donald Trump's emergence, for example, expressed a rejection by many Americans of the traditional establishment but was not an antirich crusade. The same antiestablishment attitude holds for Britons who voted for Britain's exit from the European Union. For decades Chile enjoyed the highest growth rates in Latin America and achieved the best social indicators and the least unequal income distribution of the region. Nevertheless, widespread discontent, protests, and a plebiscite led to a Constitutional Assembly to reform the Constitution.

My impression of these three events is that what bothered citizens more than the existence of megabillionaires or the concentration of income and lack of desired social services was the feeling of being excluded and belittled by the establishment. This feeling was not only caused by extravagant and conspicuous consumption but also by less exotic and more commonplace forms of exclusion—for example, from clubs, schools, universities, vacation sites—and insufficient occasions for citizens of different incomes to meet as equals.

In this book I propose that beyond income equality, there are other powerful forms of equality, many of which a good city can construct.

The Equality That the City Constructs

If equality of income is elusive under capitalism, what kind of equality can we look forward to? The forms of equality I have in mind can be achieved even with capitalism. What is fascinating—and the assertion at the heart of this book—is that a city can bring about some of them. Cities can foster at least two kinds of equality: quality-of-life equality and what I call democratic equality. And they can foster an environment in which nobody feels inferior or excluded.

"Quality-of-life" equality encompasses obvious things, such as good prenatal and early-infancy care and access to good schools, but it also means a city where everyone can access green spaces and sports grounds without owning a country house or being a member of a club, or take music or painting lessons and go to cultural events regardless of income.

"Democratic equality" is derived from a fundamental principle of constitutions: all citizens are equal before the law. When this holds true, public good prevails over private interest. This standard is explicit in some countries' constitutions, including Colombia's, and is implicit in all of them. This principle means that a bus with two hundred passengers has a right to two hundred times more road space than a car with one passenger; a golf course in the middle of a city where there are no public parks nearby should become a public park; waterfronts, particularly in urban and suburban areas, should not be private or exclusive. Democratic equality not only makes it possible but imperative that private properties should be expropriated[5] when required to build a road, a park, a school, or a cultural center.

In a good city, individuals at all income levels meet as equals. Of course, high-income citizens always come into contact with low-income citizens but generally in a hierarchical and unequal relationship. One citizen owns the apartment in a building, and the other one is the doorman; one is the company's chief executive, and the other cleans the office toilet. In a good city, all meet as equals on the sidewalk, in the park, on the bus, and at cultural and sports events. That is not as simple as it sounds. Upper-income citizens will do almost anything to keep lower-income ones from going to or passing through their neighborhoods. Many urban battles have to do with this issue, even if disguised with costumes, such as environmental struggles. I venture that the wealthy would more readily pay higher taxes than tolerate a project that might bring lower-income citizens close to their neighborhoods. I will present several examples of that in this book. The good city constructs equality across income levels and between those who have different physical abilities or ages.

The ideal city advances equality, but what should that "ideal" look like? Ever since the publication of Rachel Carson's *Silent Spring* in 1962, the world has become much more aware of our natural environment. Today, any child who grew up with Animal Planet, Nat Geo, Discovery, and school courses on the natural world could tell us about the ideal environment for a whale or gorilla. We are much less clear about the ideal environment to foster a happy child than a happy whale.[6] Ants know how to make the ideal anthill, but humans are still unclear about how to make an ideal habitat for ourselves. Ask anyone on the street to describe their ideal home, and they will certainly do it in detail. They'll tell us how high the ceilings would be, the color of the walls, the number of rooms, and whether the floors would be wood, tiled, or carpeted. But if instead we ask the same person to describe their ideal city or neighborhood, they will be less precise. How many parks would there be, and what would they look like? How wide would the roads and sidewalks be? How high would the buildings rise, and how would residents get around? Would the city have a mix of commercial and residential buildings? It's interesting that the possibility of a full and happy life probably depends more on our city than our home since we generally spend more waking time outside the house than in it. This is ever more the case as households and homes become progressively smaller. Yet we are much less clear about how our ideal city would be designed than about our ideal house.

Even those who make decisions about urban development might not have clarity about their ideal city, and as a society we have no shared vision of that city either. For example, consider the place of the car in our cities. One day I was watching a documentary on cranes in the Pantanal region of Brazil. It showed that when young cranes are learning to fly, they frequently fall from tree branches into the water, where they are devoured by hungry alligators. With a father's solidarity, I was anguished to watch parent cranes tense with fear for their offspring. Then I realized that the predicament of children in our cities is similar to that of the fledgling cranes. As soon as they step out of the house, they face the risk of being killed by a car. When we tell a three-year-old child who is just learning to talk, "Watch out, a car," she jumps away with fright. And rightly so, because thousands of children all over the world are run over every year. It is shocking that we have become so accustomed to having our children grow up under the threat of death. Is it not possible that after eight thousand years of urban life we can achieve a better solution?

Without realizing it, we began to design cities more for cars than people. The twentieth century will be remembered for the astonishing inventions that so quickly transformed the way we live: cars, planes, phones, and then "smartphones," televisions, movies, sound equipment, computers, the internet, and so many others. But in the history of the human habitat, I think that the twentieth century will be remembered as the one in which we took a wrong turn. For eight thousand years all roads and other urban public spaces were designed for people, but the more cities adapted themselves to the car from the 1920s onward—a mere second in terms of millennia—the less pleasant they became to humans. We have customized cities more for cars' mobility than for human happiness.

Happily, in the second half of the twentieth century, the damage was so apparent that we started to make adjustments. Urbanist Jane Jacobs and the citizens of Manhattan succeeded in stopping the construction of highways that would have destroyed neighborhoods such as Greenwich Village. Copenhagen began to progressively remove cars from the town center in the 1970s, and hundreds of other cities—large and small, mainly in Europe—pedestrianized at least a few streets of their centers. By the end of the twentieth century and into the twenty-first, other countries began to imitate the bikeways in Holland and Denmark. In Bogotá, we built more than seven hundred kilometers of bikeways. Paris today is moving yet further with this transformation. The Chinese, whose galloping economic development initially led them to blindly imitate the United States and Japan, began to see bikeways not as a millstone of the past but as an asset for the future. Slowly, cities began to be conceived once again for people and not just for cars. But the damage has been done: it will take decades to remake our cities.

Because the United States was the most successful society of the twentieth century, it was also the one that most "automobilized" its urban structure. By the end of the century, most people lived in low-density suburbs. The number of people per hectare fell from 325 to 50.[7] Most people who lived in suburbs needed a car even to buy a loaf of bread. Children, the young, and the elderly who did not drive or did not have a car were almost prisoners, dependent on others for their mobility.

The developing world tends to have an inferiority complex and to judge what is "right" or "wrong" according to the model of more economically advanced countries. Effectively, we often find that these societies have already solved many of the problems we confront. But the advanced countries' model is not always either desirable or the one to follow in our cities. Would it be possible to design our city not around the needs of cars but rather around those of a five-year-old on a tricycle or an older person using a wheelchair? We would have very different cities if decisions were made with these citizens in mind rather than adults with cars.

If our contemporary city is not as good as it might be, then neither are our lives because they are conditioned by the city. We make our cities and then they make us.[8] The city reflects our values and behavior, and, at the same time, it creates and conditions them. Trout in a stream are a sign that the water is clean because those fish require clean, well-oxygenated water to survive. In the same way, it is an indication that we are in a good city when public spaces are teeming with children unaccompanied by adults. Children by themselves in public pedestrian spaces are a kind of an indicator species of good quality in an urban environment. Other vulnerable citizens in public spaces, such as the elderly or in some cases women, are an urban quality indicator as well. Jan Gehl writes that in a good city people like to go out for a walk, to see people, to meet neighbors, sit at a café or on a bench in the square.[9]

One loves a city, falls in love with her architecture, geography, squares, and people. We fall in love with the intense feeling of *existing* that she stirs in us. The city inspires us, recognizes us, and allows us to express ourselves.[10]

Creating Cities That Do Not Yet Exist

In the next decades and centuries, billions of people will live in cities that do not yet exist and have not yet been designed or built. Most of these cities will be located on land that is today rural. There is a unique opportunity to make them different and better. We could have cities in which all homes are no more than a ten-minute walk from a park, a shop, or public transport. So far, cities in the developing world have not been better than the ones that preceded them—or even as good.

Today it is accepted that we have a right to drinking water, education, and health services. In developing countries, we have progressively been able to provide our citizens with what could be described as survival essentials. When I was a child, much of Colombia did not have electricity, which was the case even in some Bogotá neighborhoods. About half of the children did not have access to education, and 70 percent of the population did not have access to decent health care. When I worked at the Bogotá Water Company in 1985, almost 30 percent of households still had no piped water, 40 percent had no sewerage, and half had no rainwater drains. In 1990, in the city's lower-income areas, long queues on the street, composed mainly of women, waited for hours each day with plastic jerry-cans to buy a low-octane petrol to use as cooking fuel. Stove explosions were common, causing terrible burns to children. Today, every household in Bogotá has piped water, sewerage, and natural gas; any child or youngster has access to public education, and 100 percent of the population has health insurance that guarantees them access to modern, professional, albeit imperfect, health care. We secured what was necessary to survive. Now, the challenge is to LIVE and to be happy in cities with beautiful infrastructure and opportunities for quality-of-life enjoyment—and equality. As populations decline and it becomes viable to work from anywhere, cities where life is enjoyable will be crucial in the competition for people who can choose where to live.

These better cities of the future are not the inevitable consequence of economic development. If there is no clear vision and a state that works to achieve it, then economic development may make cities worse. But the opposite does hold true: a better city brings economic development because it attracts and retains the qualified, creative, and productive people that generate it. Furthermore, it encourages citizens' constructive behavior. I believe in the market economy, but market forces alone will not produce good cities: the state must intervene with designs, regulations, and investments. Decisions about the location of parks, the height of buildings, the width of streets and sidewalks, and even the type of trees planted along an avenue cannot be left to private initiative.

The creation of a city is an ideological task and requires a vision, seen through the looking glass of preferences felt in the soul and heart. The creation of a city is a process closer to taste than reason and closer to art than science. It expresses how we want to live. The creation of a city is a collective venture. Unlike economic development that results from a myriad of autonomous decisions, we achieve our desired city only through a shared vision and actions and rules that can only be materialized by the social organization and political process we call government. The rules that emanate from that vision, then, are ultimately political decisions.

In contrast to the market economy and economic development, if everyone in cities pursued their own selfish interests, unregulated, urban quality of life would worsen in many ways—for example, with urban development without parks. In the case of cities, the principle that what is good for the bee is good for the hive is invalid. Rather, the opposite once again holds true: what is good for the hive is good for the bee. It may be rational for an individual to use a private car to go to the office. There may be some advantage in flexibility and speed by doing so. But if everyone does the same, then we end up with bottlenecks in which everyone wastes time. Similarly, from a purely selfish point of view, somebody may want to build a twenty-story building in a residential area where there are only three-story buildings. If they did so, they could enjoy a wonderful view, but they would ruin the character of that neighborhood. And if all neighbors did the same, of course, none of them would have the view. In a city it isn't possible to allow individuals to maximize their own benefits free of regulation because all too often this would negatively affect the common good.

Our happiness is closely related to a greater realization of our potential, and a good city facilitates that. There we can paint, walk, ride a bicycle, learn music, cook elaborate dishes, practice a sport, work for a community, or create a company. The city provides the infrastructure, opportunities for learning or meeting others whose knowledge we need for our projects, and recognition for our achievements. The best city is the one most fertile for the realization of human potential and thus for happiness.

A habitat conceived for equity and human happiness does not enter into conflict with environmental sustainability but rather achieves it. In Bogotá we fought difficult battles in our search for quality-of-life equality. We rebuilt sidewalks so that people could no longer use them as car parks, started to build a network of hundreds of kilometers of bikeways, and gave exclusive lanes to buses to create the TransMilenio system. In ensuing years my city and I were given a number of environmental awards. This honored but also surprised me because my prime objective had not been environmental improvement. I had simply tried to make a more egalitarian and happier city.

What would an ideal city be like if we had a magic wand? We have one: it's called time. Fifty or a hundred years is a long time for a human but the blink of an eye for a city. If we have a shared vision, we can achieve it, even if it takes a hundred years. I was always impressed by the medieval cathedrals, which took two hundred years or more to complete, and not because of contractor problems. They planned from the start a construction time of more than a hundred years. What projects do we undertake today, to be completed in two hundred years or even fifty?

Public policy discussions and decisions, such as those related to economic policy, are ephemeral. Even the most intense political debates have less impact on people's lives than politicians might think. In contrast, how a city is made determines to a large extent the quality of life of many generations, for hundreds of years into the future. The quality-of-life equality that I envision—and that well-designed cities support—is not about income. If those of us in developing countries measure success simply in terms of income, we condemn ourselves to be losers for hundreds of years. The most important competition is about a happier way of life.

CHAPTER 1

The City Is a Crucial Competitive Advantage,
or Disadvantage

I n "post-industrial society," as Daniel Bell called it,[1] the critical factor for economic growth and the accumulation of power has been knowledge; thus the principal competition between countries and cities is for people who have knowledge and the capacity to create or simply are so good at what they do that they can choose where to live.

In developing countries, the wealthiest entrepreneurs and businesspeople hold the most power and influence. But in London or New York, there are dozens of billionaires who live in anonymity. Nobody cares what they do or think, and they are irrelevant outside the sphere of their business. Successful athletes, artists, journalists, television presenters, scientists, museum directors, politicians, writers, and senior private- and public-sector executives are much more important and influential. Their importance is derived from knowledge, regardless of whether or not they are wealthy.

In order to attract and retain productive and creative people who can choose where they live, we need quality of urban life. When economic growth gets discussed, references are usually made to tax policy, industrial policy, interest rates or exchange rates, port infrastructure, highways, or railroads. Other countries can easily replicate traditional economic policies to favor growth, such as fiscal or industrial incentives. But *a good city is a comparative advantage that cannot be imitated, and a bad one is a comparative disadvantage that cannot be remedied.*

For economic growth, just as important or even more important than economic policies are cities with low crime, good public transport, parks and other pedestrian spaces, bikeways, world-class universities, high-quality schools, cultural life, restaurants, and other amenities such as, for example, as is true of Bogotá, abundant places to dance. Governments of developing countries spend billions on interurban highways to improve competitiveness and economic growth. It is astonishing that they spend little to improve the quality of life of cities.

In an increasingly globalized world in which communications are better and cheaper than ever and a growing number of people and businesses can locate anywhere, the quality of urban life as a competitive factor will become ever more important. And yet economists who study economic growth and competitiveness have almost entirely ignored this matter.

Attracting Workers to a City

The challenge of attracting workers is a somewhat recent development. In the mid-1900s the most brilliant young people had to go and spend their lives where the great corporations of their day—notably, perhaps, the chemical or automotive giants—decided to set up shop. Many of those young people probably would have preferred to live in New York or San Francisco rather than Detroit, Pittsburgh, or Midland. But the heads of those major corporations were not especially concerned about where their young employees would have preferred to live—because they didn't have to be. Their employees would live where corporations decided to locate. Contemporary mega-enterprises such as Google, Facebook, Microsoft, and Amazon can't afford such indifference. Today, companies have to locate in cities where the young people they need prefer to live. Increasingly, too, these companies are allowing their employees to work remotely, and, to live, those employees choose the city they like best.

When working in a low-quality city is impossible to avoid, people at least locate their families in a more desirable one nearby. Every Friday before noon, caravans of cars leave Buenaventura, a city that hosts Colombia's main port on the Pacific. The caravan heads for Cali, a city with three million inhabitants that's a little less than three hours' drive away through tropical jungle and mountains. Traveling in their own cars, technicians and professionals who work in port-related activities go to Cali for the weekend to be with their families. Buenaventura lies on a bewitchingly beautiful bay, surrounded by hills covered in jungle. Its inhabitants include talented athletes, artists, and chefs, and the port generates substantial economic activity. But the city's quality of life is so severely limited that thousands of higher-salaried people who work there have their families live in Cali.

Seatech is a major Colombian producer of canned tuna. It has some twenty ships fishing in the eastern Pacific, and each fishing voyage lasts nearly two months. Although its vessels fish only in the Pacific, the company's processing plant and administration are located in Cartagena, on the Colombian Caribbean coast. This means that for each fishing voyage, the ship needs to cross the Panama Canal twice. The company's operating costs are therefore higher than they would be if the plant was located in Buenaventura, on the Pacific coast. In addition to the canal tolls and the crew and fuel costs for the additional navigation days, the ship often wastes several days waiting in a queue to enter the canal.

Why pay millions of dollars a year to transport fish caught in the Pacific Ocean to the Caribbean Sea—millions that could have been saved by operating in Buenaventura? For one simple reason: to get highly qualified people to live in Buenaventura, the company would have to pay salaries several times higher to compensate tangibly for the lower quality of life. Ships' captains and officers do not want to spend even the few days needed to unload their cargo and prepare for a new voyage in Buenaventura. After more than six weeks on the high seas, they want to enjoy a few days in a nice city before setting sail again.

If Buenaventura had a good quality of life, the port, as the powerful and permanent economic engine that it is, could transform it into a diversified, dynamic, and fascinating city. It would attract tourists, and businesses unrelated to port activity would flourish.

Buenaventura is another example of how central governments can make major investments in roads, ports, and railways but do little to improve cities, although quality-of-life improvements could be even more effective than traditional infrastructure to foster economic development and an influx of residents. The cost of low-quality urban life is quite explicit, as is true with Buenaventura. It's also evident in the higher salaries that qualified people demand to live, for example, in Lagos, Nigeria. And even when these workers, lured by very high remuneration, accept relocation to a city with severe quality-of-life deficiencies, they do so only for a limited time. They won't make the kind of long-term commitment to the place that knits together a social fabric and is important to a good city.

In contrast, many bright young people around the world want to live at least for a while in Paris, London, or New York, and for that they are willing to sacrifice some material comforts: they leave their large apartments in Bogotá, Mumbai, or São Paulo and forgo domestic servants and nannies, golf clubs and country houses. They will live in a small apartment and have fewer comforts, but they'll have Paris, London, or New York, with all that those cities have to offer in terms of quality of life.

What is abundant and all but limitless today can become scarce surprisingly fast. In the seventeenth century, lobsters were so abundant in Massachusetts that they were often used as fertilizer to increase farm production. Today, they are one of the most expensive and coveted foods, and most people can't afford them. In a world whose population has increased by billions in recent decades, population would not seem to be at all scarce. However, many rural areas and small cities worldwide have a shortage of workers because young people are leaving for larger cities. World population growth has slowed and will continue to do so until populations begin to decrease, as is already happening in many societies. Eighty-nine countries today have fertility rates below the 2.1 offspring per woman required to sustain a population's size. In a few decades, nations and cities will be competing fiercely to attract and retain people. Only eight years ago, Colombians were required to obtain visas to go to any European country. Now we don't need to. Did Colombians become better people, or did Europeans become nicer? They well know hundreds of thousands of Colombians will overstay their visas and settle there for the rest of their lives. But that is exactly why they eliminated the visa requirement: they need nurses, waiters, plumbers, engineers.

Most troubling for small cities is that the young who are leaving are the better prepared and more capable of their generation. They leave because they can't find opportunities in their home cities. In my city of Bogotá, which now has a population close to ten million,[2] some brilliant young people who do advanced research in science or technology also leave for Europe or the United States.

At the beginning of the twenty-first century, the humorist Bill Maher quipped, "There's a reason small towns are small. No one wants to live there."[3] There is some truth to that. So small cities will have to make great efforts to be especially pleasant to live in. While a "small" city in the developing world is one with fewer than one million inhabitants, many European cities of a hundred thousand have industries, universities, intense cultural lives, and an extraordinary quality of life while also being dynamic and competitive.

What can these small cities do to achieve a unique competitive advantage that cannot be duplicated elsewhere? What would draw an investor to a small Colombian city less developed than Bogotá? They would have to pay the same taxes as in Bogotá and would enjoy no advantage in terms of labor legislation. In Bogotá the investor more easily finds highly qualified employees, as well as a larger market, a richer culture, a wide variety of restaurants, and so on.

Small cities do have interesting advantages, however: less traffic, shorter distances that make it possible to move on foot or by bicycle, quick and easy access to rural areas and nature, and, generally, lower housing and living costs and a more robust sense of community. In smaller cities it is easier to participate in civic life or cultural activities, not simply as a spectator but as a creator—perhaps as a musician who performs in a local bar or venue. If smaller cities can leverage advantages such as these, concentrating on quality of life, they can become attractive places for some creative and productive people. Some studies find higher levels of satisfaction among residents of smaller cities than large ones.[4] Modern technology eliminates many of these cities' previous disadvantages. Now people can enjoy the latest films, work online with others anywhere in the world, and deliver work as quickly as if a client were across the street.

Small cities feel the effects of the youth exodus to large cities, but the situation isn't ideal for large cities either. They resent being the milk cows of the nation. Their inhabitants watch their taxes being siphoned to other parts of the country to the detriment of their own city, which is left without the funds to leverage its own progress. Some businesses do not have good cost-accounting and use funds from profitable products to subsidize loss-making ones. Usually, to be successful, a business should do the opposite: stop producing what brings losses and concentrate its funds and efforts on increasing production of profitable goods and services.

Taking resources away from highly productive cities with high concentrations of knowledge and capital in order to subsidize rural regions with low levels of productivity implies costs, not only for cities' competitiveness but also for the country's economic development. Naturally, for democratic reasons and in the interests of national unity and humanitarian principles, it is essential to build roads to access even the smallest population centers and to provide them with electricity and schools. But it is also important to be aware of the cost to economic growth when we transfer resources from the most productive centers to other less productive regions.

I'm not suggesting here that cities seek independence from their countries. I only mean to emphasize the immense importance of cities for economic

growth and competitiveness. National governments would do well to remember that their major cities are not only the locomotives of progress for
the country but also the principal source of funds to support their poorer regions, which are mainly rural.

Some of the most successful nations in recent decades are city-states, almost without territory, such as Singapore and, until recently, Hong Kong. At
first sight it might seem that it is an advantage for a country to have a large
territorial expanse. But at least in the early stages of development, in the global
south, large expanses of territory can generate more costs than advantages.

Historically, the opposite was true. Cities and civilizations rose on the surplus generated by the rural sector. Rome and Paris were built on the surplus
generated by farmers. Some city-states of the past, such as Venice or Florence,
were the locomotives of development based on trade and finance but initially were largely sustained by surrounding farming regions. However, most
of the great cities in the developing world today, such as Mumbai, Cairo, or
Jakarta, are the source of funds to develop and subsidize the rural regions of
their countries.

In all areas where knowledge and creativity are critical, few care about
the atavistic concept of nationality. The most dynamic great cities on Earth
open their doors to those who bring knowledge and creativity; in this way
they consolidate their leadership. In the industrial era, many states offered
subsidies to attract capital. In the postindustrial era, when the competition
is for creative and productive people, it is quality of life that works, not
subsidies.

Governments can regulate property, tax it, and even expropriate it. But
they can't do those things with knowledge. A society in which knowledge is
progressively more important than land or capital is therefore a more democratic society, one in which those who govern have increasingly less control.
For progress to take place, governments must concentrate more and more on
ways to improve urban life.

Cities After Covid

Might small cities and rural areas flourish in the postpandemic world? Many
people have predicted that we will no longer work in offices, that we will see
a mass migration from dense cities to more spacious suburbs and outlying

towns and villages and a significant reduction in business trips. The quarantines that forced many to sequester in small apartments in a dense city, along with the fear of crowds inherent to the pandemic, made many people dream of a life in the suburbs or even the small towns beyond them. And technology allows us videoconferences.

It seems, however, that human contact is still necessary. We travel across the world to talk about projects that could be discussed over Zoom. Unstructured meetings—different than Zoom ones, such as those that take place at lunch in a café nearby and not just with workmates—spawn new ideas and projects. As several authors have noted, ideas seem to flourish in densely populated cities. People who are different in their backgrounds, interests, and even clothing styles, those who see things through different lenses converge in cities. Robert Putnam writes that "social contacts affect the productivity of individuals and groups,"[5] and Edward Glaeser observes that "innovations cluster in places like Silicon Valley because ideas cross corridors and streets more easily than continents and seas."[6] Unsurprisingly, a high percentage of new patents are based on previous ones registered in the same city or state.

People still seek personal contact, to look each other in the eye and *feel* the capacity, credibility, and integrity of the other. When we go on a business trip to another city, we walk around it, enjoy its architecture, "get the feel of the place." By doing this, it is more likely we will imagine a new project there, or agree to participate in one, than if our only contact with the place was over a Zoom call.

The Covid-19 lockdown and remote work, much of which remains, idealized life in small villages or suburbs. I am skeptical of that life ideal. My mother had eight siblings and my father seven. I had four, as did many of my classmates. Today, most of my friends my age have only two children. As societies grow wealthier, people have fewer children and households are smaller. Half the households in Scandinavia today have just one person. Eighty years ago, the option of living out in the country or on a distant beach and working remotely, had it existed, would have been more attractive. We would have lived in homes with many siblings, and we would have had nearly twenty houses nearby of uncles and aunts with eight or ten cousins each, that is, nearly two hundred cousins. Today a child typically has one sibling or none, at most two uncles and aunts, and at most four cousins. Today, many of us live on our own, or with a partner, or, for a few years, with one or two children. Our social life is increasingly less with our family and more with our friends, and it takes place more outside of our home than inside it. Thus, we need our city even more, with its parks, cafés and restaurants, cinemas, and sporting and cultural events. Today, living and working from a home far away from the city for most of us is less attractive than ever before.

Higher levels of education and income have also diversified personal interests almost limitlessly, from dog-breeding, astronomy, yoga, and Chinese cooking to old books, local insects, and electronics. A large city means that whatever our interest, we'll meet like-minded people from whom we can learn and with whom we can share.

I have led teams large and small, and I suspect creativity is not the same without human contact. I doubt that the same esprit de corps can be created or that executives can feel as comfortable in choosing who to promote if they have only met candidates on-screen. Above all, I believe that we laugh more and have more fun at work if we have personal contact with our colleagues.

Denser cities also support the environment. In advanced cities the two main causes of energy consumption, and therefore of global warming, are heating and air conditioning and mobility. In suburbs, as land is less costly, we find larger houses than in dense cities. Inevitably, more energy is needed for cooling and heating them. And in such environments, distances are longer, and people use less mass transport and more private cars. As a result, both heating and cooling and mobility require more energy in suburbs than in a large, denser city. This would be another cost incurred if the Covid-19 escapist idealizations actually became a reality.

It is likely that many people will work fewer days at the office, for example, only four or even three. But regardless of whether they go less to the office, I suspect people will enjoy living in denser cities. People like dense cities not just for work reasons but also for leisure-time ones. Time will make clear what we really prefer. My bet is that the same things that have brought people to cities, even after plagues and disastrous bombings, will continue to do so. Moreover, I am convinced that dense cities will be progressively greener and more pleasant to walk, bicycle, and live in. My prediction is that energy savings, the variety offered by large cities, the social outlets, and the human contact at work will continue to be preferred well into the future. Beyond Covid-19, we will continue to live in densely populated cities both because they are more fun and because they make us more productive.

Town Mergers: Good for Equality, Bad for Politicians

Although some romantics deplore that developing cities will continue to attract people from rural areas and grow, studies have confirmed that those who migrate to cities quickly improve their living conditions and their children's opportunities. Of course, everything possible needs to be done to improve small farmers' lives and income, but we should not worry that people from rural areas migrate to cities. Moreover, in some cases, it would make sense to encourage and facilitate that process. The most serious poverty problems in developing countries are concentrated in rural areas. While Asian small farmers tend to live in small settlements, their fellows in Colombia and elsewhere in Latin America often live in isolation, in solitary houses perched on mountainsides or deep in the fields, far from their closest neighbors and without access to a road. That makes them even more vulnerable to criminals, such as the drug traffickers and guerrillas who have laid waste to rural areas in Colombia. Isolation also makes it difficult for the state to provide education, technical assistance, health services, recreation, or internet service. For some children the walk to school takes hours, and they often fail to finish their secondary education because there is no school within a reasonable distance. I don't know of any nation-state that has made an effort to relocate subsistence farmers from their smallholdings to new settlements or nearby towns from which they could easily ride a motorcycle to and from their farms and where they and their families could enjoy some of the advantages of modern life, which today are beyond their reach.

The vicious segregation of housing by income level can be found in almost every city in the world.[7] If high- and low-income housing are further situated largely in different municipalities, then the problem is worse. In low-income municipalities, a high level of public investment is required to provide social services, such as kindergartens and schools, health centers, homes for the elderly, and even subsidized water and electricity. Unfortunately, there are not enough funds to cover those needs because low-income earners don't pay much in taxes. The reverse is true in a high-income municipality. The capacity to pay taxes may be high, but residents need few social services because, especially in the developing world, high-income citizens use private education, health services, and so on and sometimes even have private local water supplies.

The division of a large city into a number of municipalities not only inten-
sifies inequality but also hampers the realization of metropolitan projects,
such as large parks or mass-transit systems. And "not in my backyard"
(NIMBY) projects further exacerbate inequality through the location of such
things as highways, sanitary infills, prisons, and even social housing
programs.

Some countries have powerful supramunicipal authorities that intervene
in municipalities, compensating inequalities by concentrating investment
and services in the poorer cities. Sometimes, as in Spain or Brazil, these authorities are powerful regional governments. In other countries, such as
France, the national government provides funds to regional governments. In
yet others, such as Chile, national government itself invests and is directly
in charge of many local projects and services.[8] But there are cases, as in Colombia, where municipal governments have great autonomy, and no regional
or national government provides enough services or undertakes any significant investments in the poorer municipalities to reduce inequalities, which
consequently grow worse.

Some of the towns north of Bogotá have attracted middle- and high-
income citizens. There are no informal developments there, and most growth
over the last decades hast taken place in gated communities—some quite
luxurious, with riding centers and golf courses. In contrast, south of Bogotá
in the municipality of Soacha, the opposite has occurred. Soacha has attracted low-income people and in recent decades has had the fastest-growing
population of any municipality in Colombia. Naturally, the need for public
investment in Soacha is enormous, and its tax revenues are scarce, unlike in
the high-income municipalities to the north.

The solution to this dilemma is nothing new. In 1954, Gustavo Rojas,
Colombia's only—and happily short-lived—dictator in the twentieth century,
followed recommendations of the World Bank mission headed by the economist Laughlin Currie and merged Bogotá with six surrounding municipalities. This meant that during some of the most intense urbanization stages, the
enlarged Bogotá had a relatively technical management of territorial planning
and infrastructure construction, which would have been impossible had
each one of the six small municipalities been in charge of its own planning.
The new, merged Bogotá consolidated some institutions that within a few
decades became as sophisticated and efficient as those of a developed city.
This contrasts with the institutional weakness of the perimeter towns that
were not part of the merger, as reflected in population densities that are

several times lower than those of Bogotá, governments that are unable even to operate sewage plants properly, and an almost total absence of public parks or quality sidewalks.

Even more important, the merger made Bogotá government into a powerful machine for redistribution. The city collects very high taxes in high-income areas where minimal public investment is needed, and it invests the vast majority of the city budget in the lowest-income areas, which enjoy an ever-improving infrastructure. For example, some school buildings in very low-income areas could be the envy of some of the most expensive private schools, and these areas feature better libraries, cultural centers, sport facilities, cableways for transport, and larger and better parks than those of high-income sectors. Furthermore, much higher water or electricity charges in the higher-income sectors subsidize rates in lower-income ones.

A city constituted by seven separate municipalities rather than one would never have achieved that powerful redistribution from high-income sectors to the poorest. It would also have been difficult to mount projects such as the creation of TransMilenio, which serves all seven of those former municipalities on its routes today.

Why do we not do another merger similar to the one of 1954 today? Why not merge a dozen of the municipalities on Bogotá's perimeter? Two groups would oppose it. The first is the people who live in the high-income municipalities who, like their counterparts everywhere, know that a merger means a transfer of funds from where they live to lower-income sectors, which are today part of other municipalities. The second is the professional local politicians who prefer to continue to be the head of the mouse rather than the tail of the lion. Indeed, even politicians in the poorest municipalities oppose a merger, although they know that their electors would benefit from one. Of course, both parties offer superficially sophisticated arguments to oppose the general interest, alleging noble principles such as "the environment" or their municipality's unique traditions and "culture."

But the reality is that boundaries between municipalities in conurbations are invisible to most of the people who live there. Their residents identify more with the big city than with the municipality. Nevertheless, the merger of several municipalities is seldom a voluntary process. It is usually only possible if the decision comes from a higher authority, such as a national law.

Inequality between municipalities is not exclusively a problem of developing countries. In the United States that inequality can be seen in one of its worst possible forms: children's education. North of New York City are towns with some of the best public schools in the world, where teachers not only earn much more than those in the neighboring or nearby towns but also enjoy smaller class sizes. For example, in several instances just a street separates the towns of White Plains and Scarsdale, with large houses and carefully tended gardens on both sides. A visitor would think that the value of the houses is the same on both sides. But a house on the Scarsdale side of the street is worth much more than an almost identical house on the White Plains side. The difference stems from the fact that children who live in a house on the Scarsdale side are entitled to go to a much better public school than those who live on the White Plains side.

In other municipalities in the same area but not adjacent to Scarsdale, such as Yonkers, home to people with lower incomes than in White Plains, the difference is even greater. A wider comparison between municipalities of different regions or states would find similar dramatic differences, even in matters in which all would agree on the need for equality, such as education. This is the type of inequality that could be eliminated, even within a capitalist system. For example, financing for education could be done at a national and not a local level, or there could be guaranteed minimum funding per student nationwide. However, when dealing with conurbated municipalities that are part of the same large city, a practical solution to unequal education and other kinds of inequality is the fusion of municipalities.

In addition to the inequalities engendered, the splintering of major cities and metropolitan areas into a number of towns or municipalities frequently makes mobility difficult and expensive. Low-income citizens have fewer chances to live near their workplaces: if transport systems are not metropolitan and integrated, then their travel times are longer and their commutes more expensive. In a number of cases, buses from one municipality are not allowed to enter others and passengers must transfer to other vehicles and pay an additional fare at the "border."

Manhattan is an island in metropolitan New York City, but with a single ticket you can travel on more than ten metro lines anywhere east and north of Manhattan, to Brooklyn and the Bronx, crossing the East River.[9] But to the west, crossing the Hudson River, there are no metro lines because one enters New Jersey, a different state. Across the river from New York, locations in New Jersey can only be reached by buses or trains not integrated into the Manhattan subway and bus system. This means that commuting takes longer and costs more for many low-income people who live in New Jersey and work across the river in New York.

Unfortunately, this situation is not unique. In some cases, municipalities within a large city obstruct the construction of mass-transit systems through their territories. When the Metro was being built in Medellín, intransigent opposition in the adjacent municipality of Envigado dictated that the route be changed to go through another municipality, on the other side of the river, which increased project costs.

The engineers' design for our Metro in Bogotá called for rail yards to be located on the other side of the Bogotá River, in a rural area of the neighboring municipality of Mosquera. It was evident that thousands of hectares of rural land in this municipality adjacent to Bogotá would be urbanized in the near future, and to have that rail yard in Mosquera would have been the first step for a future extension of the Metro into that municipality. Nonetheless, the regional governor and mayor of Mosquera made it impossible to extend the Metro there. Fortunately, Bogotá had alternative lots available on which to locate the yards, albeit at greater cost. The new location locked the future extension of the Metro toward Soacha, another municipality, and not to Mosquera. The two cases above exemplify the inconvenience and expense of dividing cities into many municipalities.

In Santiago and Paris, the national governments build and manage mass-transit systems that operate in an integrated fashion within and across several municipalities. In other cases, there are regional transport companies. In most countries, national or regional governments wholly or partly finance metro systems.

Berlin functions efficiently, partly because its territory is large and includes all the land in its metropolitan area that could plausibly become urban. The city limits today result from a 1920 law that expanded Germany's capital, absorbing seven towns around its perimeter. Hamburg also has an extensive territory as the result of a merger of several towns. In Germany many municipalities have expanded to achieve economies of scale and efficiency.

In 1901 municipalities around Copenhagen[10] merged with the city, which consequently tripled its area and allowed it to plan for future growth, although within Copenhagen there is still the rich municipality of Frederiksberg, which often obstructs city projects. In Denmark the number of municipalities was reduced semivoluntarily from 271 to 98 in 2007. They remain autonomous municipalities, which causes difficulties. In Belgium the municipalities of Laeken, Haren, and Neder-Over-Heembeek merged with Brussels in 1921, and between 1961 and 1983, many municipalities in other Belgian regions merged as well, which reduced the total number from 2,663 to 589. In Finland, between 1966 and 2009, Vantaa, Sipoo, and other municipalities merged with Helsinki. In Queensland, Australia, between 2007 and 2011, municipalities were reduced from 156 to 77 "local governments." Chinese cities have consolidated by gradual absorption of the territories and municipalities around them.

Although well-demarcated high- and low-income areas exist in all major cities, segregation in South Africa under apartheid was even more pronounced because it was racial as well as economic. Only whites could live in certain areas, and on the periphery were racially segregated urban areas only for Black Africans. In many cases the main purpose of the fusion of towns is equity, but in postapartheid South Africa this was especially critical. Many municipalities racially segregated under apartheid were merged by law. In Cape Town, for example, sixty-one municipalities were merged into six in 1996, and into one in 2000.[11]

In Canada hundreds of municipalities were merged in the first decade of the twenty-first century by a decision of Parliament. In the province of Ontario alone, the number of municipalities was reduced by almost half between 1996 and 2003. Five municipalities around Toronto merged with the city in 1998, increasing its population sixfold. Unfortunately, fifteen municipalities in the metropolitan area were left out of the merger, which has caused problems, especially since they are the fastest-growing areas. Although initially most of the people in the municipalities that were to be merged voted against it, a few years later most believed that the merger had been positive. Also in Canada, in the Québec province, between 2000 and 2003 the number of municipalities was reduced by more than two hundred; more than twenty of these municipalities were merged with the city of Montréal.[12]

In the cases of multiple municipalities within a single metropolitan area, supramunicipal institutions are useful for the planning and management of some services. But this does not solve the problem of equity. Only the merger of municipalities enables funds to flow from high-income areas to be invested where they are most needed. Municipality mergers are convenient for planning, efficiency, and equity—and precisely for these reasons powerful interests oppose them.

*   *   *

Beyond the Covid-19 pandemic, I believe that humans will continue to seek dense urban environments that facilitate human contact and varied learning opportunities and foster creative human interaction. Now cities will have to compete more and more for the talented workers who are increasingly free to choose where they live. Cities will particularly need to improve their pedestrian spaces, such as sidewalks and parks. Smaller cities and towns have advantages, but it is unlikely that large cities will lose preponderance. Finally, if what matters is equity and efficiency and not petty, shortsighted political interests, many municipalities around large cities should merge with the city. The merger of small towns into one urban entity can support democratic and quality-of-life equalities.

CHAPTER 2

How to Use City Land More Democratically

L atin America's process of urbanization in the second half of the twentieth century is similar to what is happening somewhat faster in Asia in the first half of the twenty-first and will happen in sub-Saharan Africa a little later. Although huge cities were also built in Asia in the second half of the twentieth century, its population is still mostly rural. The Latin American experience is instructive for Asia and Africa, not to learn what should be done but rather to learn what should *not* be done.

While Latin America's urban population went from 50 to 80 percent, the population of its major cities increased more than 500 percent.[1] In some cases, such as Bogotá, the increase was more than 1,000 percent. In many countries of Asia and sub-Saharan Africa, less than 50 percent of the population is currently urban. This means that the populations of hundreds of cities in both regions will multiply between five and fifteen times during the twenty-first century. The physical size of the cities will increase even more dramatically. More than 90 percent of what will be the cities of Africa in the year 2100 has not yet been built, and currently the land on which they will be built is mostly rural.

Cities in Latin America are still growing, and the built area of many of the larger ones will double by 2100. The same trend applies to many cities in the United States. These are places where the population is growing and the average household size is declining. The quantity of houses the United States will need to build between 2020 and 2070 surpasses the entire 2021 housing stock of the United Kingdom, France, and Canada combined.

Over the rest of this century, we will build more than 80 percent of the urban areas that will exist in the world in 2100. I suspect that nothing we are doing today is more important than designing and redesigning these cities well. That will be decisive for human happiness hundreds of years in the future. And if we don't do them well now, it will be extremely difficult to correct them in the future.

The number of square meters of buildings in cities grows faster than the population. This happens because progressively households have fewer members, which means that more homes will be needed, even if the population were to remain stable. For example, the size of households in India today is more than twice that in Germany. If we just halved the size of Indian households, then we'd need twice as many new homes for the same population. Another contributing factor to the increase in the square meters of buildings is that as incomes increase, homes tend to get larger.

Furthermore, as economic development increases, the share of nonhousing buildings increases. A small, poor village or a low-income neighborhood has few nonhousing buildings. As incomes grow, a number of buildings that aren't used for housing appear, such as offices, warehouses, universities, restaurants, larger shops, hotels, cinemas, and gyms. Economic growth also brings a larger share of road space and green areas. For all the above reasons, economic development means that the urbanized area increases much more than is proportional to population growth; there are more square meters of city per inhabitant.

Shlomo Angel estimates that as the population of cities in developing countries increases from 2 billion to 5.5 billion between 2000 and 2050, the urban land such cities will occupy will increase sixfold.[2]

Asia and Africa offer the greatest opportunities to make better cities and improve how we live. As a Latin American, it saddens me to see all the mistakes we've made and the opportunities we've missed. Most large cities of Asia, built in the same decades, have similar or even worse deficiencies, except Chinese cities.

Another reason why these cities in the late 1900s weren't built better is because these were arguably the worst decades in the history of human habitat construction. For thousands of years and up to the end of World War I, cities were built for human beings. After that they were built more for cars, and this concept peaked after World War II. No importance was given to pedestrian public space. Most of the few large parks in those cities predate the second half of the twentieth century, and many come from the nineteenth century. Sidewalks were scarce, narrow, or uneven, and bikeways were not even considered.

Another serious problem that contributed to the deformation of cities built in the second half of the twentieth century, and one not yet properly solved, was the private ownership of land. This caused speculative management of land rather than management oriented toward the common good. Consequently, a large portion of cities in the developing world were constituted by informal settlements, often located suboptimally, that had severe infrastructure and public space deficits. The high price of land and developers' haste to obtain enormous profits from the increased value of rural land also meant that many formal developments were built far from city perimeters and without desirable parks and other public spaces.

Cities: The Result of Vision or Lack Thereof

Unfortunately, we must admit that the cities we have built so rapidly in recent decades in developing countries are no better than those built previously in advanced countries, and indeed they are generally worse. The urban model I've just described accounts for some of the failure, but it's also due to the fact that ruling classes in the developing world assigned no priority to making cities pleasant for lower-income citizens. Wealthier citizens built themselves comfortable, even luxurious homes, country clubs, and roads for their cars, and some who inherited land in the areas surrounding cities made large fortunes as cities' growth reached their properties. Meanwhile, they neglected the needs of millions of poor migrants arriving from rural areas. National and local governments in developing countries worldwide failed to live up to their historical responsibility.

It was economically impossible to give everyone a car, a trip to Paris, or a color TV. But land, the raw material for a city, was there. Had it been more democratically used, cities would have been better located and would have had more and better public spaces.

In 1811, when New York had 96,000 inhabitants, its government designed and approved an expansion plan, which provided for growth equivalent to seven times the area of the city. It took until 1900 to occupy the area included in the 1811 plan.[3] In 1859, Ildefons Cerdà won a competition in Barcelona to plan the growth of the city. This city also thought on a grand scale for the future. The plan provided for an expansion of 900 percent of the area of the city, which at that time had a population of 150,000.[4] They were visionaries, even without having access to the statistical information or demographic and urban growth projections we can count on today. It's a pity that many forecasts about growth in developing world cities are based on illusions and not judicious analysis.

Cities are the result of vision, or the lack thereof. In growing cities it's not expensive for governments to purchase rural land around cities for parks.[5] This is the best investment a government and society can make. I don't know of any instance where a society has made an investment in land for urban parks and later concluded that it was a mistake. But as far as I know, this has not been done in any country in the developing world. Projects of this kind come up against the usual short-term criteria of governments and their myopia: the illusion that their cities will not grow.

Even if the benefits of buying land for future expansion and large parks were clear to them, governments—and particularly local governments—are usually under pressure to satisfy more immediate needs. To ensure that land for future parks is secured, a national law can mandate that a percentage of a tax should be dedicated to that specific purpose or that a percentage of local or regional government spending should be allocated to it.

There are goods for which private property and the market economy do not work well. One of them is land around growing cities. In a market economy, prices of goods tend to approach the cost of producing them. For example, when tomato prices rise above the cost of producing them, more tomatoes are planted, supply increases, and prices fall. This does not happen in the case of land around cities: it does not matter how much the price rises; the supply of land around the city, with access to water, schools, transport, and employment, does not increase. The basic principle of the market economy that supply increases when prices increase is not met. There is therefore no justification for land around growing cities to be managed by means of private property and the market economy.

Agrarian reform, by which the state takes over and redistributes large rural estates, has been an integral part of many revolutions. It has also been advocated since the middle of the twentieth century by democratic voices. After World War II, the US government implemented this type of reform in Japan and promoted it in Korea, Taiwan, and Latin America as well, after the Cuban revolution, as a means of constructing social justice, strengthening democracy, and countering rural guerrillas and communism.

Curiously, ideologues for social justice in developing countries never proposed, promoted, or applied a similar urban land reform, which would have been even more relevant for those rapidly urbanizing societies and more effective for the improvement of poorer citizens' lives than agrarian reform. The state could have acquired land around cities, through voluntary sales or expropriation, at rural land prices. It could have organized the city's growth and solved housing needs. The implementation of urban land reforms in Latin America in the second half of the twentieth century would have produced very different and better cities.

The problem of the high cost of land is not solved with the growth of income because that brings an increase in demand and, with that, higher land prices. Moreover, the price of land around growing cities increases much faster than income per capita. Regardless of income increases, well-located land remains out of reach for low-income citizens.

Land price increments enrich a few landowners around cities. These monopolistic owners of land, that critical resource for human life, undeservedly receive the increase in land values generated by the work of the rest of society. Each time citizens who live on the edge of the city, frequently in informal settlements, improve their home through often herculean effort, they increase the value of properties held by nearby large landowners. The same is true if a government investment brings water, sewerage, a school, or a good road to these neighborhoods on the edge of the city. Although any capitalist's investment may increase in value as society progresses, those investments are subject to risk from competition, technological innovation, and so on, but this is not the case for land ownership around growing cities. Unearned enrichment is the lesser problem caused by private property of land around cities; the bigger one is that cities grow in the wrong locations and without adequate public spaces.

A tree knows where to expand its large and small branches to receive light and air. It knows how to grow. And that's a good model for a city.

There is only one optimal site for a city to grow well. For example, thousands of hectares of rural land belonging to the municipality of Mosquera are adjacent to Bogotá. No land is as close to Bogotá's employment, education, and recreational opportunities as that of Mosquera municipality. That land is not very fertile. Although the region close to Bogotá is one of the largest flower exporters in the world, no flowers and almost no other crops grow in Mosquera. Metropolitan Bogotá is growing, and the number of homes will double in the coming decades. It would seem natural for Bogotá to grow on the land in Mosquera. But the municipal authorities of Mosquera, under the influence of speculative landowners, have obstructed well-planned development. They didn't even permit the Bogotá Metro to locate its yards in Mosquera territory.

As a result, the housing that might otherwise have been built in an orderly fashion in Mosquera is now being constructed in a piecemeal fashion and more so in scattered areas of other, more distant municipalities. This means that trips to work, study, or anywhere else are longer, take more time, and consume more energy.

Minimizing travel distances is imperative when deciding where a city ought to grow. Every additional housing unit generates more than three additional trips a day. Now the growth of hundreds of cities in the developing world in the next few decades means hundreds of millions of additional homes and at least three times as many daily trips. If a city grows farther away than it would have with effective planning, then millions of trips will be longer. If instead it grows in the optimal location, travel distances and energy consumption are reduced to a minimum, travel times are shorter, public transport systems function with low costs and high frequencies, and many people can walk or bike for their daily needs. All this improves quality of life and reduces global warming.

Ten or thirty or even more minutes of extra travel time for each of those daily trips would have enormous economic, environmental, and quality-of-life costs. This is further reinforced if we remember that once a city or part of it is built, it is difficult to demolish it in the future to rebuild it in a better location. Something so important to many generations as where cities grow can neither be dictated by the market, developers and landowners wishing to maximize the value of their rural properties nor by the mayor or council of a small municipality close to a large city. It is a matter of regional and national interest.

Planning is essential, but urban planning in rapidly growing and developing cities can produce a result opposite to the one desired: it can stimulate growth in the worst places. What happens, for example, if the plan allows development in one sector and radically bans it in another? This increases land prices where development is allowed and reduces prices where it is not. Consequently, in the absence of a capacity to enforce such a ban, it stimulates urbanization in the more affordable, prohibited areas. Land is the most critical factor for housing. Once people have land, they will build a house regardless of their income level. Poor people will establish their informal housing often on unsuitable sites such as the steep slopes in Caracas or

Medellín or the flood-prone areas in Manila or Jakarta. In many African and Asian cities, these neighborhoods occupy railway corridors, as happens in Manila, where people mount makeshift wooden platforms on wheels to propel themselves along the tracks. This is not always the case, however. Some informal neighborhoods, for example, in India and Pakistan, are well located in central areas or close to employment hubs, such as ports or wholesale food markets.

Excessively restrictive regulation of the land that can be urbanized, based on wishful thinking, frequently has unintended perverse consequences. The greenbelts that were supposed to surround some cities, as in London or Seoul, have made land more expensive and access to housing by low-income citizens more difficult. In Bogotá a misconceived environmentalist approach led to the establishment of a tree-less forest reserve[6] and the zoning of thousands of hectares to the north of the city as rural, which severely restricted development. This approach simply expelled middle- and low-income earners exponentially and banished them to other municipalities well beyond city limits.

Bogotá is high up in the Andes mountains on a plateau with hundreds of thousands of hectares of flat land. Despite that abundance of level terrain, many of its poorest citizens have been forced to solve their housing needs by settling on the steep slopes high in the mountains that flank the city to the east and south or on low-lying, flood-prone lands to the west.[7] In mountainside neighborhoods it's almost impossible to find enough flat ground for a soccer field and even hard to find the smaller area required for a basketball court. Obviously, if the democratic principle of prevalence of the public good over private interest had been observed, these lower-income neighborhoods would be located on the flat land below, where cows grazed as humans built their mountainside neighborhoods. The cows prevailed—or, to be more specific, the speculative criteria of those who owned the land on which they grazed prevailed—rather than the needs of many generations of humans.

Urban development on the higher slopes not only has and will have a high and detrimental cost to quality of life but also a high environmental cost. The use of bicycles in these neighborhoods is very difficult. Buses and other vehicles consume a great deal of energy to reach these neighborhoods. Water has to be pumped up to them, which consumes extra energy and funds. Bogotá as a whole is at an altitude of 2,600 meters, or 8,600 feet, and the higher up the housing, the colder the air, which compels many to install heating if they can afford it. Heating would be unnecessary on the flat lands a few hundred meters below.

The "Pirate Developers" of Bogotá

Driving his huge red Cadillac with white upholstery, his belly pressing against the wheel, Arquimedes Romero traveled along unpaved roads, through what was then still extensive grasslands. His car glided like a yacht, and his passengers didn't feel the bumps over potholes. This was 1990, and Arquimedes was showing one of his developments to a banker who was going to make him a loan, presumably for a project other than property development. Like all of Romero's other projects, this was a "pirate development," as these illegal subdivisions of land into small plots for sale were popularly known in Bogotá.

The upper-crust owners of large tracts of inherited land watched the city creeping toward their properties as surely as a tide rises over the shore. Despite the guards they hired, every meter that the city advanced toward their estates increased the risk that late one night the estate would be overrun by hundreds or thousands of squatting families and no courts or any other authority would be able to expel the new occupants. In the face of this threat and given that the city administration did not allow them to develop those estates because they were in flood-prone areas, the frightened landowners sold out to illegal developers like Romero.

These illegal developers protected their property with unorthodox guards who were feared. When they decided to develop, they would demarcate the plots to be sold, marking the perimeter with strings tied to stakes placed at the corners. For roads they simply threw truckloads of gravel on top of the grass. Then they would go about selling the plots, which for some reason still unknown to me were always six meters wide and twelve meters deep.[8] Buyers did not receive legal property titles, and lots had no access to electricity, water, or sewerage. Generally, there were no schools nearby.

Buyers of these plots built their houses little by little. Sometimes they would hire a stone mason or an expert plumber to do part or all of the work. They also actively participated in the community organization in order to exert pressure on city agencies, alongside some local politicians who became their sponsors, to bring them basic utilities and, eventually, paving for their roads and legal recognition. Flooding problems, when they existed, were also solved sooner or later by major or minor public works.

Government could easily have done what illegal developers like Arquimedes Romero did. But they could have done it well, with good urban design, broad streets, large parks, and land reserved for public buildings such as schools or health centers. A government entity could have sold plots of land on credit, just as the illegal developers did. But disregard for the needs of the poor and the myopia of wishful thinking that the city would not grow impeded any planning in a large part of the city.

Even aristocratic estate owners could have developed basic urban projects on their properties but with better design and generous public spaces, if only authorities had allowed it instead of banning development.

Although illegal developers, large and small, were breaking the law, the reality is that Colombian democracy tolerated them. It was such a generalized activity and so safe from any form of penalty that sometimes billboards in low-income neighborhoods advertised the sale of illegal plots. The supply of plots in informal settlements was so abundant that pirate developers had to compete with each other. Because of this, some even reserved land for future small parks. Those who bought from them did not see them as criminals; on the contrary, they often treated them as benefactors who helped them solve their housing needs. Several of those pirate developers eventually became prominent local politicians, elected to the City Council and even to the Colombian Congress. Politicians sought out those who didn't care to be elected, because they attracted large numbers of votes from those they had "helped" to obtain a plot of land and a home.

At the end of the 1990s, I met Rosalba Andrade, a smiling and dynamic woman in her mid-fifties. She was working in one of these neighborhoods, which was still only pastureland, demarcated with stakes and string and a few houses in the early stages of construction. She had a shop where she sold beer, soft drinks, and some food. There she also had a *tejo* pitch. *Tejo* is a traditional game in the mountains around Bogotá that remotely resembles the French and Spanish *pétanque*. Invariably, the consumption of beer accompanies the game. Andrade told me that this was her eighth house. She would buy a plot in a recently for-sale project, where plots of land were still marked with strings. She would erect rudimentary walls, a roof, a *tejo* pitch, and a beer counter. And she would start building a house. Once she finished building, she would rent it out and move on to the next recently staked-out neighborhood. She was certain that those developments, especially if they were reasonably well located, would make rapid progress with the support of politicians looking for votes and that her properties' value would soar.

Colombian democracy, which essentially allowed illegal developments, produced better informal neighborhoods than those in countries with dictatorships or democratic governments that did not facilitate their improvement and legalization. With some of the more autocratic governments, invasions or illegal neighborhoods in some countries could be bulldozed flat from one moment to the next or the inhabitants could be evicted. The worst results occur when there is neither legal housing nor informal development, and instead of facilitating the legalization of informal developments or improving them, authorities repress them. Housing is then built in the least suitable places, with no space reserved for roads let alone any other public space. In some cases, the only ingress and egress are narrow passages between houses, or sometimes through the houses themselves, where passersby must all but step over sleeping residents. The latent threat of eviction discourages investments to improve individual houses, to say nothing of neighborhoods overall. This situation is worse if the government promises to relocate some of these residents to free housing elsewhere, as has happened occasionally in South Africa, as housing and infrastructure improvements are thus discouraged.

Large parts of most cities in the world started out illegally. This is the case, for example, in London, Paris, and Tokyo. Housing built in squatter settlements or pirate developments accounted for almost half of all housing in Bogotá in the year 2000. In Colombia, and generally in Latin America today, there are fewer "pirate" neighborhoods, slums, favelas, or whatever they might be called, due to slower urban population growth, higher incomes, government subsidies for housing acquisition, and low inflation, all of which have made possible long-term mortgage loans. However, in some parts of Asia and most of sub-Saharan Africa, these informal settlements constitute a very important part of the cities, even the majority. About a billion people around the world live in slums.[9] Every day, tens of thousands of new homes are being built in these illegal neighborhoods worldwide. Informal developments will continue to grow until the housing problems of those most in need are solved.

In his book *Instant City,* journalist Steve Inskeep describes illegal development in Karachi.[10] The city has grown mainly over a desert, valueless as farmland and therefore ownerless as well. This was public land, and illegal developers there—unlike their counterparts in Bogotá, who had to squat on or purchase land from private estates—simply seized that public land, which they subdivided into plots and sold. In the early stages of this process, government had no capacity to oversee or protect the land, much less to recover it once it had been occupied. Subsequently, these land-grabbing developers carried out the process with the complicity of the state because illegal developers, as was the case in Bogotá, belonged to local political machines.

What does it mean to be a citizen of a country if not, before all else, to have the right to live within its borders? But that is a vacuous right if we don't have a home to live in with our family. And that home cannot be in the middle of a jungle or desert but somewhere close to opportunities for work, study, and the realization of human potential. If there is anything in a country that truly belongs to its citizens, it's the territory itself. If all resources of a democratic society should be managed so that the public good prevails, this principle should apply first to land.

I have always been convinced of the convenience of legalizing informal developments. When I started my political life, before I was thirty, I befriended many popular leaders who wanted to improve their informal neighborhoods. A bit later, as vice president of the Bogotá Water Company, I had the opportunity to visit many of those neighborhoods and effectively contribute to the improvement of their residents' lives. As a first stage, the company took water to those neighborhoods in tanker trucks. Years later it installed piped water and sewerage systems. Finally, and usually years later still, it installed rainwater drainage systems, which were a prerequisite for street paving.

After buying a plot from an illegal developer, almost always on credit from the seller at very high interest rates, all family members would take part in building the home: parents, uncles, children, and sometimes neighbors, who were often friends who had migrated from the same rural areas. The houses were built brick by brick, as money became available to buy materials from small local hardware stores, frequently also on credit. Each home became a life project and often a source of income. After they finished three or four stories, families would open a shop, a beauty parlor, or some other business on the ground floor or rent it out for those purposes. Floors unoccupied by the owner would house the children and their families or would be rented out as well.

Each of these neighborhoods tended to be formed by migrants from the same municipality of rural Colombia. When I was mayor, we organized competitions for neighborhood histories, and settlers wrote some very human, and at the same time epic, accounts of where they had come from, why they had migrated, the difficulties they had overcome, and the leaders who had motivated and organized them. They are the story of the birth of a city.

From the start, inhabitants of each nascent neighborhood would elect a community action board. The central government regulated and supervised elections for these organizations, which were originally rural. Once elected, members of the board and their president would single-mindedly dedicate themselves to seeking appointments with city agencies that could help them improve the neighborhood. Frequently, whole communities would gather at the entrance of one or another public office, banging saucepans and blowing whistles, asking to be listened to and demanding a date for a visit to their neighborhood.

Bogotá politics at this time—basically the second half of the twentieth century—was organized around these neighborhood leaders. They would offer candidates to the city council the votes of their communities in exchange for commitments to help them solve their needs. Of course, they often organized meetings and offered their votes to more than one candidate in the same election.

Influential elite voices opposed the legalization of these informal neighborhoods, arguing that this encouraged further illegal neighborhood development. Personally, I always thought that most of those who built their houses in those neighborhoods were hard-working, disciplined, and courageous. They were building their homes in this way because the state had failed in its responsibility to provide them with a legal alternative. Illegal urban development is evidence that the main obstacle to the housing solution for those who most need it is *land* because once they have land, one way or another they build their homes. And if they have the security that they will not be evicted, they keep on improving them. I have great respect and admiration for those who built their housing in those informal settlements, whose hard work contributed an important part of our city and helped forge our character. To honor and support the study of this part of our history, we built a Museum of the Self-Built City, which sits at the mountaintop terminal of a cable car with a formidable view of thousands of homes that initially sprang up as informal settlements.

A couple of weeks after taking office as mayor in 1998, I received a court order: we had to evict more than two thousand families who had squatted a terrain west of the city ten years earlier and then demolish their houses. Bellavista, which is what they called the neighborhood they had built, was located relatively close to the central wholesale food market of the city. Many residents earned their living from the market, helping to load or unload trucks or performing other tasks. As always happened with informal neighborhoods in Bogotá, some space had been left for roads, and even the land earmarked in city plans for a highway had been partially respected. Also, as usual, the houses had piped water, provided legally or otherwise, which came from the water company's mains, and they had legal power supplies. Sewerage was nonexistent or rudimentary.

The entire area had been developed below the level of the river and flooded frequently. Community organizations had constructed drainage canals, which were totally contaminated with wastewater. Every now and again a child would drown in a canal or a corpse would be dredged up. This was one of the most dangerous parts of the city, with one of its highest murder rates. In order to bring wastewater and rainwater to the river, the neighbors had installed small pumps, which sporadically broke or had an intake blocked by a dead dog. In the rainy season, either because the pumps were damaged or simply insufficient, the neighborhood sometimes would flood knee-high. Occasionally, toilets would not discharge, and wastewater would back up and overflow in homes.

I did not consider even for a moment abiding by the court order to evict these squatting families. They had been living there for more than a decade. Instead, we decided to do everything possible to avoid the eviction, to legalize their possession of the houses, and to radically improve the neighborhood conditions.

We located the owner of the land who had won in court his petition for the eviction. He was a man of about seventy. I met with him and explained that the city administration had legal options that would allow us to postpone the eviction for years. I told him that it would be best for him to sell the land to the city at a very favorable price. In other words, he could either receive cash quickly, by selling the land to City Hall, or else leave his heirs with a legal action that could last decades and might someday provide something for them. Under the circumstances he preferred to sell.

We sent social workers to talk to the community, to try to secure power of attorney from the squatting families to negotiate with the owner for the purchase of the land. This was a dangerous task because some unscrupulous lawyers were deceiving the families, demanding money to represent them presumably in order to make them the rightful owners of their lots. It came to a serious impasse when these lawyer-criminals murdered a community leader who was helping us persuade residents to empower the city administration to pursue the process. Fearful, our social workers refused to return to the neighborhood.

I visited the neighborhood and met the community. After much work we managed to buy the property and hand over title to the residents. We also provided them with funds to improve their homes. We built sewerage networks and a large pumping station to end the floods that affected the entire southwest of Bogotá. We installed pipes to replace the sewage canals and built bikeways on top of them.

We modified the route of the planned highway, moving it west to avoid demolition of a number of houses and to ensure that it would not pass through the middle of the neighborhood. In the area originally reserved for it, we built a beautiful park, a school with excellent facilities, a community center with an indoor swimming pool, and a kindergarten for three hundred children.

Through the middle of Bellavista, we built the marvelous 24 km Alameda Porvenir, a tree-lined bicycle highway, the world's first, that traverses the entire southwest, a low-income area of the city. The Alameda Porvenir had an especially strong and symbolic impact in the years after its construction, because in a society where the car connoted higher-class status, cars in the area circulated on unpaved roads in poor condition, while cyclists and pedestrians had a beautiful, tree-lined, paved road all to themselves. The lighting in Alameda Porvenir even had underground cabling, a rarity in the city at the time and today still far from ubiquitous. The people who lived in those sectors, very poor at that time, acquired a new awareness of their own importance and of the irrelevance of cars to human value.

A three-kilometer bicycle ride away from Bellavista, on Alameda Porvenir, we built the stupendous Tintal library. In the first stage we only paved one of the access roads to Bellavista, for buses to go there and back. Other roads were initially left in gravel and were paved only over the following decades.

Children and the elderly were more important than cars, and this wasn't just theory for us. In Bellavista and many other informal settlements we improved, we built parks and sidewalks before we paved roads. Cars bounced around between potholes and splashed through pools of mud while people walked along beside them on good sidewalks, and children played in parks that rivaled those in any of the world's advanced cities.

Setting aside the unpaved roads, we left a high-quality infrastructure of schools, parks, and community centers in Bellavista. Security wasn't ideal, but the area ceased to be on the list of those with the highest crime rates. Houses have been systematically improved, and a number of businesses are flourishing in the neighborhood.

Twenty years later, during my second period of office, we turned more than fifty hectares adjacent to the neighborhood into a park and contracted to construct the first line of the Metro to start its route exactly there.

I'm proud that as mayor I legalized almost five hundred informal neighborhoods in Bogotá—far more than any other mayor.[11] We did much more than confer legal ownership on residents. We improved those neighborhoods, and this effort extended down to the planting of trees and tens of thousands of colorful bougainvillea that would vine along the walls of self-constructed houses. Working with residents, we painted more than 130,000 façades, and in some mountainside neighborhoods we generated macro-murals with the façade colors. One of these covers twenty-six hectares and depicts a giant butterfly that can be seen from kilometers away. More important than the aesthetics of these façade paintings is the construction of community organization, identity, self-esteem, and a sense of belonging.

In these neighborhoods we built more than fifty schools with facilities that rival or surpass those of private schools where higher-income children are educated.[12] These schools can double as cultural centers and adult education institutions as well. Despite fierce opposition from teachers' unions, we ensured that thirty-five of these public schools in some of the poorest neighborhoods were administered by some of the best private schools and Andes University, the most prestigious higher-education institution in the country. We've seen extraordinary results academically but also reductions in school dropouts, teen pregnancies, and drug use.

Parents do all they can to get their children enrolled in schools administered through this plan. Those whose children are enrolled in these schools defend them so unanimously and enthusiastically that left-wing mayors who have followed me, after years of vociferous opposition to private operators, have renewed their contracts. But unions and populist politicians have ensured that many low-income citizens, whose children do not attend these schools, reject me and the program.

In Medellín, Colombia, cable cars were built to move people from low-income neighborhoods on the mountainsides to the Metro. The magic of these devices that seem to fly over the city sends a message that low-income citizens are important to society. In Bogotá we followed Medellín's example and built a cable car to a low-income neighborhood up in the mountains of Ciudad Bolívar locality.[13] The entire route goes above neighborhoods of informal origin. Complementary to the cable car, we built infrastructure to enhance the project's impact, boost sector self-esteem, and attract visitors. We built a large center for citizens' services at one of the stations, where residents can pay their electricity, water, or gas bills; apply to school for their children; or open a bank account. As more and more of these activities happen online, we designed the building so that it can easily be transformed into a cultural or activity center for the elderly. At other stations, we built kindergartens, parks, and centers for senior citizens. Working with the community, we painted thousands of house façades and even roofs in lively colors.

We purchased more than a hundred houses located on the edge of a cliff, many of them precariously situated, and built a pedestrian walkway from the cable-car terminal to a new park, all with breathtaking views of the city. In the park we erected a fifty-meter-high Colombian flag and a statue of Símon Bolívar, the leader of Colombia's independence. Although this sector carries his name, it had no monument to Bolívar. All of this we did for the enjoyment of the local population and to generate a sense of belonging and self-esteem. That the cable car and its surroundings have also become tourist attractions generates pride and instills confidence in the people who live there that they have the capacity to succeed.

During my first term as mayor, we built Tunal Park, which presides over sixty-two hectares and has a beautiful library. It sits across from Avenida Boyacá, the large road that passes by the station at the start of the cable-car line and is connected to it by a pedestrian bridge. The cable-car terminal station is on the same plot where we had built a TransMilenio terminal, which makes it easy to transfer from one system to the other. During my second term as mayor and concomitant with the cable-car construction, our great manager of the city's recreation and sport agency IDRD, Orlando Molano, built one of five "Happiness Centers" in Tunal Park. It includes an Olympic swimming pool, gym, auditorium, theater, music rooms, dance rooms, ceramics workshops, and more. We also improved the park with synthetic turf soccer fields with lighting, a BMX track, and a large children's playground.

Today, residents of one of the lowest-income neighborhoods in the city, perched high in the Ciudad Bolívar mountains, can take the cable car down to the TransMilenio station, from which they can transfer to a TransMilenio

BRT (a bus operating on bus-only lanes) and go anywhere in the city without paying extra. Or families can take the cable car down to the terminal station and cross the pedestrian bridge to reach the park, where their daughter can practice swimming in the Olympic pool while their son reads at the large library or plays soccer in a top-quality field.

When government and its police effectively repress informal settlements, the only alternative for the poor is to crowd into tenements. Entire families cram into a single rented room, packed into a space where they can hardly breathe and have no privacy. Of course, the tolerance and improvement of illegal neighborhoods is no guarantee that the problems of tenement living will be resolved. But without informal settlements, the problems worsen, with poor people living in rented rooms at a daily rate. This is what happened in the tenements of Manhattan's Lower East Side at the beginning of the twentieth century, where families of between three and fourteen members occupied very small apartments, without water or sewerage. For many, such spaces were not only home but also their places of work.[14]

The problem is systemic: it doesn't matter who runs the government when land around fast-growing, developing cities belongs to private owners. Informal settlements will persist as the solution to housing for many poor citizens so long as the land needed is managed to make a profit and not to solve housing needs and make quality cities.

State intervention is essential to solve the problem, through the offer of land, housing, subsidies, and financial arrangements as needed in legal, well-located neighborhoods with proper public spaces at a similar price as land and housing in illegal ones.

In cases where neither citizens nor governments have the money to pay for finished housing, governments can do the same as illegal developers: they can sell land on credit, with no public services. If there is one thing that illegal development proves, it's that once people are able to get a patch of land, they will build their homes. It may take them years to finish them, but they do it. Governments can do better than illegal developers, however: they can provide well-located land with good public spaces. This is what many governments in Africa could do today and in the coming decades, if they are able to prevent a few speculative owners from enriching themselves through the unmerited appropriation of the enhanced value of land around cities.

Another option is to offer housing in various stages of completion. During my first term as mayor, we created the public enterprise Metrovivienda, which purchased large tracts on the edge of the city, through either voluntary sale or eminent domain. Metrovivienda applied sound urban design principles and constructed the basic infrastructure and then sold large blocks of land at low cost to private developers so that they could build housing at regulated prices and within a predetermined time frame. Some of these private developers built basic one- or two-story houses, to which owners could subsequently add other stories.[15] While Metrovivienda sold land for housing at a low cost, it sold land destined for commercial use at market prices, which to some extent subsidized the housing.

This land-bank approach meant that we not only controlled the prices of the land acquired but also de facto the prices for all private land around the city. Private landowners cannot sell at a price higher than that offered by a public entity such as Metrovivienda. The competition that Metrovivienda represented also forced private developers to make high-quality urbanism part of their projects. Finally, the existence of the public land bank discouraged land speculation and promoted the development of private estates because owners realized there would be no land scarcity to support significant price increases.

When we established the Metrovivenda Recreo project on the southwestern edge of Bogotá, it was an oasis of orderly urban development flanked by a mass of illegal developments with narrow, unpaved, and recurrently flooded roads. Metrovivienda's example and competition, as well as the pumping station that resolved the area's flooding problem, stimulated numerous similar good-quality developments from the private sector.

If a land bank is to achieve its objectives, it must have the largest possible amount of land and purchase yet more as it develops what it has. In Sweden and Finland since 1904, local governments have become the owners of most of the land around the cities. As they sold plots to be developed, they bought more land. In this way they ensured that cities grew in technically desirable areas and with designs guided by the public good rather than private profit. Both countries ended up with large green areas around the cities, and they still structure their urbanization this way.

European governments commonly acquire land for expansion and then create detailed urban plans for it. L. C. Borup, the mayor for finance of Copenhagen from 1893 to 1903, decided to buy land in nearby municipalities to organize the city's future growth. He took out loans to do this. Any government that goes into debt to acquire land around an expanding city will pay an interest rate that is invariably lower than the rate of increase in land prices.

Today, Copenhagen has large parks and is better than it would have been thanks to the vision of its turn-of-the-century mayor.[16]

Cities in the developing world whose populations multiplied severalfold in the second half of the twentieth century, as was true in most of Latin America, would be much better had the state acquired the land around them in 1950. They could have grown in the best areas and could have had generous spaces for main roads, parks, schools, and other public infrastructure. Cities that are growing rampantly today could turn out much better if states acquire all or a significant part of the land needed for that growth.

The land purchase required for the optimal growth of any country's cities would have only a nominal impact on that country's finances. The land that most major developing cities need for future growth could be bought for the equivalent of a thirty-kilometer underground metro line. It is difficult to imagine a more socially and economically cost-effective investment, with benefits today and hundreds of years into the future. Unfortunately, governments are not prone to make investments whose benefits will only be visible several decades later. Also unfortunately, neither the World Bank nor the other development banks have made loans for the purchase of land for urban development or parks, and even less for the creation of land banks for future urban development.

There is no worthwhile excuse not to act since these decisions will affect millions of people's habitats for many generations. However land is financed or acquired—whether through expropriation, bonds, or other means—we cannot condemn millions of people for hundreds of years to live less happily than they would with wiser public land management. Private property is only justified when it contributes to the management of society's resources in a way that favors the public good. If, on the contrary, it becomes an obstacle to the public good, then society may choose other and exceptional ways of managing a resource, including the land surrounding growing cities. Expeditious expropriation at fair prices is not communism: it's simply democracy at work.

Keeping private property idle, or with a few grazing cows on it, while thousands of families live in overcrowded tenements or badly located informal neighborhoods is evidence of insufficient democracy. UN-Habitat states that a "ratio of 50 percent of public space is common in successful cities. Manhattan, Barcelona and Brussels have up to 35 percent of city area allocated to street space and an additional 15 percent for other public uses."[17] In much of the developing world the percentage of public space is only around 10 percent.

Shlomo Angel, in his book *Planet of Cities,* proposes that the state should acquire if not all of the land needed for urban expansion, then at least all that is necessary for a major road network and large parks.[18] Better to buy more than might be needed rather than less. But more ambitious schemes are possible, short of acquiring all land for urban expansion. For example, a ring of land 300 meters wide all around the city could be bought, anticipating urban expansion. A large boulevard with several lanes could be built in this belt, using, for example, 60 meters for motor-vehicles including a BRT. The other 240 meters could be turned into a formidable park of tens of kilometers with wide sidewalks, bikeways, sports facilities, trees, and green open spaces. In time, of course, often in a short time, the city will grow beyond this green belt, which will become a marvelous park traversing the city for many kilometers.

On what land cities grow is not a matter solely of local interest. It's intimately related to an entire nation's competitiveness, its quality of life, and its civilization. A city administration usually has neither the funds nor the legal capacity to intervene in nearby municipalities to make purchases. This is a task for national or regional authorities and eventually in alliance with the government of the central city.

The Charm—and Misery—of Informal Neighborhoods

A council of distinguished architects dictated that in Bogotá some large houses constructed by local notables imitating historical European styles are culturally valuable and can't be demolished. They concluded the same about many buildings recently designed by local architects. Personally, I think that our informal-origin neighborhoods are more interesting. They were built by their original residents, with the help of very local master-builders and without the intervention of urban experts or architects. Unlike the uniform blocks produced by large construction companies, generally lacking character or identity and often even lacking ground-floor shops, every building and space in self-constructed neighborhoods has something of interest.

To begin with, a home built brick by brick by a family with their bare hands has an identity and reflects a pride that no industrial housing unit could ever match. And even if its original builders or their descendants no longer live there, it retains its peculiar features and singular charm. On the roof, three or four stories up, these houses might have a terrace where residents grow flowers or aromatic herbs; they might have a clothesline and a space for a barbecue on a sunny Saturday afternoon. There may be an opening in the roof-terrace wall so that the dog can stick his head out and scan the street. From an open window a resident may gossip with a neighbor, who lives only a few meters away, across the narrow street—not as narrow as those in medieval cities, which were wide enough only for a pair of horses to pass, but in the same spirit. The ground floor is probably occupied by a shop of some kind, especially if the house is on a street that has become a neighborhood main street.

As there is little traffic in streets, children play there and adults chat or fix a motorcycle. Unlike in large apartment blocks, neighbors know each other, and many of them take part in community organizations for the improvement of the neighborhood and its security or in sports or cultural activities. If the neighborhood is located on a steep mountainside, its residents enjoy exceptional views of the city. The steps and small squares cut into the slope give these neighborhoods character and build community. With colorful paint, plants, and some architecture in their small public spaces, these popular neighborhoods have charm.

Over time, many of these informal neighborhoods will become especially attractive, initially for young people and artists and later for owners of restaurants, galleries, and bars. This has already started to happen. Neighborhoods that started as informal and marginal are now fashionable in the hills around Seoul and in Valparaiso, Chile. Gentrification is taking place in some of Rio de Janeiro's former "favelas." On the other hand, many informal settlements in Asia and Africa are too precarious and almost completely lacking in public spaces, so the only solution may be demolition and the relocation of their residents, preferably to new buildings in the same area.

Everywhere, but especially in Asia, poor and informal neighborhoods are also hubs for a wide range of productive endeavors, from recycling-related activities to more elaborate processes such as garment-making or ceramics. Most of the members of the more than sixty thousand residents of the legendary slum in the middle of Mumbai work there. The informal neighborhoods of Karachi, such as the large Orangi Town, produce saris and sandals. Child labor is always deplorable, but the young girls who peel tiny shrimp at Machar Colony in Karachi make a real contribution to their families' survival. Both because residents of such poor and informal neighborhoods have a strong sense of identity with their neighborhoods and buildings and because of opportunities for work at their locations, one thing is clear: they have no interest in living anywhere else.

Dharavi's excellent location adjacent to Mumbai's prime commercial district—between Matunga and Mahim stations on the Western Railway and the Sion station on the Central Railway, as well as some major roads and an upcoming metro line—have made it attractive to construction entrepreneurs and the government. Government programs, in partnership with private interests, have tried to relocate its residents to multistory buildings nearby to free the land they currently occupy for redevelopment. But so far, programs have not been successful. The new buildings have not taken into account these residents' cultural idiosyncrasies or the productive activities they perform there, so most residents have rejected them. "Our *'anskruti'* [culture] does not fit into the high-rise apartment system," said one old man sadly, looking at the apartment tower blocks.[19]

In Latin America, homes in illegal neighborhoods, although initially small, end up being more spacious than the alternatives offered by private developers or state housing programs. Regardless of whether its origin is formal or informal, low-income citizens' housing in buildings of fewer than six stories tends to function better than housing in taller buildings.

In Manila there are hundreds, maybe thousands, of kilometers of pedestrian alleys and byways in low-income neighborhoods of charming houses with terraces, plants, and shops. Neighbors know and help each other. In other parts of the city, sometimes near informal neighborhoods, developers are building tower blocks of dozens of stories, tiny apartments, and very narrow sidewalks, and neighbors barely know each other. In their spare time, they seek to escape from the city, fleeing to gigantic shopping centers. Who can lead the better life?

With some investment, Manila's popular neighborhoods could be made wonderful: hundreds or even thousands of houses could be acquired for demolition in order to open up tree-lined arterial roads several kilometers long exclusively for buses, with wide sidewalks and bikeways. Since many of these neighborhoods are clustered along riverbanks, demolitions could also clear the way for waterfront promenades. Additional demolition could make room for parks, sports facilities, schools, kindergartens, and cultural centers. As I walked through Manila's fascinating informal neighborhoods, I imagined that they could become one of the most charming and attractive sectors of the city, both to live in and to visit.

Cape Town has one of the most beautiful urban locations in the world. Compared to other cities, the amount of precarious housing in informal neighborhoods is relatively small, but those neighborhoods create disproportionately large problems for the rest of the city. For example, crime of all kinds—drug trafficking, gangs, and murders—is concentrated in Cape Flats. For many years, governments promised informal developments such as Khayelitsha, Hargeisa, and Cape Flats that they would relocate their residents to free housing elsewhere, and these promises discouraged people from improving their homes or neighborhoods or weaving a social fabric. Had the government concentrated from the beginning on the improvement and legalization of these settlements, many of the problems they face today would probably have been avoided or would at least have been mitigated.

Thus far I've described the case of initially informal developments that have been legalized and, over the years, provided with infrastructure and improved, as is the case in most of Latin America. But the reality for most residents of informal developments, especially in Asia and Africa and still for some in Latin America, is misery. Hundreds of millions of families live in subhuman informal settlements, crammed into precarious leaky housing, without piped water, sewerage, or, in many cases, electricity. One-third of sub-Saharan Africans in cities and towns do not have electricity.[20] The vast majority of the people who live in these neighborhoods do not have access to public transport, schools, kindergartens, or health centers, to say nothing of parks or cultural or sports facilities. Many do not even have dry land under their feet: their houses sit on stilts driven into the mud in shallow, stinking swamps, as is true in Makoko, in Lagos, where more than a hundred thousand people live in abject conditions.

While in some parts of the world people talk about technological innovations such as artificial intelligence or space exploration, hundreds of millions of human beings elsewhere struggle to survive in slums that grow relentlessly around developing world cities. In Latin America it is a phenomenon largely confined to the poorest countries; in Asia this grim phenomenon has been declining; but in Africa it's exploding. Almost half of the urban population of Africa today lives in informal settlements, and their population increases by 4.5 million annually. For example, two-thirds of the twenty million inhabitants of Lagos now live in informal settlements, and the city's population continues to grow at rates that lead experts to forecast that it will be the most populous city on Earth in a few decades.[21]

There is only one reason the poor crowd into inhuman informal settlements: lack of access to a well-located plot of land. Governments do not have the funds to provide them computers, air conditioning, or metros. But how land around cities is managed is largely a political decision. And clearly private ownership of such land has not produced good results in any growing developing city.

Perween Rahman, trained as an architect, worked for more than thirty years with communities in the slums of Karachi, mainly in the huge informal development of Orangi. She had obtained international support to draw up the neighborhood's plans, move forward with their legalization, and define its public service networks. But in the process of helping the poor of Karachi organize and legalize their occupation of the land and to design and install water supplies and sewerage, she came up against the parapolitical mafias that have traditionally organized the appropriation of the land surrounding the city as a way to make money and win political support.

Rahman, fifty-six, was killed on March 13, 2013, for her fight to defend a plot of land for a park.[22] Writer and journalist Steve Inskeep, author of *Instant City: Life and Death in Karachi*, had written only four years earlier about community leader Nissar Baloch, who was also assassinated for challenging the gangs of parapolitical developers. If the Pakistani state had planned and organized the orderly growth of Karachi, it would have solved its citizens' housing needs with dignity and would have created a better city. It would also have prevented the parapolitical corruption associated with illegal urbanization and the assassinations of Rahman and Baloch.[23]

At the end of the twentieth century, there were serious conflicts in two otherwise-unrelated Colombian cities, Apartadó and Arauca. In both cases there were murders in connection with the squatting on land for informal settlements. In both cases, too, the suburban land occupied had had no monetary value thirty years earlier: Apartadó was surrounded by thousands of hectares of jungle and Arauca by thousands of hectares of flatlands in the Orinoco basin, useless for farming and all but uninhabited. What happened? Apartadó found unprecedented success in growing bananas for export, and Arauca made a giant oil strike. Subsequently, they became boom towns, and the land surrounding them became a valuable speculative good. The Colombian government should have acquired tracts of land in optimal locations to accommodate the urban growth that was likely to happen in these two locations. But it did nothing. And a few years later, conflicts erupted over land— land that had only recently been worthless and was now urban!

It is astounding to watch this mistake get repeated again and again. Obviously, when a large mining, oil, industrial, or agricultural project begins in a relatively unpopulated rural area, it will spawn a new town; and if a small city exists there beforehand, it will mushroom in size. Any forward-looking government or, indeed, any company developing its own project should acquire the land to secure a properly organized and well-planned settlement with quality of life even after the oilfield or the mine is depleted.

Unfortunately, this rarely happens, and the urban growth and prosperity resulting from economic bonanzas of one sort or another usually do not bring quality of life and social harmony but rather the opposite. Often companies who own the mining, industrial, or other projects build a fenced-in enclave for their workers, antiseptically isolated from their surroundings, and ignore the urban development outside of their project. All too often companies pay dearly for such neglect, as social conflict and even violence ensue. Even in the best of cases, a wonderful opportunity to have created a beautiful and lasting urban environment is missed.

Expensive Land not Only Spurs Informal Settlements, but also Often Leads to Poor Location for the Growth of the Formal City

Traditionally, governments grant subsidies for housing construction or acquisition, but they do not intervene in the land market. This has a perverse effect: the increase in purchasing power brought about by the subsidy leads to an increase in the price of land. Thus, a significant part of the subsidy goes to the landowner, not the homebuyer.

Private ownership of land and the inability of the state to drive development hurts middle-class citizens as well as those who turn to illegal developers and deforms the structure of the city. Even without illegality, the market pushes development to where land costs least, which is often precisely the worst places for the city to grow, mainly because they are farthest from employment centers and places of study or recreation.

Toward the end of the twentieth century, Mexico seemed to be making rapid progress toward solving housing deficits that had been created by decades of population growth, migration to cities, and smaller households. It had at its disposal the powerful INFONAVIT, a megafund for social security and pensions, which channeled huge amounts of money into housing. Additional funds were provided by Mexican banks and international investors who lent money to and invested in large housing development corporations. These corporations made it possible to produce housing on an industrial scale, at great speed and at very low cost. Everything had been solved and was under control—everything, that is, except land.

As the funds provided by INFONAVIT to home purchasers had limits and the value of well-located land increased as a result of increased demand, developers began to buy large tracts far from urban centers where it cost less. Immediately, they realized that the most profitable part of their business was not the building of houses but the speculating in land—the increase in value of rural land that they bought and turned into urban land. Among the most valued and highest-paid executives of the housing construction companies were those responsible for "relations" with local governments that issued building licenses and facilitated access to utilities, making it possible to develop land far from the urban limits.

Poorer people and even some in the middle class who wanted homes of their own might have felt that projects where housing was for sale were too far away. But they also felt that they had to make use of the money that INFONAVIT and the banks were providing them in order to become homeowners. They also calculated, based on experience, that their homes would increase in value.

The result was not good. The structure of cities was distorted. No low-cost, high-frequency public transport could serve those distant developments. Riding a bike to the city was of course unthinkable. And as many residents did not have cars, they simply could not occupy their new homes. In many of these projects, almost one in five homes was still empty several years after completion.

Other factors, aside from distance, impeded the integration of these developments into the cities. Invariably, these were walled housing developments. They did not contribute public parks, only private green zones within the walls of each neighborhood. The model was based on low density. When residents needed to buy something, they had to drive. Mexico has some of the most attractive urban centers and traditional towns in the Americas, where people enjoy beautiful, busy public spaces. Unfortunately, housing project developers who galloped toward INFONAVIT funding at the end of the twentieth century were not inspired by the Mexican models.

The Mexican government became aware of the massive problem these developments were creating, although somewhat late. In 2011, the Social

Development Ministry of Mexico published a study called *The Expansion of Cities 1980–2010*.[24] It compares Mexican cities' population growth with the urban expansion of these cities. On average, while the population doubles, the area occupied becomes six or seven times larger. In vast Mexico City, the population grew 1.42 times, and the city's area 3.57 times. In Monterrey, the population increased 1.98 times and its area 4.95 times. In Puebla-Tlaxcala, the population grew 2.4 times and its area 12.4 times.

Something similar happened in Bogotá, although on a smaller scale and for different reasons. People in governments simply imposed restrictions on urban expansion,—which increased the price of land and forced hundreds of thousands of families to surrounding municipalities to find homes they could afford. Ironically, the putatively "left" and "environmentalist" governments that restricted building in Bogotá, thus expelled lower-income citizens from the city, requiring them to make longer and more expensive trips and have higher energy consumption. A larger amount of rural land per home was occupied than would have been the case if those homes had been built in Bogotá. Between 2005 and 2018, *fifteen times* more land per new housing unit was used in those municipalities than in Bogotá.[25]

Public Ownership of Land: Convenient but not Sufficient

If the principal cause of deficient urban development in the developing world is the private ownership of land and the state's incapacity to buy it or effectively regulate its development, one might assume that countries in which land belongs to the state would have ideal cities. In some aspects, they have achieved wonderful things, such as abundant parks and green spaces, as there are in Moscow. In eastern Berlin, urbanism is of such high quality that it managed to overcome a rather boring architecture. But other less positive examples illustrate that public ownership of land or instruments that give the state effective control of urban development are necessary but insufficient by themselves.

In the absence of adequate sources of income, for many years the main source of income for Chinese municipalities was the sale of land to developers. This not only led to often inadequate planning, but to corruption as well. Public ownership of land can be a powerful means for cities to grow in the right place and in the right way, but evidently it is not sufficient.

Great fortunes are made in the developing world from the increased value of land around cities as it changes from rural to urban. Not so in northern Europe, where prices of rural land acquired by the state for urban development are those of rural land in the region. No one there has expectations of increased values due to eventual development since that depends entirely on a state decision. Sometimes these countries' urban development takes place on privately owned land, but even then, urban design, down to the smallest detail, is the responsibility of state agencies, and any profit generated by the change of use is taxed.

Many European cities buy land for their growth and expansion and draw up detailed plans for its development. In the Netherlands, for example, municipal governments always have the first option to buy private land for future developments.[26] Subsequently, they sell it to private developers who are required to develop them based on government parameters. Occasionally, the public sector takes direct charge of urban design, leaving the private sector only with the design, financing, and construction of buildings. For many years now, cities in northern Europe, such as Amsterdam, Helsinki, and Stockholm, have held large tracts of public land around their urban areas.

Lagos de Torca: A Different Way of Making a City in Bogotá

During my first tenure as mayor, which ended in December 2000, we built about five kilometers, or three miles, of the Avenue Boyacá, a six-lane artery across hundreds of hectares of uncultivated farmland whose owners only awaited the necessary infrastructure to urbanize it. It was clear that the new road would immediately spur development around it. The city plan, which had been approved by the City Council, required that 25 percent of the land of new developments should be preserved for parks. As there were large holdings of fifty or even a hundred hectares, development of those lands should have generated many parks of more than ten hectares. Unfortunately, urban development around the Avenida Boyacá turned out poorly. The owners of large properties found ways of avoiding ceding the lands for parks of any significance. They split up their land into several plots and often left no public parks at all but only some small green areas inside gated developments. Sometimes they didn't even leave any green inside, only surface parking. Instead of shops at ground level, they built shopping areas designed to be reached mainly by car and a large shopping center as well.

What could have become a wonderful part of the city did not. Further, virgin land was developed to provide housing for high-income citizens, and private developers didn't even pay for most of the basic infrastructure, such as the major roads and main pipes for water supplies and sewerage. This sad outcome reinforced my conviction that to make a good city, we should be doing projects rather than issuing regulations, since private developers are specialists in bending the latter to their convenience. I believe City Hall should engage in large-scale projects in which it will have control over all urban design and some parameters of the buildings. What we had done in Metrovivienda for lower-income citizens, where we acquired the land through a city corporation we created, had much better urban design than that around Avenue Boyacá and therefore was much more pleasant to live in.

One of my main goals when I returned years later as mayor was to organize the city's growth in a different and better way. Bogotá no longer had much land to grow in. There were some 5,600 hectares to the north. Although tens of thousands of hectares in the municipalities beyond had already been developed—and badly—in Bogotá there remained those 5,600 hectares, still mostly given over to pasture and crops.

I made it clear that we were going to require owners of a large block of land north of the city to contribute their land as equity to a development corporation of which they would then be shareholders; that the urban design, down to the smallest detail, would be done by City Hall; and that landowners and developers would bear the cost of infrastructure. However, it was our wonderful planning secretary, Andrés Ortiz, and the brilliant young Juan Camilo Gonzalez, a recent Stanford graduate, who really achieved the creative financial scheme and urban design of unprecedented quality in Colombia. Fortunately, the previous mayor had blocked development of the land where the project was located. This made landowners and private developers receptive since now they would be able to develop the land, despite the fact that the project made previously unheard-of demands on them, and thus we worked constructively together as a team.

We structured an 1,800-hectare project that we called Lagos de Torca. The project would be private, but we were not about to allow owners to do as they wished with their plot. We made a detailed development design, which included dozens of kilometers of greenways, a large central park and abundant local ones, twelve-meter-wide sidewalks along the main roads, and bikeways on all roads. We then invited all landowners to put their land in a trust. Regardless of its location, all the land was appraised at the same value because without a project nothing could be built on the properties. Therefore, the value of each property was initially very similar.

Development rights had to be obtained for building, and those rights had to be purchased from the trust. The trust administered them, but those construction rights were generated by City Hall for the project, just as it authorized building anywhere in the city. In a way, those rights to build were City Hall's contribution to the project. These rights could be bought by anyone, not only by the landowners. They were an investment, and there was a market for them. The owner of the land could buy those development rights from the trust or from a third party who had bought them.

The trust paid for the land required for public infrastructure with buildability rights, and with proceeds from the sale of the remaining rights, it constructed the infrastructure, including water and sewerage networks, roads, and so on. The city was prepared to use eminent domain to acquire land from those who neither wished to contribute their property to the project nor sell it to the trust.

The city divided the land into large blocks, defining how the more than one thousand properties should be grouped. The owners within each block started construction at approximately the same time so that road networks and other infrastructure could connect them and the block to the rest of the city. If an owner had not built simultaneously with others in his sector, then the city could have forcibly taken over the property and put it up for public auction.

In the past, owners whose land was required to build a road, for example, had to sell at a low price. Conversely, those fortunate enough to have land alongside the built road made a large profit from its increased value. In Lagos de Torca, however, nobody is adversely affected. Those whose land is required for public uses such as roads or parks are paid by the trust with development rights. Effectively, that means they become shareholders in the buildings. They earn no less than those on whose land the buildings are erected.

Before Lagos de Torca, the city had borne a large portion of public infrastructure costs for new developments. In this case those who erect buildings pay for that infrastructure through the purchase of buildability rights.

City Hall also required that at least half the housing would have a controlled price and would be reserved for low-income buyers in this traditionally high-income area. Some of the walled-in, high-income communities in the neighborhood naturally found it undesirable to have lower income neighbors and tried to sabotage the project in several ways, including through legal injunctions.

The Lagos de Torca project was completely self-sufficient, despite the high cost of the land, the generous public land cessions, and the stipulated high-quality infrastructure. This was possible because half the homes were for middle- and high-income earners. On less expensive land, or with government subsidies, similar projects can be implemented, with homes exclusively for lower-income groups. The Lagos de Torca project is a way for a city to grow where and how it should.

Aside from Lagos de Torca, we proposed similar projects for the remaining 3,700 hectares of Bogotá's north. With them, in addition to Lagos de Torca, we would have managed to consolidate 5,600 hectares, with more than one million inhabitants and a large park with a total area of 1,450 hectares.[27] South of the city we structured a similar project of 415 hectares with a 130-hectare park, plus other smaller green areas, called Reverdecer del Sur.[28] For this one we were able to get the central government to contribute 100 hectares of an army battalion's land, and I even had to meet with the Catholic cardinal to get the church to contribute a large plot they owned to the project (including the Artillery School barracks).

*   *   *

Land—and how it is owned, used, and distributed—is at the very heart of city planning. The failure to plan realistically for the growth of a city and to do projects such as Lagos de Torca simply means that a city will grow where it should not and in ways that it should not. In Africa the issue is particularly critical. Over the coming decades, hundreds of millions will cram into poorly located slums with inhuman conditions, which will make life much less happy and less civilized centuries into the future. It is crucial that governments radically intervene in the use of land surrounding growing cities if this is to be avoided.

CHAPTER 3

Urban Demolition and Redevelopment

Buildings do not last thousands of years, and those constructed in poor societies deteriorate even faster. Almost all buildings will be demolished sooner or later to build better, more comfortable, better climate-adapted, or taller ones. The renewal question is not *whether* but *when* and *how*. For example, should renewal happen building by building, or in large blocks of many buildings, which generally works better?

In Bogotá tens of thousands of single-family houses have been demolished and replaced by apartment buildings eight or more stories high. As we'd expect, the new buildings are of a higher quality than the houses they replaced. However, this building-by-building renewal process increases inhabitants per hectare without generating any increase in public spaces such as roads, sidewalks, plazas, and parks.

As of 2023 Moscow's mayor Sergey Sobyanin is carrying out a massive urban redevelopment process that will result in the relocation of one million Muscovites. Buildings put up in the 1960s and 1970s Soviet era, when society was poorer, are being demolished. Residents are being given apartments in new, better, much taller buildings in new developments. Predictably, some sectors have opposed the project. Despite low-quality indoor and outdoor common areas, such as playgrounds and nonexistent community rooms, Moscow's approach is better than what happened in Bogotá because the city generates more and better public space. And it is better than what happens in the United States, where much urban growth takes place in ever fartherflung, car-dependent suburbs. In contrast the new buildings in Moscow are centrally located near where old ones were demolished as well as near mass-transit stations.

We have cities that have existed for millennia, even if few of their buildings are a thousand years old, and today's cities will probably still exist several thousand years hence. Few buildings deserve to be preserved by decree for millennia. When we contemplate a declaration to preserve a building or neighborhood by government mandate, we should bear in mind that it's a decision that implies preserving it not for thirty or three hundred years but for three thousand. Buildings are not made for eternity, even if we should build them as if they are. A few should be preserved for artistic, cultural, or historical reasons, but most are destined to be altered or replaced.

Many city sectors are reconstructed to make better buildings, increase density, or change uses. Some sectors are completely rebuilt in a couple of decades. One- or two-story houses are often demolished to make way for higher buildings. Almost all tall buildings in cities around the world are built where houses or smaller buildings once stood.

With the passage of time, societies become wealthier, and their citizens want better housing and better public spaces than what they had when the country was poorer. Sometimes, "better housing" means more space; sometimes, better protection against heat or cold; at other times, proximity to green spaces or sports facilities or being closer to or farther from shops. Occasionally a building's owners wish to change its use.

Committees of architects with infinite powers and, I hope, comparable wisdom decide which buildings to preserve forever. In some cases, a social consensus informs their decisions. In other cases, not so much: they decide to preserve buildings designed by a professor they particularly appreciated or a friend's father, or because the local "cultural" elite thinks that a building ought to be preserved because one of its members had something to do with it. Art historians would be surprised to know that in Bogotá there are more than five thousand buildings that must be preserved for eternity.[1]

A Cemetery or a Park?

For years I would have lunch with my father in a restaurant located on the top floor of the Seguros Tequendama building in Bogotá, one of the tallest in the city's center at the time. As far as the eye could see, the land was covered in buildings. Not a single park could be seen, only two undeveloped green plots. To me it seemed obvious that those plots should be turned into parks. I was already dreaming of being mayor at this time, and I was anguished by the thought that they might erect buildings there before I could turn them into parks.

The two plots were located in the central neighborhood of Mártires where drug sales and use are problems, parks are scarce, and sports fields are almost nonexistent. When I came into office, I inquired about those two properties and found that one belonged to the Ministry of Communications and the other, which belonged to City Hall, was a short-term cemetery for unidentified and unclaimed corpses. In theory, after corpses had been buried for a year or two, their remains were exhumed and incinerated. In practice, they were left there for many years.

In the first phase of this project, we managed to buy the property from the ministry and make a park there. We even installed a major sculpture by the internationally renowned Colombian artist Fernando Botero at the entrance because until then there was no work of his in any public space in Bogotá.[2]

Though the plot belonged to the city, it took longer to turn the cemetery into a park. Hundreds of remains had to be inhumed, but we did manage to close the cemetery. As my term as mayor neared its end, I wanted to leave with the park project under way. We built broad sidewalks and exchanged the high wall around it for an ornamented iron railing. And, unfortunately, that ornamented railing turned out to be the park's undoing. Up until this time almost no one knew of the existence of this plot of land or that it belonged to the city. But when we changed the wall along the airport road, one of Bogotá's main arteries, for a mostly transparent wrought-iron fence, politicians and artists with large egos discovered that piece of land.

In Colombia, a mayor can't be reelected for a term immediately following their last. When I was able to run again, I lost twice. When I was finally reelected, I found that part of the land I had recovered for a park had been used to install a building in remembrance of victims of violence. Unfortunately, many politicians seem to think it's most expeditious to erect public buildings in parks.

I also found that the previous mayor had contracted an important artist to make eight silkscreen prints alluding to violence, which were reproduced on hundreds of acrylic panels and then placed on the covers of the niches of the columbarium. It was to be a temporary exhibit for a year, but as things turned out, the artist and the Bogotá artistic elite decided that these drawings, and the columbarium structures built seventy years earlier, should be classified for conservation and maintained until the end of time. Naturally,

Global South artists are well received in the galleries and cocktail parties of Europe's artistic world when they refer in their work to the tragedies of violence in their countries. And Paris would perceive acrylic panels alluding to violence in Colombia as something rather chic.

The National Heritage Council—which had no citizen representation from the sector of Mártires and hadn't consulted with anyone from the sector—could care less that tens of thousands of low-income children and youth would be left without a park, playground, or sporting facilities. The council declared that those seventy-year-old columbarium structures, which occupy about half of the park, were cultural heritage and should be conserved for eternity. And the rest of the land should not be profaned by sporting facilities or children's playgrounds because some bones had been found there. Neither the members of the council nor the artist who produced the work—nor their friends at cocktail parties and private art previewsknow anyone in Mártires. They've never even been there. So the leisure time of children in that neighborhood, or the risk that they might be vulnerable to drug addiction in the absence of recreation and sports facilities, is of no concern to them.

The classist elites in societies are not only those privileged by money.

Cities in developing countries are not the only ones that will grow over the next few decades. Many cities in the United States, Canada, and Australia will grow enormously. Ideally, new housing should be built close to their urban centers, where employment, recreation, and mass-transit networks are concentrated. But there is no empty land around the centers; there are tens of thousands of hectares of suburbs. The optimal location for urban growth is in suburbs closest to the central city. If this is to materialize, large tracts of suburbs will have to be demolished. The alternative is growth in increasingly distant new suburbs.

For example, New York City could grow in areas around the railway stations of the lines that run from Connecticut and the north of New York to Manhattan. Those who would live in homes located there would have train services to go to work, study, or find recreation in Manhattan. But these are very affluent and restricted areas today. Densification is prohibited around the stations and in New York, as in many other cities; residents in thousands of suburbs of individual homes located close to urban centers and public transport have succeeded in passing regulations to prevent the construction of multifamily housing. Regulations prohibit not only multistory buildings but most often even the subdivision of existing homes into two or more units.

If regulations were to allow it, individual houses could be demolished and replaced by well-designed, six-story buildings, for example. It would be a way to form neighborhoods with charm and plenty of trees with broad sidewalks, bikeways, greenways, shops in walking distance, and lively public spaces. These places would satisfy the democratic principle of prevalence of the public good because millions would have access to better-located housing and shorter commutes.

Homes in those multistory buildings would be smaller than those built in distant suburbs and therefore would consume less energy for heating or air conditioning. Because residents would travel shorter distances to work or other destinations and have easy access to public transport, less energy would be consumed for transport. Less energy consumption for heating, air conditioning, and transport means less global warming.

Studies done at the University of California, Berkeley, found that the construction of housing through the redevelopment of suburbs close to centralities with jobs, services, and public transport is the most effective way of reducing greenhouse gases that generate global warming.[3] It also prevents the appropriation of farmlands for development and ameliorates traffic congestion.

From a democratic perspective, regulations that impede the demolition of individual houses to replace them with multistory buildings means that lower-income people are forced to live increasingly farther from work and waste ever more time commuting. Real estate agents in California use the expression "drive till they qualify"[4] to describe how lower-income prospective buyers must take a car and drive farther and farther away until they find a home within their budget.

California needs millions of additional housing units. Governor Gavin Newsom has said that the housing crisis is his priority and was able to get the State Senate to approve legislation in 2021 to make it possible to build two dwelling units on land where previously only one was allowed. Higher densities were permitted near public transport corridors such as bus and train lines.[5]

Other US cities are also taking steps to tackle the housing problem. Minneapolis has issued regulations that allow any house to be subdivided or demolished, with up to three residential units built in its place.[6] A recent regulation in Oregon for cities of more than 25,000 inhabitants allows for houses to be subdivided or demolished in order to put in their place up to four residential units.[7] It's a start.

Everywhere, most of those who live in suburbs close to urban centers would initially oppose their redevelopment. However, it's possible that the quality of projects, with abundant parks and exceptionally good pedestrian infrastructure, as well as the profit to be made by contributing their houses to redevelopment projects, might convince them otherwise. Moreover, they would receive beautiful new apartments. For those who oppose the scheme, there remains the possibility of expropriation. Turning the inner suburbs of American, Australian, or Canadian cities into denser urban environments is crucial for quality of life, equity, and sustainability and can significantly contribute to a reduction in global warming.

It is better to totally redevelop large tracts of suburbs and not simply to change zoning laws to allow multistory buildings and higher densities. Otherwise, densities will be higher, but there will be no more parks, wider sidewalks, extensive greenways, or roads to accommodate BRT, for example. A more ambitious redevelopment makes it possible not simply to increase densities but to create a different, better city.

Urban Renewal in Developing Cities

Cities in developing countries tend to be denser and to have fewer suburbs, but this isn't because they have been better planned. Neighborhoods in popular sectors were built with high densities because those who made them had neither money nor cars. And high-income neighborhoods became dense because cities had fewer roads and more traffic jams than those in advanced countries, and that made people want to live close to their jobs.

Such was the case in Bogotá. Traffic jams made it too painful to live far from the city center, and it was difficult to protect individual homes from thieves. Owners sought to enrich themselves by demolishing their houses and replacing them with high-rise buildings or selling them to others to do it. Unfortunately, this process took place on an ad hoc, house-by-house basis, not by blocks or larger areas and without any planning by city administration. Thus, although density multiplied several times, no parks were created or enlarged, and the process didn't even yield wider sidewalks.

Although it's too late in many parts of the city, there are now regulations and mechanisms for urban redevelopment, whether in old industrial premises or in residential neighborhoods, to generate more and better public space. Many places prohibit the demolition of one or two buildings to construct one high-rise building, and a prerequisite for redevelopment is that several build-ings in a relatively large area must be brought together to form a larger area to achieve a significant increase in pedestrian public space. As in other parts of the world, these regulations allow a majority of neighbors to proceed with a redevelopment project even if a minority opposes it. The system has worked successfully, for example, in Spanish cities.

There are a number of ways to guarantee the rights of owners and ten-ants. But redevelopment processes of this kind are always easy prey to popu-list political interests on the one end and vulnerable to powerful owners who might oppose them.

Bogotá has a decaying sector of some six hundred hectares, surrounded by three main roads—Calle 80, the NQS, and Avenida Caracas—all of which have TransMilenio, and Avenida Caracas will soon have the Metro as well. The sector, which was once residential, now hosts a disorderly commercial area, largely specializing in vehicle parts, that often spills onto the side-walks. Many people would like to live there because it's close to an area with high-value housing, the main financial center, many jobs, a wide variety of recreational activities, and the city's most central and largest park, the Simón Bolívar. Originally, neighborhoods in this decaying area were com-posed of single-family houses. Over time, some of them gained extra sto-ries, and others were replaced by mediocre three- or four-story buildings. Neighborhood parks are almost nonexistent.

We structured a program to redevelop this sector, generating pedestrian public space, making it possible for local inhabitants to remain there, and at-tracting new residents. The central focus of its life would be a linear park covering 10 hectares along 2.1 kilometers connecting the El Virrey park, which is the main park of higher-income groups, with the Simón Bolívar park, the city's central park. We called the project "Entreparques" (between parks) because it would connect the two.

The project would generate other improvements to pedestrian space, such as the widening of sidewalks and creation of several new, smaller parks. At the end of the operation, the sector would increase its park areas from 3.6 to 14.8 hectares. Adding the parks together with the wider sidewalks and the land for public facilities such as schools, the project would create a total of 25 hectares of new public space. The project would also create 34,000 homes where today there are only 2,800 occupied residences. The project plan pro-vides for the continued existence of around 5,000 commercial-use buildings in the sector.

The driving force for redevelopment of the sector is an important increase in the permitted height of buildings. But to access those greater heights, owners must make some payments to the city. The proceeds are used to acquire land for parks and to construct the infrastructure of pipes, roads, and other needs.

The project requires that new, taller buildings consolidate properties of at least eight hundred square meters. This of course means that several neighbors would have to agree on the project. The goal here is to avoid lot-by-lot redevelopment through the reconstruction of individual buildings, which does not generate any additional public space.

Unlike our other urban redevelopment projects, in which the city's urban renewal corporation (ERU) purchased the properties, Alameda Entreparques depended on decisions made by local residents. The city could expropriate owners who refused to participate in a project only when owners of more than 85 percent of a given renewal area had agreed to support it. Naturally, a project that depended so much on the initiative and will of the owners would take several decades to complete.

This project, like all our others, was attacked by ex officio political opposition. They alleged that some dark capitalists planned to take over the buildings in the sector and expel the residents. Although the process was voluntary and contingent on owners' initiatives, the populist caricature worked for an election campaign. We didn't manage to secure the project by law or start it, and my successor as mayor buried it.

And naturally, the easiest thing for many of those in government is to implement only uncontroversial projects or simply to do nothing. The reconstruction of parts of the city affects some who don't wish to contribute or sell their buildings. Frequently, then, even when projects comply with the democratic principle of benefiting present and future majorities, they will always be vulnerable to populist opposition. There are many plays and films that caricature the process, portraying those who lead redevelopment projects as evil capitalists and those who have to sell their buildings or move as victims of a heartless system.

There are almost limitless opportunities to remake parts of the city differently and better. This is especially true in cities of the developing world built when societies were very poor; when knowledge about the design of a good city was sparse; and when the state's technical, legal, and economic capacity to execute good urban planning was weak. Furthermore, these cities were built hurriedly to accommodate oceanic migration waves from rural areas. The Indian architect and wonderful human being Charles Correa once said, "We all live in ugly cities but love them." In developing cities the prime objective of urban renewal should be to generate more parks and, generally, more and better pedestrian space. This will be possible if there are laws that ensure the public good prevails and state institutions provide leadership and managerial capacity.

Expropriation, use of eminent domain, or whatever name is given to forcible purchases is nothing special in democracies with market economies. Curiously, there is almost no opposition to the acquisition of housing to make way for roads for cars, but when a project's purpose is to improve the city and the life of its inhabitants, it provokes populist attacks. It is of course desirable that projects should be implemented with the support of the largest possible number of owners and that it should be made easy for residents to stay in the sector.

Does urban redevelopment favor the public good? Will present and future majorities benefit from the project? Will people live better? Will there be better public spaces? Will there be more tourism and investment? If the answers are yes and society as a whole is going to be better off, then urban redevelopment projects must be implemented even if some feel that they are negatively affected, despite efforts to avoid that. Whether some private interests, either businesspeople or purchasers, benefit from the project should not be the decisive criterion of its worth or whether it should proceed. If the public good is to prevail, it makes no difference whether an expropriation's purpose is urban redevelopment or a new road.

In 2005 there was a major national debate in the United States in relation to a Supreme Court ruling that supported the expropriation of housing and other property for a redevelopment project in New London, Connecticut. A private developer would be in charge of the project, which was going to generate parks with a large waterfront as well as housing.[8] So even the country that epitomizes capitalism and private property not only uses expropriation, or purchases through eminent domain, but also uses it for urban redevelopment programs, even private ones. The *New York Times* editorial about the New London case recalled that the newspaper's own building had been made possible as a result of expropriation for a private project.

Redevelopment projects are so convenient to society that on many occasions governments will subsidize private enterprise to carry them out because otherwise they would not be viable. A subsidy used in the United States is tax increment financing (TIF), in which the government agrees to hand over part of the increase in property tax generated as a result of investments made over several years to those who make investments in the redevelopment of a deteriorated sector.

The voluntary or forcible acquisition of property by the state is also used to capture the surplus value generated by a public investment, such as occurs in areas surrounding the stations of a new mass-transport line. If property around stations is acquired as a location for housing or services, it not only makes it possible for society to benefit from the increased value of the area but also ensures that more people will benefit from the new mass-transport line. The state could appropriate the increased value generated by a public investment through taxation. This is not easy to do, however, because owners of neighboring properties generally do not have the capacity to pay those taxes. Another mechanism that we used in the case of our own Metro line is to charge for redevelopment licenses near stations.

Demolition for Revival: Bogotá Reborn

In the United States many prefer that government stand aside, letting redevelopment occur on a house-by-house basis. Or they prefer not to redevelop at all. Almost always, regulations prohibit several-story construction in residential zones with houses. Rarely do authorities exercise leadership to redevelop a sector. They do not even intervene in cases where sections of the center or areas close to it have completely collapsed and are semiabandoned.

This attitude is partly owing to the deeply influential urbanist Jane Jacobs, who became a legend with her book *The Death and Life of Great American Cities* and through her leadership in opposing the construction of major roads that would have destroyed an important part of southern Manhattan. She criticized the demolition of densely populated dynamic neighborhoods, with a wealth of relationships and traditions, and their replacement with badly designed projects and towers, surrounded by featureless and vacant green zones unrelated to the buildings. Jacobs was so lucid and potent in her criticism that authorities in the United States have since been afraid of undertaking redevelopment projects to improve or densify urban areas.

I visited Birmingham, Alabama, in 2012 and was surprised to find hundreds of hectares of well-located neighborhoods near the center, such as Titusville, which had seriously decayed, beset by uninhabited houses, closed schools, and an abandoned stadium. Not even when confronted with these disastrous circumstances had the state intervened to generate urban redevelopment. Beyond the blight was a (missed) opportunity: at a distance that can easily be covered by bike, one reaches the center of Birmingham where, for example, the University of Alabama's prestigious medical center is located. Instead, thousands of people make long commutes from distant suburbs to the center, when they could probably live in these more centrally located zones. True, any intervention risked affecting residents who remained in these decaying, semi-abandoned neighborhoods. Nevertheless, it seemed to me that the worst that could happen to them was to do nothing.

Deteriorated sectors often recover without state intervention. Where there is a location favorable to market trends, they attract new residents or investors who improve existing buildings or demolish them to erect more valuable ones. But sometimes the decay is too severe and tends to spread to nearby areas with its concomitant social problems and crime.

The demolition of a sector of a city is a delicate operation. Special care needs to be taken to protect residents, and there is always the risk of mistakes. The only way to avoid mistakes is to do nothing, and politicians know this full well. Consequently, some of them specialize in doing precisely that.

In the United States there have been successful redevelopments of decaying central zones, such as the Baltimore, Pittsburgh, and Austin waterfronts, where abandoned ports and industrial facilities once stood. Similar redevelopment has occurred in cities such as Hamburg in its former port area, and London on properties where the 2012 Olympic Village was constructed. But if a city is growing, industrial installations for "brownfield development" quickly run out. To achieve a better life for present and future generations and by the rationale of the prevalence of public good, it is necessary also to redevelop low-density residential zones located close to the center and to mass-transport lines. Major redevelopments have been successfully implemented in residential sectors of French and Spanish cities, and we can learn much from them.

Communist-era architecture in eastern Berlin buildings was monotonous, and when the wall came down, the buildings were in poor condition. But they had a human scale, around six stories, and the urban design was pleasant, with broad, tree-lined sidewalks and many parks. Eastern Berlin embarked on a new life and progressively became an increasingly attractive sector. The Berlin example is interesting because it suggests that for urban resilience, urban design is more important than architecture.

Other urban sectors with good urban design and low-rise buildings have been reborn out of serious decay. This is true for neighborhoods in central Washington, D.C., Philadelphia, and Greenwich Village in New York, among others.

It would also seem that low-rise buildings become more valuable over time or hold their value better, and when they lose value, they are more likely to be rehabilitated and recovered. One reason for this may be that the rehabilitation of a building of five or six stories is technically and financially simple. Further, there are fewer owners to negotiate with, and they tend to know each other. In contrast, rehabilitation of decayed buildings of fifteen stories or more is technically, financially, and socially complex, and so the processes of decay are difficult to reverse and tend to deepen until the buildings are demolished.

I know of several cases in which high-rise buildings for low-income citizens in developing world cities quickly deteriorated. Residents are not culturally accustomed to this type of housing, and it's not uncommon for coexistence problems to arise and for them to stop paying their building administration bills.

Just as important as redeveloping badly decayed sectors is preventing others from falling into that predicament in the first place. A "vaccine" to prevent urban decay, and a treatment that might reverse it, is to provide quality pedestrian space—well-maintained, clean, and with lighting—that creates a feeling of order and lures neighbors from their homes. We did such projects and complemented them with "software," such as the enhancement of community organization and takeovers of "sectors of fear" with cleaning operatives, façade paintings, and cultural events with music.

There are cases in which the decay is so all encompassing that it can only be reversed by large-scale physical intervention by government. When I came to office in 1998, the historical center of Bogotá had endured decades of continuous deterioration to such an extent that no new private buildings, or even public ones, had been constructed for years. The only exception was the reconstruction of the Palace of Justice, after it had been burned to the ground in a guerrilla action that killed almost a hundred people, including eleven of the seventeen justices of the Supreme Court. Hundreds of thousands of university students studied downtown, but they went to classes and returned home to their neighborhoods as quickly as they could. Neither students nor their professors lived in the area if they could avoid it. Many buildings stood vacant, and most others were underutilized and had been improperly maintained for years. There were thousands of empty offices, and many government institutions, including several ministries, had moved elsewhere.

The historical center of Bogotá had ceased to be a place of integration and had instead become a barrier that separated the city's more prosperous north from the less prosperous south. Public transport to reach the center, or traverse it, was chaotic. Gaggles of old buses occupied the entire space of the two wide boulevards that pass through the center. They wended their way more slowly than a person walks, stopping in any of the three lanes, sometimes blocking all three, to pick up passengers for which they competed ferociously. Private cars were often stripped of windshield wipers, mirrors, and even lights while stopped at a traffic light or in a traffic jam.

One of the main causes for this deterioration was the so-called "Cartucho." It was sort of an independent republic of crime that had been growing for more than sixty years until it came to occupy a twenty-three-hectare area. It was a place of unimaginable horror caused by the human deterioration of thousands of addicts who wandered through darkened streets, covered in filth, many with serious health problems in addition to their drug dependency. They crowded together to consume drugs for days on end in crumbling buildings abandoned for decades by their owners. The Cartucho was a life-destruction factory. Those who entered to consume drugs once often ended up losing every resource they might have had materially or socially and became homeless.

It's incomprehensible that Cartucho was located only a hundred meters from the Plaza de Bolívar, the historic heart of the country and Colombia's most important institutional center, as Congress, the Palace of Justice, the mayor's office surrounding it, and even the Presidential Palace is only one block away. The location deeply symbolized the state's impotence; indeed, the headquarters of the Bogotá Police was across the street from one corner of Cartucho, and the army barracks responsible for the security of the presidential residence was one block from another corner.

The sector was dominated by organized crime and had the highest murder rates in Colombia—probably the highest on Earth. All kinds of crime and depravity were committed there: during my time in office, a four-year-old boy was raped and castrated. Neither the police nor the army entered this area at the lowest circle of hell except during large-scale operations, and those were very sporadic.

Few families—and as time passed, fewer and fewer—lived around the Cartucho, despite neighborhoods with much potential for redevelopment in this most central of city sectors. The Cartucho continued to expand and seeded similar horrific areas nearby. When they needed money, any addict who was a habitual criminal—and many were—had only to walk two short blocks to the Plaza de Bolívar and its vicinity, theoretically the most important tourist sector of the country, and beg threateningly or simply mug somebody.

There was nothing on which to leverage Cartucho's recovery, neither in its society nor in its buildings. Radical surgery was needed. Given that the Cartucho problem was of a magnitude and importance that deserved presidential, national government intervention, I had met with three presidents before I became mayor to try to persuade them to demolish that sector. Aside from the dramatic urban and social damage it caused, Cartucho was a national security risk. I was not able to convince any of them to demolish it. Dozens of presidents and mayors had come and gone, and all had looked the other way. The risk of a very visible failure in an operation to take control of the sector, possibly with the loss of lives, was too high. Even greater was the risk of being unable to prevent criminal organizations from returning to take over the sector a few days or weeks later. So everyone had chosen the same course of action: inaction. And meanwhile Cartucho continued to slowly asphyxiate the cultural, historical, and institutional center of Colombia.

We decided to face up to the powerful mafias that controlled Cartucho and to demolish more than six hundred buildings. This was a long, difficult, and dangerous task, headed by Elsa Patricia Bohorquez, who even managed to persuade some of those who had been leading criminals in the sector to collaborate in the process, which included police operations, the purchase of property abandoned for decades by its owners, and demolitions. Equally important was the social care provided to the drug-dependent homeless, many of whom were able to be rehabilitated.[9]

We succeeded. On the site of Cartucho, in the center of Bogotá and Colombia, there is today the Tercer Milenio (Third Millennium) Park of almost twenty hectares, named because it opened in 2000. A significant portion of the funds invested in the project was destined for social work, such as the rehabilitation of drug addicts, the relocation of some residents, and of micro businesses. We wanted a center with people living in it—with families and life. The Bogotá center lacked parks. This factor also made it difficult to attract families. The Plaza de Bolívar is charming but small. We therefore decided to make the large Tercer Milenio Park on the land opened up by the demolition of Cartucho.

When I came back to office eighteen years later, I found that another area of concentrated crime and drug distribution and consumption, similar to Cartucho, had sprung up. The "Bronx," as it was called, was much smaller than Cartucho, but its criminality was even more intense. The police would not enter the two-hectare area, which was only five blocks from the Presidential Palace. Like Cartucho, the Bronx had existed for decades but had grown during the years after my first term as mayor. In addition to the sale and consumption of drugs, there was sexual exploitation of minors, kidnapping, and even murder. A year before, two agents of the Prosecutor's Office who entered that circle of hell had been detained by criminal organizations for eight hours. For decades presidents and mayors had avoided taking any kind of action due to the high risks involved.

After weeks of careful preparation, we entered the Bronx one night with police special forces and succeeded in taking control with no casualties. In the Bronx, we demolished dozens of buildings. We acquired a neighboring, beautiful centenary building that housed some army offices, formerly the school of medicine, and started a project to make a creative district, including a center of higher education. In a few years this nucleus will become one of the city's most iconic architectural places.[10]

In my first term as mayor, I would have liked to buy and demolish not only the buildings in Cartucho but also those of nearby deteriorated sectors to build housing projects. But my period of office was only three years. During my second term of office, which lasted four years, we acquired and demolished the greater part of the San Bernardo neighborhood, a few blocks away from the Bronx and adjacent to the Cartucho, now Tercer Milenio Park. There, two blocks from the Presidential Palace, we teamed up with private developers and built more than four thousand apartments.

A lack of mass-transport service had exacerbated the center's progressive decay. In addition to the TransMilenio BRT route down the Avenida Jiménez, we built the twenty-five-kilometer Avenida Caracas line that connects the city's northeast to the southeast through the center. The city administration later constructed two additional TransMilenio trunk routes through the center so that Tercer Milenio Park is completely framed by four transit lines. And in my second term of office, we contracted the first Metro line in Bogotá, which also crosses the center, running between the former Cartucho and Bronx and along the edge of the park.

We made numerous additional interventions to recover the center's dynamism and its function as a place of local and national unity and a tourist attraction. We restored churches, recovered plazas, built a school, recovered two traditional marketplaces, and contracted the construction of a university, a creative district, and thousands of apartments. Today a number of private investments have been made, universities have expanded, and new buildings have been built; old office buildings are being restored, and there are new towers and large housing projects under construction.

Parks as the Catalysts of Redevelopment

Although the conversion of the Cartucho into the Tercer Milenio Park had some idiosyncrasies, given the area's nature and criminal activity, as a general rule the development of parks through the demolition of one or more blocks may be a powerful means of revitalizing and improving a sector's quality of life. Our Global South cities developed with little planning, in poverty, and through many illegal practices. The main consequence of this has been a dearth of public space. Over time, sectors with these deficiencies deteriorate because they lose residents whose incomes increase, as they migrate to other parts of the city or the suburbs that are better endowed with green spaces.

Parks opened by the demolition of built areas powerfully improve their surroundings. They are a catalyst for the improvement of the city that brings families, cafés, and shops to neighborhoods and stimulates the improvement of buildings. Unfortunately, such projects are rare. By contrast, demolitions to make or widen roads for cars are frequent, despite the fact that they sometimes negatively impact sectors through which they pass.

Now, there are successful examples of major urban demolition to build roads when care has been taken with pedestrian borders. One good example is Georges-Eugène Haussmann's work in Paris in the second half of the 1800s, although cars hadn't yet been invented. Haussmann was also financially creative in ways that developing cities might adopt. Not only did he acquire and demolish the buildings essential to opening his major boulevards; he also acquired those on the new roads' perimeters to generate lots for sale. Profits created by the increased value of those plots made it possible to finance major roads. Toward 1850, when Haussmann was engaged in his grand projects, the per capita income of Paris was comparable to or lower than that of many developing cities in 2022.

Cities have a magic wand to generate value: to charge, or to require generous cessions of public space, for changes in land use from rural to urban or for the construction of higher buildings. It's possible, for example, to foster widening of sidewalks by authorizing high-rise buildings to compensate for the reduction in built area.

Bogotá had several wide roads of six to ten lanes. TransMilenio operates in some of them and will occupy more in the future. Although these roads are wide, they hardly qualify as boulevards because the sidewalks are very narrow and afford no pleasure for pedestrians. So we issued a regulation to freeze the height of existing buildings. However, high-rise building was permitted for projects that consolidated a certain number of buildings to generate a large plot of land and that left sidewalks twelve meters wide.[11] So, over time, these major roads with a mass-transport service will become real avenues, with wide, tree-lined sidewalks, bikeways, and ground-floor shops. They will be pleasant for walking.

Should "Gentrification" Be Stopped?

There has been much criticism of gentrification—the process by which, for whatever reason, some relatively low-income sectors become attractive to higher-income citizens who can afford higher rents or prices. The resulting rise in property value leads some owners to sell and, gradually, low-income tenants to leave because they are unable to pay the higher rents. Others, with higher incomes, can buy or rent a home in the traditionally low-cost sector. They not only buy; they make improvements to the buildings. Should the city try to stop that?

Any improvement of a sector, such as upgrading of a park or sidewalk, is likely to increase property values. Governments are generally unsuccessful in trying to forestall gentrification. They cannot prevent a city sector from becoming attractive or fashionable and therefore more expensive. Nor can a government prevent owners who wish to sell from doing so. It's also questionable whether governments *should* try to impede a process that improves a sector. It would seem to be more effective to construct equity using the state's power and public funds improving low-income sectors around the city rather than trying to impede so-called gentrification. Increments in tax revenues generated by gentrification can be channeled into improvements in the living conditions of the lower-income population.

Iconic Buildings Reflect and Strengthen Society's Values

High-quality public infrastructure not only improves life but also sends a symbolic, unconscious, and powerful message that citizens of the sector are important. Handsome and somewhat majestic school buildings in low-income neighborhoods, such as dozens we built in the poorest sectors of Bogotá, strengthen neighborhood pride and a sense of belonging. They build values: they express that education and children are important more eloquently than any television campaign. It is not so evident that children are important if one remembers, for example, that in Colombian cities a very significant percentage of children in the sectors most in need seldom or never see their fathers, and many don't even know who their fathers are. For a child who lives in a humble dwelling and who sometimes contends with material wants as well as inadequate stimulation at home, it opens a world of possibilities to arrive at a beautiful school where importance is given to knowledge and to that student's life. In fact, we find many children in the poorest sectors do not want to go on vacation from school.

We built three large libraries, aware that in purely functional terms it would have been better to build fifteen smaller ones. But small ones would have been at greater risk of losing operating funding in the future. And, more important, large and imposing libraries reflect and construct values. They show that knowledge is important, that the most respectable citizens of our society are not those who *have* but those who *know* and teach.[12]

When a very poor person enters one of these beautiful buildings, they feel respected and valued and that they belong. They can enter the formidable library or sports and cultural center simply because they have a Colombian identity card, not because they have money or a fancy degree. In this way citizenship begins to acquire meaning, beyond simply being able to live within Colombia's borders. Unlike a shopping center that sells expensive goods beyond their reach where low-income citizens feel uncomfortable, they feel no pressure in a public library and are entitled to everything that the library has to offer. The mere existence of a stupendous library in a low-income sector is an expression of respect for the intelligence of the residents.

A library whose beauty surpasses that of a nearby shopping mall also sends a message about social priorities and values. In order to defeat corruption and drug trafficking, it's necessary to despise drug traffickers and other criminals' materialism and conspicuous consumption. When the young hero of the neighborhood is not the one who arrives on an expensive motorbike wearing jewelry and brand clothing because he sells drugs but one who rides an old bicycle, reads, paints, and engages in sports, we will have taken an important step in the right direction.

Buildings reflect and construct the values of a society. Think about how, from kilometers away, anyone can understand what was important to any small village in the west for millennia before 1900: religion. Churches towered against the sky and above all the other buildings. Medieval cathedrals were not only monuments to God: they enhanced a society's self-esteem and dignity and celebrated the human capacity to create. Their immense beauty, unlike that of kings' palaces, was accessible to all, even the humblest. Cathedrals constructed equality in religious ceremonies to which citizens of all walks of life attended, as equals before death and before God.

At their inception many opposed the construction of these medieval cathedrals, arguing that it was better to spend the money distributing alms to the poor. Should those societies have distributed alms instead of building the cathedrals that still inspire us? We hear similar arguments today when any important work is undertaken, particularly if a significant part of the funds is to be used to make beautiful, majestic projects or simply to make the city more pleasant for pedestrians. Beyond the delight that cathedrals have provided many generations, it's probable that the tourism, economic activities, and employment they still generate today may have more effectively reduced poverty than the distribution of alms.

Often, the most beautiful and impressive buildings in developing societies are airports. They seek mainly to impress businessmen and tourists from abroad. For the design of an airport, an internationally known "starchitect" is usually engaged, and billions of dollars are invested in its construction. In some way an airport is a symbol of a country's power, strength, and aspirations. However, in developing countries, most people do not go to the airport. Why not have a city's best buildings in the popular sectors, indeed, in neighborhoods that were initially illegal and are in the process of improvement?

Most cities are identified by iconic buildings, some of which are new, such as the Sydney Opera House or the Gateway Arch in St. Louis, Missouri, not to mention the many towers with which businesses, architects, and cities vie for preeminence. There are buildings that have singlehandedly changed the perception and almost the identity of cities, such as the Guggenheim Museum in Bilbao. If a beautiful building can have such positive impact in a city, then one can have an almost indescribable effect in a low-income neighborhood. Such buildings can be, for example, sports and cultural centers, transport terminals, libraries, hospitals, plazas, or parks.

*   *   *

In a city, each building, each pedestrian space, each corner speaks. They all have something to tell us—sometimes rather loudly. A city with no sidewalks, with wide roads and few intersections, where the man in the street must dash across to avoid being run over by a car, expresses that human life is not important. So do decayed and deteriorated sectors beset by political inertia. A good city does the opposite: there, every detail expresses that the human being is sacred.

CHAPTER 4

City Life: Better Than the Suburbs

When you travel from a typical, dense city in the developing world, with its sparse green areas and abundant traffic and noise, and arrive for the first time in any US suburb, with its idyllic houses surrounded by immaculate gardens, it seems heavenly. But soon you notice something odd. In this patch of perfection, there are no people on the street; occasionally, a car passes. If we spend enough time there, we may see a lonely jogger or someone walking a dog. If we want to go to a café or buy a loaf of bread, we find that we have to drive there. And you begin to realize that your disorderly and less than impeccable city has some advantages.

There are many reasons for living in a suburb, as hundreds of millions in rich countries do. Suburbs are quiet and peaceful and have abundant green spaces, trees, and gardens. The suburban ideal came from nineteenth-century England, whose cities had experienced a century of industrialization and pollution. For hundreds of years, life expectancy was higher in rural areas than in cities.[1]

From the beginning of the nineteenth century, the noise, pollution, and congestion of urban centers led some to build houses on the outskirts, with large gardens and close to open countryside. But the exodus only accelerated with the expansion of the railways in the mid-nineteenth century and the arrival of electric tramways toward the end of it. The population of so-called Outer London multiplied several times in the second half of the nineteenth century, while it shrank in the city center. Yet the suburbs of the second half of the nineteenth century and the first decades of the twentieth were different from those that followed, after the arrival of the car. They were precursors of the twentieth-century developments insofar as they were largely composed of individual houses, often with a small garden, but they had a much higher density and were structured around railway lines, tramlines, and pedestrian mobility, with shops close to home.

This urban-suburban form also became popular in other European cities and in the United States. The designer of New York's Central Park, Frederick Law Olmsted, designed a suburb with generous gardens and curved streets in the outskirts of Chicago and defended life in the suburbs as the "most attractive, the most refined, the most soundly wholesome form of domestic life."[2] Toward the end of the nineteenth century, the population in the city centers was falling and the suburban population growing. Increasingly, people no longer lived close to their places of work.[3]

Ebenezer Howard, considered to be the father of the concept of suburbs, published his book on the "garden city" in 1898, proposing minicities with a maximum of thirty-two thousand inhabitants that were self-sustaining and surrounded by greenbelts.[4] He succeeded in creating such a place, Letchworth, which still exists, though of course it never succeeded in achieving anything close to self-sufficiency.

Although originally conceived in England, suburbs mainly proliferated in the United States after World War II, and Canada, Australia, and to some extent the rest of the world followed its example.[5] The suburbs mushroomed with the arrival of the car, which enabled more people to reach more distant areas with less expensive land. Suburbs began to be constituted exclusively of individual houses with large gardens. Without the need for a link to rail stations, they no longer had pedestrian access to a central area or to shops. In 1956, President Dwight Eisenhower secured passage of the law that allowed the federal government to finance highways throughout the United States, including urban and suburban zones. These highways promoted low-density suburban expansion much more powerfully and effectively than any argument, plan, or regulation about urban development.[6] From the middle of the twentieth century onward, the shopping center or mall, accessible only by car and surrounded by dozens of hectares of tarmac for parking, replaced the city center or high street, not only for shopping but also as a meeting place. Suburbs prospered based on the family car, and increasingly, families found they needed more than one. As suburbs have very few inhabitants per hectare, they aren't feasible sites for public transport to serve them with a high frequency.

Initially, suburbs were built for high-income earners, as is still mainly the case in developing cities, but over time they were also made for the middle class.

Residents of any given neighborhood tend to have similar incomes and habits. But in a dense city, different kinds of people generally are less isolated from each other than in the suburbs. It's possible for those in some low-income neighborhoods to walk or bike to a high-income neighborhood or to reach them by a short public transport ride.

Suburbs are particularly homogeneous in social terms, and those from other segments of the population only go there to work, as domestic staff, gardeners, and providers of other services to the residents. The large gaps and buffers between neighborhoods of different incomes that suburbs create intensify inequality and exclusion, making it impossible for lower-income citizens on foot or a bicycle to reach higher-income neighborhoods and vice versa. People of different incomes thus do not meet as equals in public spaces.

The Case Against Suburbs in the Developing World

In the developing world, suburbs acquire especially perverse characteristics because they are enclosed by walls that may be several kilometers long. In exceptional cases, where the neighborhood is not walled, each house has its own wall; in some cases, such as in South African suburbs, these walls are topped with rolls of razor wire, like high-security prisons. Latin Americans like me are offended by the border wall Trump managed to partially build to impede access for immigrants from Mexico and other Latin American countries. However, within our countries, we raise walls around our neighborhoods with a similar intention: to keep out lower-income citizens.

The long walk surrounding these walled-in developments for someone needing to be on one side or the other is a flagrant affront to democracy, especially as it limits mobility for the elderly and vulnerable and is not a democratic urban design in which the public good should prevail.

There are Texas-type or California-type developments in all Latin American cities, in many African ones, and in almost all of Asia. Enclosed suburban neighborhoods in the developing world seek not only security but also exclusion of others, particularly low-income citizens. These "gated communities" in countries like India, where there is little crime, are reminders that their principal purpose is to keep out the poor.

Ironically, the suburbs, largely created to escape to low-traffic environments, only function because of cars. One of their main attractions is the low level of traffic: in any given neighborhood, homes along the roads with less traffic are more valuable than similar ones on streets with more traffic. To maximize the value of the land, suburban developers invented the "cul-de-sac," closed-off streets to minimize traffic and thus create higher value for houses there.

Road construction rather than planning office decisions is more powerful defining where cities grow and often also how they grow. Therefore, when a road is being built, it's advisable to think of the urbanization it will spawn and the best way to organize or prevent it.

Urbanization along interurban roads as they leave the cities transforms them into urban roads. But these roads do not have the minimum urban requirements, such as sidewalks or traffic lights. Therefore, they become the backbone of urban development while destroying the quality of the urban life they themselves have incidentally created. The Pacific CA-9 road, for example, historically linked Puerto Quetzal, Guatemala's main port, to the capital Guatemala City. In the second half of the twentieth century, Guatemala City grew many times over.[7] An important part of this urban growth was concentrated around interurban roads, such as CA-9, that led out of the city. But, although this is now a de facto urban road, the design continues to be that of an interurban highway, without traffic lights, pedestrian space, or bikeways. It is a dangerous barrier where many pedestrians are run over and killed each year. Governments have almost always failed to make these roads more human—in other words, to make them urban. On the contrary, their interest is to make them more accommodating to fast-moving cars, widen them, and replicate them. The fact that there are offices, schools, shops, homes, and tens of thousands of human beings who live around those roads rarely concerns government officials. Recently, the Guatemalan government built a larger, parallel road to the CA-9, the Via Alterna del Sur, or VAS, a southern bypass that also links Guatemala City with Puerto Quetzal, as well as extending southeast into El Salvador. The VAS runs through urban and suburban areas as well as rural areas close to the capital that already have begun to get urbanized. Once again, the new highway was not conceived as the largely urban road that it is already becoming.

Highways through port cities tend to be particularly inhuman and dangerous. They bring enormous, noisy trucks traveling at high speeds close to neighborhoods or even through them, like barbarian invaders brandishing their clubs. Central governments that want to improve the efficiency of overland freight build these roads with trucks exclusively in mind, completely disregarding the children who live, study, and play on both sides of them.

Other highways are built to improve intraurban mobility. Most frequently they are "beltways," or "ring roads," around an existing urban area. But if there is something we can be certain of in relation to ring roads, it's that they are not going to remain peripheral rings: the city will grow around them, on both sides, because they stimulate urban growth. Many cities actually have a number of concentric ring roads, like Beijing, which has six. Therefore, when a ring road is built, it's convenient to design it as an urban road and not as an interurban highway, as a boulevard with sidewalks, bikeways, trees, and, as much as possible, traffics lights and at-grade intersections.

Those who most complain about traffic jams on the highways are suburban residents who have to drive long distances every day. But they are precisely the ones who cause the bottlenecks. As graffiti on a wall alongside a particularly congested section of road reads, "You are not in a jam; you are the jam."

No matter how numerous or how large the highways are, car-dependent suburban development ensures they will become congested. Not even the richest cities can solve that problem. In the San Francisco Bay Area, which headquarters some of the most creative and powerful companies in the world, including Apple, Facebook, Google, and Visa, travel times doubled in the first couple of decades of the twenty-first century, and they continue to increase, despite the network of enormous highways. For a growing number of people, the criterion to choose a company for employment is the travel time between it and home.

As land is relatively abundant and costs less in the suburbs, homes are much larger than those in dense cities. In dense cities such as Barcelona, London, Tokyo, or Bogotá, homes are relatively small. Spatially, there are limits to what people can store in small refrigerators and cupboards. They venture out frequently to buy food. They walk to grocery stores, bakeries, butchers, fishmongers, flower shops, wine merchants, and dry cleaners. On the way they see people, and sometimes they meet a neighbor. They consume very fresh products and don't buy much, no more than what they can carry in a couple of bags or a small trolley. Shopping for food is different in the suburbs: residents drive to the supermarket and often to hypermarkets farther out and buy what they need for a fortnight or more. And for that, they usually have not just one large refrigerator but often more than one.

A suburban resident goes less often to a theater, a restaurant, or a museum and thus low-density cities have fewer restaurants, theaters, and, generally, less cultural activity. For example, a restaurant that serves a more unusual or exotic cuisine can survive in a dense city because enough people live relatively close who might enjoy it. An ethnic restaurant does not survive as easily in an American suburb; there, hamburger, pizza, and barbecue joints or Americanized Chinese food tend to predominate. The same applies to Russian-language or sculpture classes and hundreds more: it is more difficult for such activities to subsist in low-density environments.

Initially, residents of the suburbs worked in urban centers and took transit to work. For example, in the case of Manhattan, people who live in the suburbs but still work in the center of the city can drive or take a shared taxi to a commuter train station and then take the train to get to work. During a second stage of suburban development, offices and other places of work follow homes and migrate to the suburbs. Sometimes these offices are located in villages served by public transport, but in other cases, anywhere next to a highway, they are in so-called "office parks" impossible to reach by any means other than a private car. The growth of places of work far from urban centers has been so great that most of the recent commute time increase in metropolitan areas has not been from the suburbs to the center but from suburbs to suburbs.[89]

The compact growth of villages or small cities that are more or less distant from the principal city is different from suburban development. These villages or small cities can be served by quality public transport. And many of the places in those villages can be reached on foot: there are shops, life on the street, and public spaces, which also distinguish them from suburbs.

Suburbanization increases distances and travel times.[10] Robert Putnam said that the length of the journey to work is a predictor of social isolation. "There's a simple rule of thumb: Every ten minutes of commuting results in ten per cent fewer social connections. Commuting is connected to social isolation, which causes unhappiness."[11] He then explains that the reason for unhappiness is not so much the journey in itself but the deprivation it causes: "When you are commuting by car, you are not hanging out with the kids, sleeping with your spouse (or anyone else), playing soccer . . . arguing about politics, praying in a church, or drinking in a bar. In short, you are not spending time with other people."[12] In our postpandemic world, there may arise a greater risk of isolation than that stemming from long commutes. Many don't drive but are quite content to self-isolate at home in front of a Zoom screen for hours, day after day. This of course makes it much less likely that they will go for a beer with workmates or develop friendships at work or probably anywhere else as well. People like to see people and be with people, so in a low-density suburb without people in public spaces, they drive to the mall.

The typical density of an American suburb is around 20 inhabitants per hectare; in Bogotá, the figure is 210 inhabitants per hectare. So if Bogotá were to have the structure of an American suburbanized city, it would occupy eleven times more land than it does today and traveling distances would be proportionately greater.

In four or five decades, metropolitan Bogotá will double the 2.7 million households it has today. If we suppose that in each home 1.5 people travel to work or study, this means 8.1 million more journeys. It is unimaginable that those journeys should be made by each individual in a car, but if they are to be done by mass transport, on bicycle, or on foot, then the city must grow compactly. In India the number of households in cities will quintuple; in Nigeria or Uganda it will increase tenfold. And the number of journeys will grow at least three times more than the growth in the number of households. Any low-density suburban development in these cities undercuts the possibility of having mass transport, minimizing travel times and transport costs and ameliorating global warming.

A car-dependent suburb causes the greatest harm to the most vulnerable members of society: the old, children, and the poor who have no cars. The absence of low-cost, high-frequency public transport and, in many places, the total absence of public transport leaves those who cannot drive a car stranded.

Many suburban neighborhoods in the United States, including Scarsdale, New York, where I lived with my family, have no sidewalks because their creators thought it would be more countrified and sophisticated not to have them. There are still individuals who need to walk in those streets without sidewalks: domestic employees and nannies who take care of the small children, children themselves, the young with no driving licenses or access to cars, and the elderly, who can no longer drive. There are sad cases of lonely old people imprisoned in their suburban homes because they can no longer drive who wait days for someone to visit them or drive them to the market. There are also many traffic accidents caused by the elderly, who do not resign themselves to the isolation. In contrast, the elderly in dense cities walk or take public transport to go meet friends, sit at a café or on a park bench to talk about politics and sports, or visit their grandchildren.

In Mamaroneck, on the coast of Long Island Sound, about five kilometers from where my family used to live, Harbor Island Park has a seafront. It would have taken me a half an hour to reach it by bicycle with my children, that is, if it hadn't been suicidal to try because the road to the park, like many in the area, is narrow, with no sidewalks and, naturally, no bikeways. The speed limit is thirty-five miles an hour, but nobody heeds it. The route passes through green areas, with gardens and trees, but they can only be enjoyed through a car window. Latin American maids who work there must risk their lives walking to work and back. The road design does not respect human dignity. This is a habitat exclusively for those with cars. Often, cars did not even stop for children at the crossing on the street across from my son's elementary school.

Once, while I was in South Africa, I was riding a bicycle through one of Cape Town's wealthy suburbs, and I stopped to talk to an old woman who was walking along the edge of the road. It had no pavement, only a track worn through the grass by countless journeys on foot made by those who, like her, had to walk. She told me that she was seventy-four years old and that she used to walk more than two hours each way to reach the house where she worked. The suburbs for high-income families in Cape Town were made for adults with cars. The same happens to domestic employees who work in wealthy US suburbs. In both places pedestrians with humble occupations have worn paths in the grass alongside main roads without sidewalks.

Private car expenses are substantial and include depreciation, maintenance, fuel, insurance, taxes, and parking. For a low-income family, having a car may mean going without some basic needs. In the more suburban and car-dependent United States, transportation costs for the quintile with the lowest earnings represent 29 percent of their income, while in Europe for households in the same quintile, such costs add up to only 7.5 percent of their income.[13] In any case, cars mean less money for sporting or cultural activities, better food, or travel. The cost of transport in an extended low-density city, where most trips are made by private car, is more than double that in cities where use of public transport, bicycling, or walking are predominant.[14] And even those who drive in Europe with its more compact cities, drive less than those in the United States. The average American drove around 23,000 kilometers in 2022, about twice as far as the typical French citizen.[15] The public cost of road infrastructure for the mobility of suburban residents also implies that less is invested in health, education, parks, or sports or cultural infrastructure.

What Is a Desirable Density?

In developing cities, the first to go to the suburbs are high-income earners. Later, suburban neighborhoods get developed for middle-class and lower-income groups. High-income citizens might seek suburban greenery and a quasi-country feel, as well as safety and better schools for their children and themselves, while lower-income citizens move to the suburbs looking for lower-cost spacious homes in addition to the greenery.

The city expands into the suburbs until traffic jams every day make the suburbs less attractive and the central areas more so. When this happens, houses in central areas begin to get demolished to build several-story buildings. For example, around 2000 in Manila, many high-income earners were migrating to increasingly distant gated communities. Ten years later, tall apartment towers began to be built in central zones of the city, advertised everywhere, from stands in shopping centers to flyers handed out to drivers at traffic lights.

These examples raise the question, what is a desirable density?

The answer is one in which we can have low-cost, high-frequency public transport, with few subsidies. It's one that makes it possible to reach many destinations on foot or on bicycle. It's one in which mobility does not consume too much of our time so that we can spend time with family and friends and pursue enjoyable activities. A desirable density makes real estate expensive and large homes rare and makes land too costly for surface parking.

When we speak of high densities, often we assume this means low incomes. However, one of the highest-income areas of the world, the Upper East Side in Manhattan, has New York's highest density.[16] Whatever the case, we do not need to have buildings such as those of Manhattan or Hong Kong to have a desirable density. With four- to six-story buildings, it's possible to achieve densities high enough to have shops accessible on foot and low-cost, high-frequency public transport.

In *The Triumph of the City,* Edward Glaeser makes a formidable case for density and decries regulations that restrict high-rise construction in certain sectors, mainly because they make housing more expensive in places where people want to live. Although I believe that the densification of some sectors is convenient, I do not agree that unlimited building heights should be allowed anywhere. The making of a beautiful and humane city cannot be left to momentary economic incentives because it's also a matter of human, social, cultural, and artistic criteria. Architecturally, the construction of high-rise buildings in some of the most charming, attractive, and valuable sectors of cities would destroy precisely their charming distinctiveness. That said, Glaeser presents some powerful data: for example, he finds that the higher the density of a county in the United States, the higher the income.[17]

Less dense, car-dependent suburbs inevitably generate parking-dependent shops. In the suburbs, when shops are not in malls, they are located on streets made to be driven on, not walked. The archetypal commercial road of this kind in the United States is lined with "strip malls," open-air parking, and a skyline littered with luminous billboards and signs, mounted on tall posts. The same shops that could be found in the dense city can be found here. Some restaurants and cafés even have tables on the sidewalk, though facing parking lots rather than sidewalks with pedestrians.

One study of hundreds of parking areas in ten cities in the United States showed that on average, during the busiest hours, only 56 percent of parking capacity was used.[18] There are some even more troubling figures: in the typical suburbanized, car-dependent American city, there are thirteen parking spaces for every car. Malls' parking lots are designed for the day of maximum demand—usually the day before Christmas.[19] It has been estimated that there are more than 500 million parking spaces in the United States, occupying 9,298 square kilometers, an area larger than the states of Delaware and Rhode Island combined.[20] In the mid-twentieth century, Lewis Mumford wrote that "the right to have access to every building in the city by private motorcar in an age when everyone possesses such a vehicle is actually the right to destroy the city."[21]

Some of the "new urbanists" in the United States have proposed that parking spaces should, at the least, be located behind buildings, where cars would not be visible. This would frame the street with buildings and sidewalks, ideally broad ones, that would be attractive to stroll.

Those who can choose where to live and prefer a suburb are not stupid. In the United States they want good public schools generally absent in the city centers, and there and in the rest of the world they seek green spaces, spacious homes, trees, birds, and safe environments for their children to play. However, it's within our power to make cities that offer both—everything that people seek in the suburbs as well as the advantages of a dense city.

Neither the Suburbs nor Manhattan

"The principles and techniques of true urban design can be relearned from the many wonderful older places which still exist."[22] So write Plater-Zyberk, Duany, and Speck in *Suburban Nation*. The new city they propose does "not look so different from our old American neighbourhoods before they were ravaged by sprawl."[23] These authors express the new urbanist position that criticizes suburbanization. The authors, like other critics of the suburbs, idealize the city that prevailed in the early twentieth century and propose it as an alternative. They miss its compactness, the possibility of being able to walk to commercial areas, and the feeling of community it fostered. The Charter of the New Urbanism nostalgically states, "We stand for the restoration of existing urban centers and towns."[24]

I am skeptical about the idealization of the traditional city. People voted with their feet—or in this case their cars—and left for the suburbs as soon as the car made it possible for them to do so. The "traditional" city that new urbanists yearn for is actually like a suburb insofar as it was formed by single-family houses. But it is denser, has shops and other destinations accessible by foot, and the public transport that suburbs often lack. On the downside, it has fewer green areas and more traffic. Its pedestrian quality is not particularly attractive: it has narrow sidewalks and the omnipresent threat of cars.

In American cities new urbanists point to new buildings in central areas, mostly inhabited by the young, as evidence that new generations no longer wish to live in the suburbs. But these buildings have narrow sidewalks and are frequently on busy streets. That people do not want a suburban life does not mean that they want to live in traditional urban centers with traffic and noise, narrow sidewalks, and few parks. It is quite common for single, young, high-income earners; young couples without children; or even couples with small children to choose to live in a city. But many of them move out to the suburbs once the children reach school age.

Furthermore, although there are developments inspired by the traditional city revived and endorsed by New Urbanists, and young people who live in dense high-rise developments, the reality is that most of the new housing being built in the United States continues to be located in low-density, car-dependent suburbs.

There are desirable models other than suburbs, the "traditional city" of the New Urbanists, or the dense Manhattan-type city. For example, not all wealthy cities move predominantly by car. Atlanta and Berlin have similar populations and similar per capita incomes. But the percentage of the population that moves by public transport or bicycle in Berlin is five times that of Atlanta. The Barcelona superblocks project is turning one out of every three streets into pedestrian areas, allowing only the residents' cars to enter to access their parking garages. The new city may be dense, with buildings of five or more stories, but it could have different ingredients: large areas reserved entirely for foot or bicycle traffic; roads on which more than half the space is only for pedestrians and bicycles; roads that are only for buses or trams, pedestrians and cyclists; greenway networks, dozens or hundreds of kilometers long, with pedestrian and bike infrastructure; and street grids with alternating roads—one for motor vehicles and the next for pedestrians; or at least one pedestrian-and-bicycle-only road every ten regular streets. Anybody's life would be happier if a couple of blocks from home they could access a greenway network to walk, ride a bike, or simply sit on the bench beside a path without cars passing by.

It seems possible that cities could be made with the features demanded by those who prefer dense cities, for example, shops and a range of activities accessible on foot and ubiquitous, high-frequency public transport. And they could have as well most of what those who prefer the suburbs seek: abundant green space, pedestrian and bicyclists' safety, and freedom for their children to be on their own in public spaces.

Most developing world cities have nothing equivalent to a Gothic cathedral, the British Museum, or the Louvre. But because most of them are located in tropical equatorial zones, in their expansion zones they could create breathtaking ample pedestrian street networks, dozens or hundreds of kilometers long, shaded by huge tropical trees. Beyond constructing quality of life and being useful for sustainable mobility, they would be icons that would strengthen identity, character, and self-esteem. London or Paris could not create anything like that today.

Despite the twentieth-century deformation of cities to conform them more to the needs of cars than humans, we never stopped longing for pedestrian spaces free of the threat of cars. We looked for them all over the place—in malls, on university campuses, in Disney parks, in video games, or in the pedestrianized historical centers in Europe. We've created more and more urban environments made for the human being who walks, rides a bike, and plays.

Masdar, in the United Arab Emirates, was designed by Foster and Partners, theoretically to function without cars and consume little energy. However, it was not very successful in reducing car use or energy consumption or, indeed, in attracting its target population of fifty thousand. Cities that start from zero on virgin land and are completely designed by architects tend to feel rather sterile, lifeless, and featureless, at least in their early decades. This is true of Canberra, Islamabad, and Brasilia, among others in the twentieth century, designed more for cars than for pedestrians or cyclists. The new administrative capital of Egypt, yet to be named, and Naypyidaw, Myanmar's new capital -both under construction, follow the pattern. Nusantara, Indonesia's new capital being built in Borneo claims to have a design more friendly to pedestrians, bicyclists, and public transport. So does the Line, in Neom, Saudi Arabia, a radically different concept, a linear city 170 kilometers long, made of two lines of parallel skyscrapers with a green public space 200 meters wide in between. Public transport and other infrastructure will run underground. It seems more appealing to leave a wider margin for spontaneity.

Cities in the developing world, most of which will grow between two and ten times their present size in the coming decades, have a unique opportunity to be designed to foster happiness. Never in the past was there such an opportunity with so much available experience, and there will not be one in the future.

An urban development for fifty thousand people was made on the site of the 2012 Olympic Games in London with ingredients that could inspire many developing cities. The heart of the project is a 226-hectare park, with long branches that extend it into the built areas. Most of the sports infrastructure used for the Olympics is now open to the public. It's a development made around public pedestrian spaces, with both hard and soft surfaces, served by nine underground and rail lines and a number of bus routes. It has universities, schools, kindergartens, and many shops and restaurants.

In Toronto, also on the land that was used for a sporting event—the 2015 Pan American Games—a satellite city of six thousand homes was built called the West Don Lands, with over nine hectares of parks and exceptional pedestrian spaces, including a beautiful waterfront.[25] Also in Toronto, a similar city, Port Lands, is being constructed. Both developments have been implemented on land previously occupied by industry. The large parks and waterfronts generated by both developments not only benefit those who live and work there but all citizens of Toronto.

During my term as Bogotá's mayor, we conceived and initiated the developments Reverdecer del Sur and Lagos de Torca for around 180,000 and 400,000 people, respectively.[26] These developments have dozens of kilometers of greenways; some roads exclusively for pedestrians, cyclists, and BRT; and wide sidewalks and bikeways on all streets. Each of them has a park of more than 130 hectares and many smaller ones.[27] We required that every block contain shops. City blocks cannot have an area larger than 1.3 hectares so that blocks will be short and more pleasant for pedestrians. Although these are projects designed and controlled by the city administration, the investment is private. With a larger degree of public investment, an even more ambitious pedestrian structure could be achieved.

The idea of cities in which most people move around on foot, by bicycle, or on public transport initially sounds improbable to some, but there is nothing exceptional about it. It's what happens today in some of the most advanced and admired cities in the world: Berlin, Manhattan, Tokyo, Zürich, and Amsterdam, to mention only a few. In Manhattan, only two out of every ten people have a car, and only one out of ten uses it for daily journeys.[28] When they need a car to go on a trip, to the mountains or a beach, they rent one. It is cheaper to rent one a dozen weekends a year than to have a car. In Zürich, the wealthiest city in Europe, four out of every ten[29] use public transport and two of ten ride bicycles.[30]

*   *   *

To talk about new city models in which mobility on foot, by bicycle, or on public transport is predominant is actually not a "new" model at all. What is new, and plausible, is to have cities that are more radically pedestrian, with more spaces for pedestrians and cyclists, and with networks of greenways crisscrossing them in all directions.

CHAPTER 5

The Challenge of Urban Transport

Mobility in developing cities is a very peculiar challenge because unlike matters such as education, health, or housing, which improve and are solved as incomes rise, mobility can worsen with rising incomes. Likewise, and contrary to what we might initially imagine, the solution to mobility is more a matter of equity and urban design than money or engineering.

Whenever I'm invited to a city to share ideas on transport, I begin by pointing out that we must first make clear what kind of city we want: the solution is very different depending on whether we want a city like Houston or Amsterdam. Furthermore, in order to know what type of city we want, we must first have clarity about how we want to live because a city is only a means to a way of life. Therefore, when we speak of urban transport, the issue is not really mobility or even urban design. It's how we want to live. And we wouldn't normally consult a transport engineer about how to live happily.

The Causes of Mobility Problems

Only a minority use private cars in the developing world. Even the wealthiest developing cities have only one-fifth the number of cars per thousand inhabitants of Germany or the United States; cities in most of the developing world have less than one-tenth that number. Nevertheless, traffic jams are epic—and growing—in developing cities. Not in our wildest imagination is it possible for road space to increase more quickly than the number of cars. Today there is a consensus that major cities cannot solve the mobility challenge solely through private cars. Mobility based on the private car is a paradigmatic example of an unsustainable model: the greater the economic development, the worse the problem can become.

Although it may seem strange to say, the main cause of traffic jams is not the number of cars. It's the number and length of car journeys. Ten cars traveling one kilometer each generate the same road space occupation and therefore the same amount of traffic as one car that travels ten kilometers. If someone who drives two kilometers to work moves farther away, increasing their trip to ten kilometers, this is equivalent to having four more cars.

The only solution to mobility in large cities is mass transport: high-capacity, high-speed transport. This may consist of trains, subways, buses organized as bus-based mass-transport systems (BRTs), trams, or a combination of all these modes. A good mass-transport system has wide coverage -it goes to all areas of the city where most journeys begin and end, has a high frequency of service, and has a low cost per passenger.

For a mass-transport system to have those three qualities, the city must be compact. In a spread-out city, it's difficult and costly to cover all sectors. Distances, and therefore trips, are long, which leads to higher costs, and since there are few people per hectare, it isn't possible to maintain high frequencies because trains or buses would go almost empty.

The most important prerequisite for good mass transport and good mobility is thus density. Metros, BRTs, trams, and even taxis work well in a compact city. And many journeys can be made on foot, by bike, or on scooter. No mass-transport system will work well in a dispersed, low-density city; taxis there are very expensive, and few journeys can be made on foot or by bike. On the other hand, all mass transport systems and other sustainable means of transport such as bicycles work well in a dense city.

For mobility, therefore, much more important than choosing between trains or buses is to get the city to grow in the right place. For most rapidly expanding developing cities, it would be much more useful for mobility to use the US$5 billion of a typical 25-kilometer subway line, to buy land for the city's expansion in the right location. In suburban environments such as California or Texas, people cannot use public transport to reach a railway station and cannot go from the station at which they arrive to their destination by public transport, then the train loses much of its justification. A high-speed train is being built in California, but most people there live and work in low density places with little or no public transport coverage, which means it will be difficult for the train to operate as efficiently as its European counterparts.

Los Angeles, for example, has a less effective mass-transport system than New York City in part because it stretches indefinitely in all directions without the obstacle of a river, whereas Manhattan streets rapidly come up against the waterfront. In island cities such as New York and Hong Kong or others such as Paris, London, and Shanghai that are crossed by major rivers, water creates bottlenecks in the few roads that lead to tunnels or bridges. This spurs the construction and use of mass transport. Therefore, the problem of lack of road continuity in cities with rivers fortuitously forces them to have better mass transport systems sooner rather than later.

Bridge and tunnel bottlenecks lead to discussions about building additional river crossings. Unfortunately, motorists often win when they want a new bridge or tunnel. I have witnessed such discussions in Kiev, Florianopolis, Valdivia, Montreal, Istanbul, and other cities. It would seem that the sooner cities decide not to build more bridges or tunnels for cars and decide instead to make them exclusively for mass transport, pedestrians, and cyclists, the better the cities become. A good example of this is the Tilikum bridge over the Willamette River, completed in Portland, Oregon, in 2015 and reserved for pedestrians, cyclists, buses, and trams. Cities such as New York, London, Paris, and others decided long ago not to build any more car bridges or tunnels across their rivers.

Some realities are counter intuitive. Just as the Earth does not revolve around the Sun, traffic jams are not solved by building more roads. There is no "equilibrium level" in the relationship between cars and urban road space that, if achieved, would eliminate traffic jams. If there was more space for cars in London, Paris, or New York, then there would be more cars. If there was less space for them, then there would be fewer. Therefore, when we decide how much space we assign to the car, we are deciding how much we want cars to be used in the city.

When we're in a traffic jam, it seems that more or wider roads will solve the problem, but this isn't the case. There is no city in which more or wider roads have averted or solved traffic jams. Chinese cities have networks of very wide roads. Beijing has many urban highways; furthermore, in accordance with urban design regulations, there is one arterial road every five hundred meters and one eight-lane road every kilometer. And yet traffic jams grow worse every year.[1] It would take many decades for any developing city to build road infrastructure such as we see in California, Texas, and Florida. Nevertheless, in those states, time lost in traffic jams increases yearly.[2]

It has been said that trying to solve traffic problems with more roads is rather like trying to solve obesity by loosening one's belt. More roads not only fail to solve the problem but exacerbate it. Wider roads encourage citizens to make more and longer journeys, whether to go to a larger park or supermarket or a more comfortable cinema. More road space generates what has been called "induced journeys"—trips that wouldn't be taken absent the wider and faster road. In other words, each road widening generates its own traffic.[3]

A widened road relieves the bottleneck for a spell. But the widened road attracts more vehicles, and momentarily reduced travel times encourage the construction of car-dependent new housing and workplaces farther away, thus bringing more traffic and longer journeys. The road then becomes congested once again. But the widened road or the highway over it has now created a more serious problem: it has stimulated a low-density expansion of the city, which makes any prospective mass-transit system more expensive and less efficient.

In the United States over a twenty-year period, the number of kilometers traveled increased ten times more than the population increased.[4] Similarly, in Canada, another nation with immense and abundant urban and suburban highways, commuting times have systematically increased. An interesting exception is Vancouver, where commuter times have not increased despite a large increase in population and buildings. Experts agree that this is because Vancouver is the only city in Canada that has systematically prevented major highways from crossing it and has most actively stimulated densification and the use of public transport.[5]

The roads in the giant city of Lagos are completely jammed. The city center stands on an island, and therefore there are bottlenecks to access the bridges to enter and leave it. Authorities could at least build BRTs, or trams and bridges for them, but they have not: they continue trying to solve the traffic problem by widening roads and making more bridges for cars. I was in Lagos one day when they were opening a third lane in each direction on the arterial Ozumba Mbadiwe road, which had previously been totally blocked. One day after the inauguration of the expansion, the traffic jams reverted right back to their earlier state.

Traffic jams are a prime indication that a road is ripe for bus-only or tram-only lanes. Some places, such as California, are already testing truck-only lanes.[6] Strange as it may sound, traffic jams may be collaterally useful. If we believe that density and use of public transport are two desirable goals, then traffic jams are a means of achieving them. They encourage citizens to want to live in central areas close to their work and to use mass transport.

Now, any city needs a road network, and not just for public transport. Cars are not going to disappear. But it is simply necessary to keep in mind that no amount of road space will do away with traffic jams.

Restricting Car Use to Solve Traffic Jams

It might have been justified to build highways to solve traffic problems before we understood the futility of this approach. But today the promise many politicians make of solving bottlenecks by making more or wider roads is almost as populist and ineffective as promising to solve poverty by printing money. Almost all developing cities need more roads. But if the new roads or road widenings do not include BRT lanes, the investment will be useless in terms of improving mobility.

Those who drive cars often believe that solving mobility is synonymous with resolving traffic jams. In fact, mobility and traffic jams are two different problems, with different solutions. Mass transport solves mobility but not traffic jams. As it is counterintuitive that more road infrastructure does not solve traffic jams, it's also true that mass transport, sadly, does not solve them either. Contrary to the illusions of the wealthy in developing cities, no mass transport, whether it is a metro, bus, train, or tram, and no matter how excellent it may be, will resolve bottlenecks. Moreover, some cities with extensive metro networks endure some of the worst traffic problems in the world. This is so in São Paulo, Bangkok, Mexico City, Cairo, and Caracas.

In New York there are daily jams en route to the tunnels and the George Washington Bridge that cross the Hudson River to New Jersey. However, no one would dare propose more or wider roads or an additional bridge or tunnel for cars. Here, any discussion on mobility starts from the premise that the only purpose is to improve public transport, and what is discussed is simply the best way of doing so. Many years ago, in cities such as London, Amsterdam, Zürich, Paris, New York, and Berlin, an explicit or implicit decision was made: that no more roads would be built to solve bottlenecks. Investments would only be made in the expansion and improvement of public transport.

The only way to solve traffic jams is to limit car use. For many drivers in developing cities, "transport policy" means facilitating car use. For transport commissioners in advanced cities, "transport policy" means the opposite: reducing car use. For decades these commissioners in London, Copenhagen, Paris, and Vancouver have been removing space from cars and handing it over to pedestrians and cyclists.

Restricting car use to improve urban mobility and reduce traffic jams doesn't mean restricting car *ownership*, although there are places that do restrict it. Singapore and most major Chinese cities limit the number of cars for which plates can be issued. To buy a car, the purchaser has to pay a fee, sometimes through an auction, similar to how taxi licenses are awarded in many cities.[7]

Restrictions on use, on the other hand, include a ban on driving on certain days or at certain times based on plate number, as is done in several Latin American cities; fuel taxes; or parking limitations. Or a fee for entering certain central sectors is levied, such as is done in London (the well-known congestion charge), Singapore, and Stockholm and, more recently, was approved for New York. But the simplest way of curtailing car use is to restrict parking on the street and even on private property.

A mayor may explain to those who protest parking restrictions that his intention isn't to negatively or unfairly affect drivers but to reduce traffic jams, and thus to ensure that traffic flows better. More parking brings more traffic jams. Even so, drivers will probably be unpersuaded. Every time a street parking space is to be eliminated, those who use it angrily claim that the city must solve their parking needs, as if it were a fundamental right comparable to freedom of expression or voting. Although some might be surprised to know it, a person who buys a car doesn't acquire a right to parking provided by the city, just as someone who buys a refrigerator doesn't acquire the right to an apartment for it, which the government should provide. Therefore, a mayor can reply to those who demand a parking solution, "To ask me where you should park is equivalent to asking me where you can keep your food or your clothes. . . . It's not the government's business." There is no constitutional right to park.

If a government is inclined to provide public space for parking, then it should first assess the alternative uses for that space, such as wider sidewalks, gardens, or bikeways. Those who want to use it as a bike path or for seating have as much right to the space as those who want to park there. Jan Gehl reminds us that "a parking lot for only 20 or 30 cars fills the same amount of space as a good little city square."[8] In a city where most households do not have cars, for whatever reason, it would be unlikely that a democratic assessment would support use of the space for parking cars.

A first step in learning that public street space is valuable and scarce and has alternative uses is to change for street parking. The most obvious limitation is to ban parking on public roads. But there are also cities that restrict parking in private buildings. For several decades now, parking spaces have been prohibited in office buildings in the center of London, except for some for people with physical disabilities. Iconic buildings such as Norman Foster's forty-one-story "Gherkin"[9] and Renzo Piano's seventy-two-story "Shard"—the highest in Europe when it was completed in 2012 and a building where almost ten thousand people work—have eighteen and forty-eight parking spaces, respectively. Curiously, regulations in developing countries usually require the opposite: a minimum number of parking spaces in buildings. World-renowned architects Richard Rogers and Legorreta designed the Bancomer tower in Mexico City, built about the same time as the Shard. But there, regulations required 2,813 parking spaces.[10]

Until recently, hundreds of cities prohibited the construction of housing buildings unless they had parking spaces, but at the same time, they permitted car-park buildings to be built with no housing. The plan for Bogotá that we devised in my second term as mayor allowed buildings to be constructed without parking spaces for the first time. This significantly reduces apartment costs, especially in the case of smaller buildings. Those who would not otherwise have been able to afford an apartment in certain parts of the city—for example, the young—could now do so. Our plan not only allowed apartment buildings without parking spaces but also penalized builders when they exceeded a certain number of parking spaces by reducing the allowable area for construction.

Some cities in Spain have leased out underground spaces below streets for private investors to build parking spaces, with ownership reverting back to the municipality after a number of years. Although this does not reduce the number of parking spaces—or, therefore, congestion—it does liberate road space, which can then be turned, preferably, into wider sidewalks and bikeways rather than extra vehicle lanes. In Bogotá we also structured some projects for private investors to create underground car parks and thus generate plazas and other pedestrian spaces above them.

During my first term of office in Bogotá, we established a restriction on the use of the car based on plate numbers, which we called *"pico y placa"* (literally, peak and plate). Cars with plates ending in even numbers could not be used on certain days during peak times, and cars with plates ending in odd numbers had restrictions on the other days. During my second period of office, and based on the same system, we created a tropicalized congestion charge; we made it possible to pay something over $1,000 a year to be free of the *pico y placa* restrictions. It was an incipient mechanism to charge for road use, which of course might have become more finely tuned and sophisticated.[11]

The option to pay to avoid restriction, like the London congestion charge, can be criticized as an odious measure that cedes road space to the highest-income citizens. However, in the case of Bogotá, these higher-income earners were already evading the restriction, either by purchasing another car with a different plate number or by putting armor on their car, as armored cars were exempted from the restriction. If they paid for noncompliance, then at least money could go to the city administration coffers to subsidize public transport instead of being spent on an additional car or armoring.

A risk of charging for car use is that it may strengthen the car even more as a status symbol and thus stigmatize public transport. It can create the perception that "winners" use cars while "losers" use public transport. Another criticism is that roads, which were made through the work and effort of many generations and belong equally to all citizens, will be used exclusively by a privileged minority. Under these circumstances, the public space of the city could worsen inequalities rather than lessening them. With the congestion charge, lower-income citizens are not only excluded from expensive restaurants and shops, or from luxury country houses or access to powerboats, but also from using their cars on public roads. This may be so, but a congestion charge, unlike access to a weekend home or a private club, can occasionally be paid by lower-income citizens.

All privileges are odious, more so when they imply citizens' exclusion from a space they always felt entitled to. Precisely to avoid the disagreeable sensation produced by not having rights that others enjoy, Disney parks for many years did not have systems to pay extra and avoid lines. They reasoned that children don't understand why others take preference over them and didn't want to have first-, second-, and third-class customers. They wanted a classless society, at least for a few hours, in which everything had been paid for in advance and everything was within reach of everyone. The pedestrian environment, in which nobody had a more expensive car than anybody else, and the informal clothing also contributed to this effect. Unfortunately,

Disney has now begun to allow payment for preferential access and jumping the queue for its attractions. It may happen that this will begin to erode the "Disney" atmosphere. People pay not only to see Mickey Mouse but also for not feeling inferior.

A congestion charge can be seen as a first—and equity-advancing—step toward charging for the use of road space. Cars occupy a valuable space that belongs to all citizens, including many who never, or almost never, get in a car. This is especially valid in developing cities. Those who use cars on roads that belong to all members of society, would pay not only the cost of maintaining the road but also an additional amount that could for example go to subsidize public transport.

The simplest way to charge for the use of a car is a fuel tax. It discourages car use and encourages a transition to smaller vehicles that consume less fuel or to electric vehicles. In developing countries where the poor do not have cars and many high-income citizens evade taxes, a fuel tax is impossible to circumvent. Unfortunately, research finds that car use is relatively inelastic to increases in fuel prices, but, above certain levels, the tax achieves some reductions, especially if there are good public transport alternatives. Another disadvantage of fuel taxes is that they are also paid by rural residents who cannot avoid using their vehicles. But there are many ways to subsidize the rural population to offset the higher cost of fuel.

To the extent that electric vehicles will progressively replace fuel-powered ones, this fuel tax will become ineffective to reduce car use. Charges for car use could be made more sophisticated with satellite tracking systems, charging different rates on different roads and at different times. A high rate would apply for use of an arterial road during peak hours; a lower rate for a local road; and a very low rate or no charge at all for traveling, for example, at 2:00 A.M. In some societies, tracking systems are opposed on individual liberties considerations, given the information the state may collect on individuals' movements. But the technology is there, and many private systems such as Waze already track vehicles. In many developing countries there would likely be no objection to tracking-based charges, and tracking could also help to combat crime.

However, regardless of the specific mechanism, there is a clear international trend: to charge for car use and to use the proceeds for road maintenance and to subsidize public transport. Those who use private cars should not only pay for the use of roads, valuable public goods that are expensive to maintain and administer, but also for a number of social costs they cause: traffic and the consequent loss of time, accidents, danger to pedestrians and cyclists, and global warming. By the same logic, those who use public transport should be subsidized: they help reduce traffic levels, risks to pedestrians and cyclists, and noise, and they contribute generally to improve everyone's life in the city, as well as to reduce global warming.

Car users benefit from public transport use by others. In developing cities, daily car users are higher-income citizens while those who use public transport are lower-income ones. It is therefore convenient, fair, and equitable to charge for the use of the car to subsidize improvements to public transport.

Solving the mobility challenge requires behavioral changes in how, where, and when we use cars and how, where, and when we use mass transport. It isn't solved simply with investments and technology. A solution is only possible if those who could use a car decide to use public transport or a bicycle instead.

This sort of change is always difficult. Like most of my contemporaries, I found it difficult to change from a manual typewriter to the computer. As vice president of the Bogotá Water Company in 1985, I decided to purchase computers in lieu of typewriters. We sent hundreds of employees to courses to learn how to use a computer. My secretary proudly attended the computer courses. When she finished them and returned to the office, she put her wonderful new computer on one side of her desk, a flowerpot on top of it, and went on working on her IBM electric typewriter. I am sure that she, along with others of our generation, found it hard just a few years later to imagine working without a computer.

The use of the car is addictive. We can step into it practically straight from our bedroom. It is a private space from which we can see the world, in which we adjust the seat to our body, listen to information or music that we want at any time, talk privately on the phone, set the temperature exactly as we like, choose our route and to some extent our speed, and arrive very close to our destination.

As with so many educational processes, the use of public transport by those accustomed to the car requires some carrot and some stick. The carrot is good-quality public transport, which is comfortable, clean, safe, and, most especially, quick and reliable. And the stick is disincentives to car use, such as a reduced number of parking spaces or traffic congestion.

We've seen that market economy principles do not work well in the case of land surrounding cities, and the same is true of mobility. If each person seeking to maximize their own benefit acts selfishly and decides that it's more comfortable to travel in a private car, there will be traffic jams, time lost, and costs to the quality of life, as well as excessive energy consumption. Hence, there is a justification for the state to intervene to discourage the use of private cars and promote the use of public transport.

Without government intervention, cars have been losing appeal, particularly as a means of daily transport. Advertisements for cars show them in the middle of deserts, on mountains, or on an endless stretch of shoreline, in stunning natural landscapes, apparently with no other vehicle within a hundred miles. And indeed it would be very pleasant to have a car in an environment of that sort, but the reality is that the sophisticated vehicles that are modern cars spend a large portion of their time crawling through or idling in heavy traffic.

Mass Transport Systems

All mass-transport systems are good. Rail systems are stupendous, and they are the first that come to mind when the term "mass transport" is mentioned. Nevertheless, their investments and operational costs are so high, especially when the system is underground, that they cannot reach all sectors of a city. Even wealthy cities such as New York or San Francisco struggle to properly maintain their metros and even more so to build the new lines they desire.

Service quality in European or US metros is high, but the operating cost per passenger, partly covered by fares and partly by subsidies, is ten times that of the TransMilenio BRT in Bogotá. If we assume six round-trip weekly journeys, the monthly cost per passenger of those systems is greater than the monthly minimum wage in all developing countries.

Often, as in London, buses carry 50 percent more passengers than the Underground,[12] even though that system serves routes with the highest demand. The fastest-growing routes in New York in recent decades have not been radial, from the outskirts to the center, but those peripheral to it. However, existing metro lines today are mostly radial, running from periphery to center. New York is a long way from having the financial capacity to build the peripheral metro lines required to meet this demand.

The cost per kilometer of one of the most recent New York underground metro lines, the Second Avenue line, was equal to the cost of building sixty thousand social housing units in Bogotá. Other metros have been much less expensive, such as recent lines in São Paulo and Paris that were ten times less per kilometer.[13] But even a relatively low-cost elevated metro, such as the one we contracted for when I was mayor of Bogotá, has a cost per kilometer equal to seven thousand social housing units in our city.

Operating costs of passenger rail systems are high. Few cover their operating costs, and even fewer do so if we factor in depreciation. The subsidy required per passenger increases as the system expands. This happens because the first line is built along the corridor with the highest demand per kilometer; the next line has a similar cost per kilometer but serves a lower number of passengers, and the one after that a lower number still.

BRTs have far lower investment and operational costs than rail systems. A BRT operates on a road's center lanes, which are assigned exclusively to it. If there are no traffic lights, BRTs can achieve speeds similar to those of a metro. With a passing lane at stations and a mix of express and local services, capacity has been observed to exceed forty thousand passengers per hour in each direction, which is somewhat less than a single tracked metro, yet more than most metros reach.[14]

Many citizens consider themselves transport experts, since they use different forms of transport, or have used them. The absolute, dogmatic certainty with which some dictate that rail is the only solution is curious. When evidence to the contrary is overwhelming, and they are left without arguments to justify a preference for rail, they state as an indisputable truth that their city or region needs "multimodal systems." This generally means that the rail option must be chosen for the route under discussion, regardless of the more economical choices that would perform equally well. As a final and irrefutable argument, they cite as proof of rail's superiority the fact that advanced cities have it. In fact, every time a public transport solution is to be implemented on a given route, the reasonable and responsible approach is that various systems should be evaluated on a case-by-case basis with a cost-benefit analysis in terms of capacity, investment cost, operational cost, speed, comfort, flexibility, urban impact. Unfortunately, often this is not done, as there are passional preferences involved, and the public generally does not care much about costs involved. Although it would seem to be elementary, decisions to spend billions of dollars are often made in cities with many unmet needs, without the slightest effort to compare alternatives.

Emotional and politically motivated decisions tend to be more the rule than the exception.

Studies to evaluate the construction of metro lines almost invariably overestimate demand and underestimate costs. This last point is particularly true with underground metros. Cost overruns frequently reach 100 percent, 200 percent, or even 500 percent, as occurred with line 9 of the Barcelona Metro.

In comparison to metro systems, buses seem to be unsophisticated and even rather boring. But when they operate on central lanes as BRTs, they can achieve capacities and speeds similar to those of metros, with investment and operating costs that are several times lower. BRT lines in Bogotá are costly because they involve substantial demolitions in a dense city to generate wide sidewalks and the reconstruction of private vehicle lanes. Even so, the cost per kilometer of the TransMilenio BRT is ten times less than an elevated metro and about fifteen times less than an underground one. Furthermore, the availability of mass transport and the improvement of pedestrian public space increase real estate values in sectors through which TransMilenio passes and stimulate investment in redevelopment projects.

A BRT is the most efficient way to use scarce road space. Let's imagine for a moment that due to an earthquake or some other event, a city only has fuel to mobilize 5 percent of vehicles. How would we redistribute it? Obviously, we would allocate that fuel to buses and trucks. Otherwise we couldn't survive: there would be no way of distributing food or going to work. Now, if road space is the scarce item, isn't it rational to distribute it in the same way? Most metro lines carry fewer passengers than those that can be easily accommodated by a BRT.

With a BRT system the exclusive bus lane needs to be the central one, against the median strip, because if it were one adjacent to the sidewalks it would prevent vehicles that need to drop off freight or passengers from doing so; and vehicles turning right onto roads at an intersection, often waiting for pedestrians to cross, would block the bus lane and hamper BRT operation. Buses need to be boarded from a station on the median strip, with a platform at the same level as the floor of the bus, to avoid the need to climb up or down steps. For payment, cards should be validated when entering the station, not when entering the bus. This prevents time lost while boarding. On a regular bus, passengers board one by one, climb up steps, and then validate their card or pay by cash. If a passenger's card is not validated because its credit has run out or the passenger pays by cash, the operation takes even longer. The BRT's large articulated and biarticulated buses have two and up to five wide doors like those of a subway car. When the bus stops at a station, dozens of passengers can alight and dozens enter in a few seconds, just as they do in a subway.

Ideally, stations have doors for passengers that open when buses arrive and close when they leave. Although buses of various sizes can be operated as BRT in a large-capacity system such as TransMilenio, two- or three-bodied buses are used, with a capacity of up to 250 passengers.

To achieve the highest speeds and capacities, BRTs must have two lanes in each direction, or at least an overpass lane at stations, so that buses on express routes that only stop at a few stations can overtake those stopped at a station. Also, a bus that has already completed the boarding and alighting process can pull around a bus in front of it that has not yet completed it.

It is helpful to have points for the sale and charging of cards not only at stations but also at many other places such as convenience stores. Each bus is satellite-tracked, and its location shows up on a large screen in the control center. The control center tells the bus to speed up or slow down to avoid bus bunching and projects images from each bus's security cameras. Electronic panels at stations provide information on the arrival time of the next bus.

Ideally, buses are owned and operated by private contractors who win competitive bidding processes based on cost per kilometer. This competitive system ensures the lowest possible operating costs. It is desirable to have several contractor companies operate a city's BRT buses in case one of them fails. Publicly owned bus operators are generally inefficient. Too often personnel are selected for political criteria rather than qualifications, or civil service rules make it impossible to hire qualified staff. They tend to have labor unions that end up demanding disproportionate salaries and benefits and abusing public transport's monopoly. Public operators don't have a strong financial incentive to properly maintain the buses, and there are even instances in which employees steal bus fuel or parts. Bogotá and other cities have had unhappy experiences with public companies running their buses. It used to be a joke, but not entirely so, that a bus would leave the north of the city with one engine and arrive at the south with another.

Although buses may belong to several private enterprises, as frequently occurs with aircraft in some airlines, their color and image should be uniform. People should perceive a single public-service enterprise, which can easily become part of the city's identity. Preferably, the land for the depot, where the buses are garaged and receive maintenance, should be publicly owned so that the operator can be replaced if necessary.

Even after putting a BRT in operation on all the feasible main roads of a city, there may be certain critical areas where lack of road space and extremely high demand justify a metro. Even if the BRT system is operating below capacity, a wealthy society may forgo other investments and choose to construct one or more metro lines. What does not seem rational, however, is that a city with poverty and unmet basic needs should decide to build metro lines before it has optimized, technically as well as democratically, the use of its road space.

São Paulo's former mayor, Fernando Haddad, who fought many battles for more democratic mobility, including hundreds of kilometers of bus lanes, once told me that "it took a hundred years of industrial revolution to reduce one hour of work. We achieved that with a few cans of paint marking out exclusive lanes for buses." Although a BRT is much more than a lane printed on the tarmac—indeed, it requires a physical separation to prevent cars from entering the bus lane—Haddad's claim is suggestive.

BRTs are the only way to attend to mass transport needs in large developing cities and resource-limited developed cities during this century. Even if one, two, or half a dozen metro lines were to be built, the greater part of public transport of these cities will be provided by buses. It might be remembered here that a traditional bus service has little in common with a BRT system, which has a much higher speed and several times the capacity. A good BRT, like TransMilenio, is much more like a metro than a like a traditional bus service.

Any urban road with three or more lanes in each direction, and many with two, should have BRT-only lanes. It is a matter of rational allocation of scarce resources. A doctorate in transport engineering is not necessary; any group of citizens who analyze the issue will find that the most efficient way to use scarce road space is with bus-only lanes. One BRT lane with an overpass lane at stations can move more than thirty times as many people as a regular lane for cars, without traffic jams. But at peak times, when most major urban roads are clogged, a BRT lane mobilizes eighty or more times as many people as a car lane. What democratic or technical justification could there be for any urban road with three or more lanes in each direction not to have BRT?

There are and will continue to be buses on all major roads of developing world cities for hundreds of years. BRT is just a name given to the most efficient way to operate those buses, so that they go fastest, achieve the greatest capacity, consume the least energy and occupy the least road space. Any other way of bus operation will result in buses going slower and therefore creating a need for more buses, which in turn means that buses will take up more space. Operating in exclusive lanes next to the median strip, with payment and boarding at stations, and overpass lanes at stations, buses achieve their maximum speed and capacity.

Developing world inferiority complexes make it difficult for us to imagine solutions other than those we see in advanced countries. Nonetheless, it's convenient to recall that what makes a mass-transport system is not whether the wheels are metal or rubber but the speed of the vehicles. And obstacle-free corridors are what make high speeds possible. Metros also achieve velocity because they only stop at stations spaced relatively far apart. A bus operating on a corridor without traffic lights, with stations every kilometer, achieves speeds similar to those of a metro.[15]

If a bus has a commercial speed of fifteen kilometers per hour, and we manage, for example, by building underpasses, to double its speed to thirty kilometers per hour, then we double its capacity, because the same bus makes two journeys in the same time. The added bonus is that if the speed is doubled, operating costs are also almost halved because the bus makes two trips for basically the same cost for which it previously made one.[16]. This is so because once we start a bus, the cost of the driver's time and of fuel consumed are very similar, whether the bus is standing still or traveling at fifteen or thirty kilometers per hour. At double the speed, we also cut dramatically the size of the fleet we need to service the demand.

More important than the speed of trains or buses is the total trip time. On a typical TransMilenio route, the average speed is around 25 kilometers per hour because the bus stops at traffic lights and at all stations, which are generally closer together than those of a metro. On a typical 15-kilometer segment, a TransMilenio journey takes six minutes more than a metro. However, overall trip time is a more important the average speed of vehicles. BRT-based trips can take less time than metro-based ones because for the cost of 10 kilometers of metro, 100, 150 or 200 kilometers of BRT can be built. This means that for a given investment, much more kilometers of BRT can be built, and therefore more people can find BRT stations closer to their trips' origins and destinations. That saves time: it takes less time to walk to the station at the start of the journey and from the station to the destination at the end.

BRT-based trips can also take less time because buses can change "lines" or corridors. When metro passengers need to change lines, they must exit the train, walk often several hundred meters to the platform of the other line, and then wait for the next train.

Many BRT buses can leave the system's exclusive lane and operate on some segments of their route on ordinary streets. This allows buses to go closer to the origin and destination of trips, saving passengers' time, something that rail-based systems of course cannot do. In Bogotá some buses have high doors to the left to collect and drop off passengers at stations when operating in the exclusive BRT lane and regular bus doors on the right, which open when operating as ordinary buses and collecting passengers from the sidewalk.

Another BRT advantage is frequency of service. Metro trains have a high capacity of, say, 1,500 passengers. During off-peak hours, such as a Sunday afternoon, it isn't possible to dispatch many trains per hour because they would run almost empty. Operators reduce frequencies to minimize costs, so stations accumulate passengers. Consequently, in off-peak hours it may be necessary to wait a quarter or half an hour, sometimes more, for a train to arrive. Since buses have a lower capacity, typically eight times less than a train, at off-peak times they can run eight times more frequently than trains to serve the same demand. Waiting times and therefore trip times are shorter.

Access to a BRT station on the surface is quicker and simpler than going underground, sometimes very deep, to a metro station. Some metros have no escalators and passengers must walk up or down stairs, which many find difficult. Mechanical escalators break down; there are few elevators, and they are often difficult to find, and frequently, as is true in New York, they also break down. Some underground stations are not cleaned often enough and smell like urine, and some are stiflingly hot in summer.

In any case, there is no pleasure in walking long distances underground in narrow tunnels. And in cities where crime is rife, which is unfortunately often the case in parts of the developing world, descending deep into metro stations, especially at night, is not something done without a dose of fear. This problem is even more pronounced for women, the elderly, and children.

Driverless Electric Buses: Similar to Trains

Soon all buses will be electric. In my second term as mayor, we acquired more than seven hundred gas-powered buses and nearly five hundred electric ones. Technology will replace drivers, something even simpler in corridors with exclusive lanes. For urban operation with frequent stops there is not much difference between a train and a convoy of electric, driverless buses on a road without traffic lights.

Arriving at Newark Airport, a passenger can reach a destination in Manhattan faster going by bus than by train. Here, to reach the train station, the traveler must first walk to the airport's AirTrain, which takes them to the train station. From the AirTrain station to the train platform, the traveler must walk a long stretch and wait a while, sometimes quite a long while, until the train arrives. When the passenger exits the train at Penn Station in Manhattan, they must walk a considerable distance to the street. And from there they walk a couple of long blocks to a metro line, unless their line happens to stop at Penn Station. Instead of doing all of the above, the bus traveler needs only to walk a few yards to the bus, which stops right outside the baggage claim. The bus starts on its way a few minutes after boarding because there are frequent departures. Unlike the train, which only goes to Penn Station, the bus makes several stops next to metro stations in Manhattan. This illustrates a couple of advantages of buses: they can pick up passengers closer to where their trips start and take them closer to their destinations, and they are more frequent.

The highway from Newark to Manhattan gets clogged every morning. But buses have an exclusive lane for four kilometers before entering the Lincoln Tunnel and while inside it. This exclusive bus lane moves more passengers than any other road in the United States. It mobilizes more passengers than the six lines of the PATH train or the three lines of New Jersey Rail, which connect New Jersey to Manhattan.

It is evident that the exclusive bus lane in the Lincoln Tunnel is formidably effective. Why then is there no exclusive lane for buses in the opposite direction from Manhattan to New Jersey in the afternoon, when the same people who came in by bus in the morning also leave Manhattan in the evening? Better still, why not have exclusive lanes on the highway all the way to and from Newark airport?

Generally, mass-transport lines are constructed on the highest-demand corridors, where the city is most consolidated. However, in cities still in the making, whose area will multiply over the next few decades, it is possible to imagine mass-transport systems as the very scaffolding, or backbone, of new urban areas even if initially they carry few passengers. Bus-based mass transport facilitates this strategy, given its lower cost than rail and its adaptability. In Bogotá we left a wide median in a large new road through a yet undeveloped area to be upgraded to BRT when demand develops.[17]

Something that has not yet been done but that has delightful potential is to structure a city around a network of roads exclusively for buses, cyclists, and pedestrians. Barring that, *any* major road built in a city would be more functional, more democratic, and *would add more value to its surroundings* if from the start it includes infrastructure for BRT, bikeways, and wide sidewalks.

Now, if for any reason transport demand in a corridor increases greatly, it is easy to build a subway when this happens and either take the BRT out, or leave both the BRT and the subway.

Why Did New York Build a Subway Rather Than Bus-Based Mass Transport?

A BRT is not an inferior system, put in place as a stopgap while enough money is collected to build a subway. So why then did the world's great cities, such as London, Paris, and New York, not make bus-based mass-transport systems rather than subways? Since subways are considered the most "prestigious" mass transport and are so deeply coveted in developing cities, it's important to have an answer for this question. One reason is that although buses are technically simpler than trains, they were invented more than half a century after the inauguration of the first metro line. The London Underground was opened in 1863 for locomotive trains. In 1890 it became a true subway, the world's first, when electric trains began to operate in those tunnels. The first suburban train started operations in Mumbai in 1867. The first overhead urban train began service in New York in 1868.[18] Modern buses only began to operate in the mid-1930s. And only in 1974 did Jaime Lerner, in Curitiba, Brazil, create a BRT system, which for the first time took real advantage of the potential of the bus as a mass-transport vehicle. And only with innovations, which we incorporated into Bogotá's TransMilenio, did it reach a capacity comparable to a subway.

As Dinesh Mohan tells us in his article "Mythologies, Metros and Future Urban Transport," the technology for pneumatic tires and diesel engines was developed between 1920 and 1940, which made it possible to manufacture the first large buses. Before that, a large vehicle could only run smoothly and without jumps on rails. At the beginning of the twentieth century, most roads were paved as they had been two thousand years earlier in imperial Rome: with cobblestones placed on a stone, gravel, and sand base. A bus with solid rubber tires bouncing over cobblestones would not only have provided an uncomfortable ride but also would have rapidly broken down.[19] The use of asphalt, a petroleum by-product, only became widespread after 1930, and general use of oil only began in the twentieth century, so much so that in World War I many British warships and all German ones were still coal-powered, while merchant shipping continued to be so several decades longer.

The historical centers of European cities formed over hundreds of years, when everyone walked everywhere, except for a few rich, who rode a horse or traveled by coach. Consequently, these cities have a labyrinthine network of narrow streets ill-suited for bus-based mass transport. The only way of rapidly traversing the center of London or Paris quickly is on underground metros, riding below streets and buildings. The case is different in more recent cities, mostly formed in the twentieth century and, especially, in the second half of the century, as is true for developing world cities. Most of their growth occurred after the appearance of motor vehicles, and despite deficient road networks, at least a few major arterial roads traverse them on which BRT can operate.

The fundamentally radial structure of metros serves the older cities relatively well, with their historical and stable urban centers. However, newer cities that developed after the car tend to have several central nodes whose relative importance changes. Some decay while new ones arise. Here, the demand for transport is much less radial and more mercurial as the city evolves.

BRTs adapt well to the suburbanized American city and to developing cities, both of which do not have one center, but rather several centralities, with new ones appearing every so often. To concentrate enormous sums in rigid metro systems in such cities to carry people to locations whose relative importance changes over time is a risk.

Cities' centralities are not changing as much as travel patterns are. Travel demand growth is not from the outskirts to the center but peripheral to it. For this, rather than heavy radial rail systems, lighter ones such as BRT are more appropriate. Not only cities and travel patterns change; work patterns do as well. In mid-2022 the London Underground carried 33 percent fewer passengers than three years earlier.[20] The New York City subway was two-thirds as busy as it was before Covid-19.[21] In both cases it is neither due to relocation of housing nor to a desire to avoid public transport because it is rush-hour trips that have declined, not those for shopping or recreational purposes. Once again, BRT is more adaptable to such changes than rail.

All the same, high-income citizens in all developing cities want subways and demand that governments build them. But generally, they have not the slightest intention of using them. They simply believe that low-income earners who use buses, collective taxis, or motorcycles would use the metro and thus free up road space for their cars. Mexico City has the second most extensive metro network in the developing world after Delhi; however, middle- and high-income citizens rarely use it, and most of them have not even ridden it once.

Metros are formidable, have great capacity, are fast and reliable. But they are expensive and do not mobilize more than 20 percent of the population of any developing city. Even in the most advanced cities, rail systems have never managed to mobilize more than 50 percent of the population. This leaves developing world citizens unfazed: it often seems that, rather than solving mobility, they just want a metro.

That higher-income citizens should use mass transport and mingle there with other members of society as equals is an objective of any democratic city. It is also evidence of a system's quality and a guarantee that it will be maintained and improved, since they have more clout in public decisions. They will ensure that vehicles are clean, safe, and run with adequate frequency.

Many drivers in developing cities argue that they do not use public transport because it is bad, but if it were good, they would use it. The New York City subway has no electric escalators, enormous rats scurry between rails, stations heat up like ovens in summer, but higher-income citizens from Lahore, Lima, or Bangkok in New York on business or tourism, who in their own cities would never go near public transport, use the New York subway. Once they return to their home cities, they even boast to their friends about their expertise in navigating the system. In the New York or Paris metros, these people travel side by side with low-income citizens of those cities without a second thought. But it is unthinkable for them to do so in their own cities, and they'll do everything in their power to avoid it.

Developing countries are not only economically backward but also more unequal societies. To suggest that those who have cars should leave them at home and instead take the bus or the train together with lower-income citizens would initially seem as aggressive as a proposal for communism. And this captures one of the core aspects of urban mobility: more than a technical or economic challenge, the solution to mobility is a political and equity challenge. The most valuable resource a city has is its public road space. "The street is the river of life of the city, the place where we come together, the pathway to the center," William H. Whyte described.[22] Diamonds or oil could be found under a city's ground, yet their value would not approach that of the land between buildings—road space. This land belongs to everyone equally: to children and the old, rich and poor.

There is no technical formula to distribute road space. A society may allocate all of its road space to cars, without even leaving space for sidewalks; on the contrary, it could allocate it exclusively to pedestrians. There are no scientific or technical arguments to justify one or the other: it's an ideological and political issue. In downtown London there are roads in which the space allocated for sidewalks surpasses the space for cars. London's authorities did not ask permission from any transport engineer to distribute road space that way.

All cities in the world today provide more road space to cars than to people—indeed, often more to *parked* cars! Who decided that valuable street space should be used to park cars and not for wider sidewalks and bikeways? What criteria were used for that decision? Were children consulted? Did people without cars vote on it? Did anybody vote on it?

One of the most crucial ideological and political issues of our time is how to distribute urban road space between pedestrians, bicyclists, public transport, and private cars and other vehicles. Inequality is reduced by taking space away from cars and handing it over to the most vulnerable or lower-income citizens in the form of wider sidewalks or bikeways. If all citizens are equal, as constitutions say, then every one of them is entitled to the same amount of road space. One citizen on an old bicycle is entitled to the same amount of road space as one in a luxury car fresh from the dealer.

Rather than stale and obsolete debates such as those about state or private ownership of enterprises, which fascinate some old style leftist politicians, we should debate equality and democracy in our time. Ironically, politicians who are ostensibly leftist, moved by populism and opportunism, often align with those who oppose bus-only lanes or bikeways. In other words, those who oppose the reallocation of any space to a non-car purpose are not all fanatics of the extreme right. It's curious to see how some politicians' leftist positions are unshakable until the moment when their own mobility by car is affected. In Soviet Russia or Communist China, egalitarian criteria did not extend to the cars of Communist Party elites. On the contrary, elites were frequently escorted by motorcycles, with whose support they ignored traffic lights and naturally flouted parking prohibitions. While ministers in Holland or Sweden move around in public transport or on a bicycle, even city councilors in Bogotá travel in large cars with a driver, escorted by a police officer on a motorbike.

The Democratic senator from New York, Charles Schumer, was bravely supporting Obama's expansion of health care to benefit the poorest Americans while his wife, a former New York City transport commissioner, actively opposed the creation of a bikeway in the exclusive sector of Park Slope in Brooklyn because it took space away from cars.[23] In Brisbane, pressures from influential neighbors and politicians forced its BRT to follow a much longer route than ideal. In San Francisco, highly educated citizens who support all liberal causes opposed a BRT on Geary Avenue to protect parking on that road. Near there, in Palo Alto, home to Stanford University and one of the towns with the highest education levels in the world, the citizens' political leanings and liberal positions only lasted until the Santa Clara Valley Transport Authority proposed bus-only lanes on a road in the town center. The project met with ferocious opposition.[24]

Any solution to mobility in developing cities is intricately linked to equality, as it requires that higher-income citizens use public transport or a bicycle. It also requires an equitable distribution of road space, giving priority to public transport. As traffic jams will only grow worse, sooner or later, higher-income citizens will have to use public transport. And the sooner a society achieves this, the better will be its quality of life and social harmony. In the developing world today, there is something similar to the class conflict that Marx envisioned. It is not between capitalists and workers, but between those who own cars and those who do not: there is a conflict between them for public funds and road space.

Some interesting doctoral theses could be written that analyze press editorials and news reports in the developing world, which reflect the car-centric and class-ridden vision of those countries' elites. They solely demand more roads, wider roads, and road repairs; taxis upset them because there are too many of them or because, allegedly, taxi drivers breach traffic regulations; public transport buses, jeepneys, and bicycles annoy them; and motorcycles exasperate them. At the end of the day, they look favorably only on their own cars and those of people like them. They demand metros they have no intention of using, and they oppose BRTs, the widening of sidewalks, and the allocation of road space to bikeways.

How Did We Make TransMilenio?

When I became mayor in 1998, it was clear to me how difficult the challenge of mobility would be. Unlike many for whom becoming mayor is simply one more step up the political career ladder, I was passionate about making Bogotá a better city and had studied and dreamed about that for many years. Years before, I had written articles on the unavoidable need to structure mobility around buses on exclusive lanes. Even if a few subway lines were built, they would only mobilize a fraction of the population.[25] In 1983 I published an article proposing the creation of a bus system operating on exclusive lanes—a BRT system. I wrote, "Buses must operate on exclusive lanes in the main arteries . . . There are ways to ensure that bus transport in Bogotá be that which a civilized society deserves, and not [an] affront to human dignity. However, in order to achieve this, political decisions are necessary that cannot be avoided simply with the promise of a Metro."[26]

In a 1985 article I emphasized that passengers should pay with tickets and not money to prevent bus drivers from collecting money from each passenger. As drivers kept part of the money for themselves -sometimes they paid the bus owner a fixed amount and kept all the money paid by passengers, they stopped anywhere and everywhere to pick up passengers. To me it was evident that a driver's income should not be based on the number of passengers carried. A change was needed to remedy the chaotic competition and frequent bus accidents this caused. I also wrote about something that hadn't yet been mentioned in Colombia, which I also implemented as mayor: "Bikeways and bicycles could be fundamental in Colombian urban transport and as a means to humanize cities."[27]

Before TransMilenio, Bogotá did not have anything that an advanced country would recognize as a traditional bus service. More than thirty thousand buses, belonging to a similar number of owners,[28] competed ruthlessly for passengers. That competition, which the public called the "pennies' war," was fierce. Buses raced against each other, picked up and dropped off passengers anywhere, often in the middle of a major road, even if those passengers were small children and their caregivers.

Drivers would drive with one hand and take payment and give change with the other. They had developed the skill of stopping to pick up passengers while straddling the street, thereby blocking its three lanes to prevent other buses from overtaking them. This savage competition led to equally savage conflict: drivers carried metal bars, which they brandished when fights broke out between them. I once saw a driver angle his bus in front of another, forcing it to stop. He then jumped down and paced around the bus imprisoned by his own, breaking each and every one of its windows with an iron bar, with all the passengers still inside. These barbaric races caused pedestrian fatalities. Rosa, who worked with me, lost her only daughter, eight years old, when a bus ran off the road and killed her.

Then, in the mid-1980s, I learned about the BRT system in Curitiba, Brazil, created by mayor Jaime Lerner. The system amazed me, and I became ever more convinced that it was the appropriate solution for our needs and possibilities. I didn't understand why it hadn't been adopted by dozens of major cities around the developing world. In my campaign leaflets, I promised a radically different bus system, but in order to implement it, I had to wait several years to be elected mayor, following several electoral defeats.

True, Curitiba was a relatively small city of six hundred thousand, and some might have thought that it was not a relevant example for large cities of several million. But there were two more important reasons: the first was that higher-income groups in the developing world—the car-driving minorities—had no interest in giving up scarce road space to buses. The second was the enormous political clout of people linked in some way to traditional transport systems in developing cities: very politically powerful organizations of owners of old buses, minibuses, and jeepneys, as well as drivers, mechanics, and the families of all of them, which add up to tens of thousands of votes. In Bogotá these people had the power to paralyze the city completely when they went on strike.

TransMilenio was inspired by the Curitiba model but has different elements that significantly increase its speed and capacity and make it more suitable for a large city, namely, its operation in the center lane, next to the median; the passing lane at stations for express routes;[29] the operational design, which included fare collection systems; and bidding for the system's operation. Today, with 114 kilometers of lines, TransMilenio carries 2.5 million passengers daily. Dozens of additional kilometers are under construction. Another TransMilenio innovation was the name itself. Before, no bus-based systems had been given any particular name. I was convinced that a name would give it character and contribute to the city's identity and sense of belonging. Today nobody in Bogota says they are going by bus; they say they will go by TransMilenio, and more often than not, they will refer to it by the shortened affectionate name of "Transmi."

Representatives from hundreds of cities have visited Bogotá to learn about TransMilenio, and systems inspired by it are operating in more than two hundred cities today. Many more TransMilenio-like BRTs will be needed in the world's large cities, particularly those that will multiply their size several times in the coming decades, especially in Asia and Africa.

For a BRT, a metro, or any other form of mass transport to work well, it must operate on the highest-demand routes, which generally are those with the highest volumes of traffic. Some governments put BRTs on alternate routes, with less volume, to try to avoid the conflict inherent to the removal of cars from a couple of lanes in order to assign them to a BRT, which results in less effective BRT performance. For the first two TransMilenio lines, we chose the two roads that most concentrated traditional public transport. On one of them, Avenida Caracas, two central median lanes had previously been assigned exclusively to buses, but the buses that operated there were the traditional ones, with doors to the right, steps to climb in and out, and a driver who competed with other buses for passengers. Therefore, although those lanes were exclusively for buses, the same chaos occurred here as on other roads.

It was unimaginable to anyone that we would be able to remove the powerful, semiformal transport companies from these lanes and territory. The first young manager of the TransMilenio project, a brilliant engineer, recommended putting the BRT on some road with fewer traditional buses where we'd have a greater chance of winning the conflict.[30] But I chose Avenida Caracas. I was convinced that any other future mayor, less passionate about the project and more political, would never confront the powerful traditional transport operators there.

We had a short time to accomplish this task as my term was only three years and immediate reelection was not permitted. We worked on several fronts at once: transport engineering, which led to important adjustments to the Curitiba model. Almost simultaneously buses had to be ordered and civil works started to convert two avenues into BRT corridors. Such work allowed us to remove traditional bus operators from those roads. They did not yet feel seriously threatened, however, as neither they nor anyone else believed it would be possible to implement anything like what became TransMilenio.[31]

Parallel to the physical facets of the project, we negotiated with some traditional bus operators to operate the new system. When the civil works were almost finished, traditional bus operators held a series of massive strikes, one of which lasted several days. They paralyzed not only Bogotá but also other regions since they had forged alliances with local bus operators in all the major cities of Colombia. Some populist politicians joined forces with them. The president kept calling me, often late at night at home, pressuring me to accept their demands. Fortunately, in Colombia, mayors have a high degree of autonomy, and I stood firm.

Although initially it seemed impossible, we secured an agreement with most of the traditional bus operators, thanks to the remarkable negotiating skills of Ignacio de Guzmán, the new project manager, who had been an important leader in the formation of some of Colombia's major business groups.[32] During the negotiating process, Ignacio was the "good cop" who invited the traditional bus operators to become major shareholders in the new system, while I, as mayor, was closer to the "bad cop," telling them we would do it one way or another—with them or with other operators. Ignacio's training as a Jesuit priest for five years probably was more useful for these negotiations than his subsequent career as a lawyer.

A few months after TransMilenio started operating, a friend told me that she often used to drive her secretary home after work. One day, when she offered to do that, the secretary answered, "Thank you, but today I must be home early, so I had better take TransMilenio." This was revolutionary in Bogotá. Suddenly, those who took public transport—mostly low-income earners— were traveling faster than those in cars!

Citizens in wheelchairs and those with baby strollers had never been able to use public transport before because they were unable to climb up the narrow steps of public transport buses, and even if they had been able to do so, they would not have been able to pass the turnstiles to enter the bus. They were immobilized, with no access to the city. TransMilenio set them free, making it possible for them for the first time to move around their own city.

TransMilenio is a public company that belongs to the city administration. It holds competitive tenders for private companies to operate their own, or third-party, buses. In the first tenders, companies that had more traditional bus owners and operators as shareholders and those willing to scrap the largest number of old buses scored extra points. Operators are basically paid by the number of kilometers their buses run. The tenders stipulate the type of bus to be used, including environmental requirements, and award additional points for gas- or electricity-powered vehicles. The issuing of fare cards as well as the fare collection system are also contracted to private enterprise.

In 2009, after visiting Bogotá, the great British architect and urbanist Richard Rogers wrote me: "I was asked what I thought the advantages were of either building a new subway system or continuing to invest in a city-wide network of buses building on the excellent TransMilenio. Bogotá has a large gap between the wealthy and the poor and any system that is developed must serve both these groups for the least amount of money per kilometer. Without doubt, the best investment is in a well-designed comprehensive bus network. Subways work best where there is wealth to meet the necessary investment, e.g., London, New York, Tokyo, Madrid and Paris. I therefore strongly recommend that you extend the existing bus network system rather than building a subway."

However, we did decide to build a metro line to reinforce TransMilenio in a corridor with a particularly high demand and to effectively integrate low-income sectors into the rest of the city. In my first term as mayor, we began work on TransMilenio and simultaneously on the metro line, mostly financed by the national government. Unfortunately, the government did not follow through with the agreed-on funds, and we couldn't fill the gap. Twenty years later, in my second mayoral term, we did contract the first metro line for Bogotá along a route with a high transport demand—demand that will continue to increase, as the line runs along one of the city's main growth axes.

On an eight-kilometer stretch on Avenida Caracas, the Metro runs above TransMilenio. The Metro thus operates as an express line and the buses as a local one. The scheme was proposed by Andrés Escobar, the Metro manager, who had seen that in Santiago at peak times trains only stop at every other station. This means that Metro stations can be farther apart, and therefore trains achieve higher operating speeds and hence higher capacity. Metro stations that are approximately a kilometer apart are physically integrated with those of Transmilenio, which are five hundred meters apart. On this segment, the capacity of Metro and TransMilenio together is more than a hundred thousand passengers an hour per direction, which is among the highest in the world for a mass-transport line.

The Metro line begins its route in a low-income sector to the southwest of the city. It transforms the life of hundreds of thousands of people who live in that area close to the stations or can access it by TransMilenio. As happened with almost all of our projects, populist politicians did everything possible to block it. It didn't concern them that many low-income sectors would be harmed, in this case left without a mass transport, which would take them to the city center in twenty-one minutes, and in some cases, low-income citizens had supported proposals that would harm these politicians. The alleged objection was that we would be building an aboveground line and not an underground one. In addition to the financial infeasibility of an underground line, it's generally more pleasant for passengers to travel aboveground.[33]

TransMilenio has now inspired and served as a model for similar systems in hundreds of cities around the world, from Istanbul, Tehran, and Dar es Salaam to Guangzhou and Mexico City. In Pakistan, for example, Peshawar built a BRT line and Lahore built an elevated one. In Karachi, working with my friend the engineer Ashar H. Lodi, I proposed that as part of the BRT project the government pedestrianize a stretch of Jinah Road in the historical center, a suggestion that was undertaken. The area became a lively pedestrian street surrounded by beautiful historical buildings, with a BRT running along it.

Although there are more than three hundred BRTs in operation worldwide, many do not work as well as they should because governments tried to reduce the economic or political costs of their implementation. For example, optimal BRT routes have been discarded by saying it would be impossible to create bus-only lanes because the road is "too narrow" or "too congested." Of course, it's precisely the most congested roads that most need BRTs.

Even in the extreme situation in which very narrow streets require a bus-only lane to exclude all other vehicles, the democratic and technical decision is to do exactly that: assign the scarce road space to buses and keep cars out. When we were building TransMilenio, we were told that Avenida Jimenez, an arterial road in the historical center, was too narrow to accommodate the system. We replied that indeed it was very narrow. But that as Colombia was a democracy, we would instead get cars out and convert it into a road exclusively for pedestrians and TransMilenio, the majority users. And so we did. A number of democratic cities—Utrecht, Zürich, Melbourne, Denver, Dar es Salaam, Pereira, and San Diego, to name only a few—have streets in the center that are reserved exclusively for buses or trams, cyclists, and pedestrians.

In terms of comfort, many TransMilenio buses, as is also true with many metros, are too crowded, especially at peak times. In São Paulo or Santiago some metro trains carry more than ten passengers per square meter at peak hours. The *oshiya*, or "pushers," in the Tokyo system push passengers into carriages to permit the doors to close. There are ways of increasing TransMilenio's capacity, such as increasing its speed by building underpasses at intersections. In any case it is quite possible that the capacity of a line will become saturated: that is one of the reasons why we contracted for the construction of a metro line that runs above TransMilenio for several kilometers.

Matters such as the name of the system, the bus color, the design of the stations, the quality of adjacent pedestrian spaces, and signage are important to make a BRT attractive. When the system is built, it seems pragmatic to have the first lines pass through middle-income and, if possible, high-income sectors, so that the system is not identified as a "poor person's transport." Indeed, in Bogotá, buses used to have that connotation.

From the outset, many who would never use a traditional bus have been using TransMilenio. This is helped, of course, by the fact that trips on TransMilenio take less time than by car, and no time or money is wasted finding somewhere to park. We also introduced a system to restrict car use by license plate numbers, which leads many car owners to use TransMilenio on days when they cannot use their cars.

London is associated with its double-decker red buses; New York, with yellow cabs. Likewise, the red TransMilenio buses have become part of the Bogotá identity, and they appear in all videos about the city.[34]

Many innovations have been adopted through time to improve TransMilenio. During my second term as mayor, noticing passengers tended to concentrate toward the doors, overcrowding those spaces, it occurred to me that seats in buses should not face forward, leaving too narrow a corridor in the middle, but rather with the back of seats against the bus walls and windows. In a regular bus that takes turns often, this may be uncomfortable for passengers that may be thrown off at a turn, but TransMilenio buses basically operate in straight roads, similar to a rail track. We ordered new TransMilenio buses to have this seat arrangement, which leaves more corridor space and encourages passengers to go farther from buses' doors. The new arrangement also contributes to reducing pickpocketing, an unfortunate problem in Bogota's buses, as seated passengers face those standing and thus contribute to controlling thieves.

Beyond its efficiency as public transport, TransMilenio is a powerful symbol that public good prevails. When cars appeared at the beginning of the twentieth century, they accentuated inequality.[35] A mass-transport system like TransMilenio restores equality in speed in a very visible way. A child can make funny faces from the window of the bus at people in barely moving cars. Unconsciously, this constructs equality and legitimacy. An underground metro could take passengers at high speed, but despite all its attributes, it would not have the same symbolic power. TransMilenio, running swiftly alongside expensive cars stalled in traffic, is a powerful image of democracy at work.

CHAPTER 6

Choosing a Mass Transit System

Public transport sets us free in a city. As has been true since the first historical appearance of trams, mass transport today gives people a greater choice of neighborhoods to live in and the possibility to have larger homes farther away, or one with a park nearby. Most people do not have the option of living in walking distance to their place of work, mainly because housing that close is too expensive for them. It may also be that one member of the household lives close to their place of work but another works at the opposite end of the city. None of the putatively self-sufficient satellite towns built thus far function as such. Although initially many residents have worked there, most changed jobs within a few years and now must travel long distances every day. Exclusively residential sectors are inconvenient; it is desirable that there should be employment everywhere. However, it would be utopian to think that most citizens will be able to live close to where they work: what is democratic is not to propose a utopia where everyone can move around on foot but to offer ubiquitous mass transport at an affordable price for all.

A good public transport enlarges the area in which people can look for work. It contributes to the flow of knowledge, the city's competitiveness, and its capacity to create jobs. It also makes it possible for people to access education, beautiful places, and cultural and sports activities. A ubiquitous mass transport makes real a citizen's right to the city.

Public transport is an expression of freedom. Life on foot, free of the worries of a car and its parking and fuel expenses and the tensions that it brings, allows us to dream, imagine, engage in contemplation and creation. Life without a car in a city in which we find good public transport everywhere is liberating. If we are not driving, we are free to chat, read, think, and jot down ideas. We can have a couple of beers with a friend and not worry about driving home. As public transport users, we enjoy seeing people on the street on the way to the station or in the bus or train and watching the city as we go. We feel empathy with someone with tearful eyes, or we smile at others' laughter; we see people who look interesting to us or are dressed creatively. On the way to public transport or while on board, we meet neighbors and acquaintances and sometimes even strike up a conversation with strangers.

The Privilege of Surface Travel

In Bogotá, millions of Coleoptera beetles, which we call *winter cucarrones*, simultaneously emerge from the ground twice a year in any area with grassy gardens, parks, and pastureland around the city—and start to fly. There are so many of these reddish-brown beetles that you can hear their buzz everywhere. They emerge out of the darkness of the ground, after many months there as larvae, find partners in flight, and ecstatically mate in midair.[1] A few hours later, they die. Although perhaps not as intensely as the Bogotá *cucarrones* experience it, we feel a liberating relief when we come out of a metro tunnel into daylight. The noise of the train fades, and we can appreciate the daylight, views of the sky, the city, its buildings, and the green trees. Surface travel, with natural daylight, is more pleasant and interesting than travel through a dark tunnel, with the deafening rumble of the train bouncing against the walls. When I was a student in Paris, I worked in a hotel at night and left, tired, in the early morning. All the same, and although I had to attend lectures later, I preferred the bus or the overhead Métro, which meant a longer trip home but allowed me to travel on the surface.

Public transport users are exemplary citizens. They help to reduce traffic, energy consumption, and accidents. Why send them underground, leaving the surface to private cars? Should we not be rewarding them? Moles are at home underground; human beings are not. That's why miners are paid more or work shorter hours than those who work on the surface.

It is true that the only way of passing quickly through a city's historical center is in an underground metro. But in most modern cities, the historical center is only a tiny fraction of the whole. And generally, there are major roads that pass alongside it. The image of public transport users going underground, while a higher-income minority enjoys daylight in their cars on the surface, does not seem very democratic. It seems that the possibility of using surface public transport, for those who prefer it, is a right, even if there is a metro line running below.

Although it's more pleasant to travel on an elevated metro line than on an underground one, the latter is better for a city than the former. Elevated lines can only be built on wide roads and, even then, they require as a complement enlargements and improvements of public pedestrian space. At all events, the negative impact is much lower than that of elevated highways since metro structures are narrower.

The Equity and Efficiency of Public Transport Subsidies

Realizing the full liberating potential of mass transport subsidies might also be in order. Generally subsidies carry the risk of poor allocation or wastefulness. If water is distributed at too low a price, there is the risk that beneficiaries will establish car-washing businesses; free food risks ending up as pig feed. Subsidies to public transport, however, have several environmental and social benefits and not much risk of waste. Transport consumption is price-inelastic: people will neither reduce their transport consumption much if it's expensive, nor will they increase their consumption if it's cheap. They consume what they need, no more and no less. Even if it were free, public transport use would not change much, and people would not spend the day riding around in buses or trains.

High public transport fares restrict recreational trips, such as those to a park, downtown, or a cultural event. It sometimes keeps youth from being able to study. Therefore, subsidies to public transport tend to be an efficient social investment. Now, it is true as well that the finances of many developing cities, which must make investments in the construction and operation of roads, parks, schools, hospitals, kindergartens, and support for the elderly who have no social security, are usually unable to subsidize transport, and, when they do it, the expenditure comes with severe opportunity costs.

For the above reasons, I like the idea of free public transport, the funding for it coming mainly from taxes on car use.

In Bogotá the TransMilenio BRT operates basically without subsidies. Other buses in the integrated system receive a subsidy of some 50 percent of the fare paid by users. Some transport subsidies are adopted for political reasons and do not actually favor the truly neediest—for example, subsidies to students or to the elderly, many of whom are not poor. A more effectively focused subsidy would benefit, for example, those who board public transport in low-income neighborhoods. A lower fare could be charged there.

In some cities, such as Paris or New York, the cost of a metro ticket is the same regardless of whether the trip is long or short. By contrast, in other locations, such as London or Washington, DC, the metro fare depends on the distance traveled. If applied in Latin America, that policy would be prejudicial to low-income citizens, who usually need to live farther away from their work.[2] If the same fare applies regardless of the length of the journey, those who make the shorter journeys, who usually have higher incomes, subsidize lower-income passengers. And this is equitable.

Of course, what is most equitable and rational environmentally is that car users pay for public transport quality improvements and operational subsidies. Internationally, the trend is to charge increasingly more for car use, not only for road construction and maintenance but also to subsidize better and cheaper public transport.[3]

In Bogotá, during my first term as mayor, we set a surcharge of 25 percent on fuel, half of that earmarked for road improvement in poorer neighborhoods and the other half for mass transport.

Trams Are Sexy and Buses Aren't

Perceptions are an important factor in transport. "Australian men won't use a bus," someone told me in Perth. While a large Harley-Davidson bike is identified as a "man's ride," buses are not, at least in Perth. Governments contemplating mass transit must consider the status or image of the various options. In many places, buses are perceived as inferior to any vehicle with metal wheels. For some reason, means of transport have always been strongly charged with status connotations. Fine horses, powerful motorcycles, expensive cars, yachts, and private planes have conveyed status. In mass transport, trams especially are in fashion today.

Local governments in the United States say that they invest in trams because they stimulate private investment in decayed central areas while buses do not. This may be true for conventional bus routes, which can be eliminated at any time, but, once again, the BRT is a different animal from a traditional bus route and has not been sufficiently tested or compared with trams in this respect. Trams have less capacity and cost more than a BRT.[4] However, local governments reason that buses do not have sufficient "sex appeal" to renew the luster of central areas, as they are identified with low-income citizens—mainly African Americans and Latin Americans.

There is no solid evidence that trams stimulate private investment and urban improvement,[5] to say nothing of evidence that trams more effectively prod investment than a good BRT. Walter Hook found BRTs to be more effective than trams in stimulating private investment in decayed urban areas.[6] It is certainly possible that improvements in sectors of Portland, Oregon, were attributable not to trams but to other factors. Clearly, in Salt Lake City, one of the first American cities to have modern trams, the impact has been insignificant: decades after the tram system was put in place, the city center still looks bombed out, with plenty of empty lots being used for parking.

Dozens of other US cities, including Dallas and Denver, have invested in trams. No argument will convince the public that they can achieve the same and more with a BRT at a much lower cost. Although governments who implement trams disguise their reasoning with arguments about capacity and cost, it's really a matter of emotion and passion, rather like what motivates someone to want a luxury car. If somebody wants a Rolls-Royce, they can certainly buy one, but it's worth remembering that it does basically the same thing as a Ford. The same applies to a society that wants to buy a tram system because it looks better than a bus-based one or because its citizens believe that it will attract more high-income passengers: if that society has the money, what a splendid idea! But BRT systems perform the same function.

It's curious that trams are a "sexy" or sophisticated option because in the first half of the twentieth century the entire world saw trams differently. They were rather seen the way buses are today: as antiquated, low quality, and for the poor. The first trams, horse-drawn, began operating around 1830. For many decades that was the only form of public transport. They were always overcrowded. In 1864, a passenger in New York complained that "people are packed into them like sardines in a box, with perspiration for oil."[7] By the end of the nineteenth century, electric engines began to replace horses. But trams continued to be full, especially in central areas, where roads were crowded with trams, horse-drawn carriages, and pedestrians, as was the case on New York's Broadway. There, frequent bottlenecks would bring traffic to a standstill for ten minutes or more.[8]

In the 1930s almost all cities in the world with more than a hundred thousand inhabitants had trams, which higher-income citizens, now beginning to shift to cars, did not use. Then came buses, which at the time, in contrast to trams, were seen as modern and attractive. A couple of decades later, they had replaced most tram systems around the world.

There is an oft-repeated tale that General Motors, the megaproducer of cars and buses, was largely responsible for the disappearance of trams because a couple of companies in which it held shares bought up tram systems in some cities to scrap them and promote car use and, to a lesser extent, bus use.[9] In reality, GM only bought some twenty tram networks, and in some cases the company even initially expanded the tram lines. The progressive and rapid disappearance of trams did not take place in those cities alone but in hundreds of cities around the world due to their poor image and the perception of buses at the time as superior. And in many ways, they were. John Kay writes, "Trams were phased out because they were inferior to buses as a means of public transport. They still are."[10]

In their own defense, trams are pretty. Furthermore, they travel on the surface, so passengers can enjoy natural light and views of the city. Generally, a tram gives a smoother ride than a bus, so it's easier, for example, to read on board. On the negative side, when a tram or a light train breaks down, those coming behind it cannot leave the exclusive lane and pass the broken-down vehicle as a BRT bus can. Regarding investment and operating costs, trams are much more expensive than a BRT. *The Economist* concludes that "cash spent on streetcars displaces spending on other, more cost-effective forms of public transport like buses, which offer cheaper and more-efficient service but are considerably less sexy."[11]

Harvard professor and author of *The Triumph of the City*, Edward Glaeser, writes, "For decades, economists like me—and other budget nerds—have argued that buses are vastly more cost-effective than trains. Yet trains cause hearts to flutter, while buses elicit groans. . . . For better or worse, the obvious economic benefits of buses won't win hearts and minds. We need tough medicine on the city streets that reduces stops and competing traffic. But we also need a heavy dose of design—some beauty in our buses. It isn't free, but costs far less than building miles of rail."[12] I agree with Glaeser on the importance of making buses attractive, with stations of quality architectural design. Naturally, for them to provide a service equivalent to a rail system, they need to operate as BRT systems. The most important attraction of TransMilenio, as with any mass transport system, is that it makes journeys faster than by car.

Although less attractive than trams, in some cases, however, buses are more attractive than other rail. High-income earners in Mumbai would never consider riding their city's packed trains. In South Africa, trains are associated with low-income citizens, and one of the justifications for building BRT systems in Johannesburg and Cape Town was to attract middle- and higher-income citizens to public transport. In Mexico City, many middle- and higher-income citizens who would not use the metro are using the BRT buses that now operate there. In many European cities, higher-income citizens, if they're not in a hurry, tend to prefer the bus to the underground metro to feel safer, enjoy the views of the city, and avoid the descent into a tunnel.

BRTs Enhance Property Values

A metro enhances the value of the sectors through which it passes. The increase in value of properties close to metro lines and particularly to stations is so large that sometimes lower-income citizens and some medium and small businesses must move to other neighborhoods. Many new businesses need to locate some distance from metro lines to find affordable rents. A metro attracts housing projects, shops, and offices to its surroundings. Most urban redevelopment projects implemented in cities with metro lines have been located close to them, so much so that sometimes the accumulation of new projects along a metro line have exceeded the line's capacity. This happened in London, where residents of new developments such as Hale Village complain that trains come in full at peak times, so they must let several of them pass before they can find room on one.[13]

A BRT also enhances the value of properties around a line. Additionally, its lower cost makes it possible to have several lines for the same price as one metro line and therefore cover more areas of a city. The relative increase in value of the sectors it crosses is thus lower. In Bogotá, major housing construction companies' commercial strategy has been to publish city plans showing TransMilenio lines and emphasizing their projects' proximity to them. The chief executive of one of the largest developers promoted projects in this way and acknowledged that their market research showed that the most important factor for buyers choosing housing was proximity to Trans-Milenio.[14] Although TransMilenio only operates on 25 percent of Bogotá's arterial roads, all the shopping centers that have opened since it began operation have been located on its trunk lines.

Several studies have confirmed TransMilenio's positive impact on sector values.[15] University of California, Berkeley, researcher Nick Tsivanidis found not only that TransMilenio increased values around it but also that its effectiveness significantly increased the city's productivity and income. Tsivanidis' study concludes that TransMilenio allowed residents to change where they lived and worked, due to the reduction in travel times and that productivity went up as workers found better matches with firms and employment agglomerated more in central areas. According to Tsivanidis' study, TransMilenio increased Bogota's real income by 2.2 percent and GDP per capita by 2.98 percent. TransMilenio can explain between 2.8 percent and 12 percent of the observed GDP growth between 2000 and 2016.[16]

The Political Cost of a BRT

Although a BRT costs much less in literal terms than a metro, its political cost is high, a factor that should be taken into consideration. Car drivers, especially in the developing world, have economic and political power and are not prepared simply to relinquish "their" space to a BRT.

In 2016, when I began my second term as mayor, we had 114 kilometers of the BRT TransMilenio in operation. Assigning road lane exclusivity to the BRT was accepted at that point as efficient and democratic. Higher-income groups that drove cars and felt inconvenienced did not dare oppose the creation of new BRT lines—at least publicly—although some discreetly promoted court actions and supported politicians who opposed the BRT.

This attitude peaked when some from the country's most powerful sectors opposed the BRT we intended to build in Carrera Septima, or Seventh Street. The Septima is the main road that crosses the wealthiest sector of Bogotá, where at least half of the hundred thousand richest and most powerful citizens in the country have their homes. They opposed the plan not only because it would take space away from cars but also because TransMilenio would in some respects mean that their sector would lose exclusivity and resemble other sectors in the city. However, the line would not only pass through the six-kilometer stretch of their sector. It would serve many more groups in middle-class and indeed some low-income sectors in originally informally developed neighborhoods on the steep hillsides to the north of Bogotá. Having TransMilenio in the northeast would have made Bogotá the first city in the developing world in which higher-income citizens use public transport. They would have had to choose between spending one or two hours by car for some trips or fifteen to twenty minutes by TransMilenio. High-income citizens would have shared the bus as equals with low-income ones. Moreover, high-income and powerful riders would have exerted pressure for TransMilenio to be comfortable, safe, and effective.

But once again politicians who opposed us, despite their putatively left-wing convictions, aligned themselves with high-income groups, even if their opposition meant hundreds of extra hours of travel in public transport every year for lower-income citizens. Part of the problem stemmed from the fact that my name was associated with TransMilenio, and by attacking our BRT, they were vicariously attacking me politically. As is typical in Global South politics, they also invented slurs. They convinced many that I was the owner of TransMilenio or that I had sold Volvo buses after ending my first term as mayor.[17]

During my second term as mayor, my political adversaries tried to convince the public that it was possible to choose between TransMilenio and a metro on any line because the costs were equivalent.[18] Many—either ill-informed or politically biased—also believed that metros and trams never run full and that a few lines of them would eliminate traffic jams in the city.

A few judges' politically biased decisions suspended the Carrera Septima BRT bidding process three days before the award date. During her election campaign, the woman who succeeded me in office made it almost a religious tenet that no more TransMilenio projects should be built and especially not the Seventh Street one. Few bothered to review any numbers or to present any analysis to rebut these populist ravings. Once elected, the mayor discarded the project, supposedly to make a radically different one. But the evident desirability of the BRT imposed itself, and a new project including TransMilenio moved ahead, albeit with a few changes, such as a full lane assigned exclusively to bicycles.

Another three lines of TransMilenio that we'd contracted, with a thirty-kilometer extension that did not cross such exclusive sectors, were supported by the new mayor. Her government in 2023 is proceeding as well with two new TransMilenio lines. New BRT lines and expansions under construction will increase the TransMilenio network by more than 60 percent, even with an avowed enemy of TransMilenio as mayor. Given a minimum objectivity, the system's benefits are overwhelming. Since 2000, when TransMilenio began to operate, it has been expanded by almost all subsequent administrations.

Challenges to BRT Implementation

The advantages of BRT seen in Bogotá can hold true in other cities world-wide. But implementing a good BRT is a difficult political challenge. Delhi metro moves 15,300 passengers per kilometer, while TransMilenio moves 20,600, a similar amount, given the Delhi metro's more extensive network. And as lines are chosen in terms of demand, each additional line normally moves fewer passengers per kilometer than the previous one. Neither the central nor local governments in India have the resources to use metro lines to solve the mobility of hundreds of cities that will grow exponentially in the coming decades. Unfortunately, a BRT that began to get constructed in Delhi had severe design problems and failed. However, when India's current prime minister, Narendra Modi, was governor of the state of Gujarat, a BRT was built in Ahmedabad, an important Gujarati city, which works well and can serve as a template for other BRTs in India.

In developing cities, the politically influential operators of traditional informal transport form a powerful obstacle to BRT. In Manila, similar to the pre-BRT situation in Bogotá, there are more than a hundred thousand jeepneys, and if each owner, driver, mechanic, and others related to the operation has the vote of their spouse and a couple of friends, they can easily muster half a million votes, a figure that would make any politician think twice. Traditional transport operators, who mobilize most of the population, can also put pressure on government by going on strike and thus paralyzing the city, as often happened in Bogotá before TransMilenio. Occasionally, traditional transport drivers are even armed, as was the case with the "minibus-taxis" in South Africa. The owners of informal transport are more or less illegal and in some cases quasi-criminal, but they are entrepreneurs who work hard. When BRT systems are built, many of them can be engaged as share-holders in BRT operating companies, as we did with TransMilenio.

Many developing world cities have abandoned railway lines along their growth axes because interurban roads run parallel to them. Why not use these neglected railway lines? In Karachi an announcement has been made that with Chinese assistance, passenger trains will operate along some fifty kilometers of the so-called Circular Line.[19] It is hoped the project, announced several decades ago, will finally materialize. However, it can be problematic to put surface trains to work in urban areas. Although the investment cost is relatively low, operating costs per passenger are high, several times higher than a BRT's. Underpasses at street intersections can be difficult to design and costly to build, and ugly walls and railings must be constructed along the rail corridor, which become obstacles that divide cities over many kilometers and impede pedestrians walking across the rail lines using paths that they have carved out through decades. Spaces adjacent to those railings tend to deteriorate and generate security problems.

Unlike metros, which may have stations every kilometer or less, suburban train stations are more than three kilometers apart, which does not serve well the transport needs of dense cities.

In an urban or suburban rail corridor BRTs achieve speeds similar to those of rail. They have lower construction and operating costs. It's easier and less expensive to construct underpasses or overpasses for buses at intersections than for rail systems because buses can use bridges and tunnels with steeper gradients and shorter spans. BRTs can have stations closer to each other than trains or metros, do not require walls or railings on both sides, and have a higher capacity than suburban trains or light rail. Unlike trains, BRTs can enter and leave the former rail corridor and operate on other roads; therefore, they can collect or disembark passengers close to the origin or destination of their trips, thus saving time.

The advantages of BRTs in rail corridors are such that proposals have been made in Britain to convert some urban and suburban railway lines currently in operation into bus corridors to achieve greater capacity and flexibility at lower cost.[20] The proposers estimate that the cost of fares could be reduced by up to 40 percent, increasing capacity and improving comfort. There are several BRTs operating on former rail lines, for example, in Los Angeles and Pittsburgh in the United States and in Cambridge, England.

I have spent so much time discussing transport in this book because it is a crucial determinant of a city's form and vitality. Also, as I mentioned earlier, transport solutions tend to be counterintuitive and have more to do with equity and political decisions than with engineering or financial resources. There should be a rational benefit-cost analysis comparing rail and nonrail solutions before transport investments are made. To start, road space should be allocated democratically, keeping in mind that all citizens, regardless of whether they own a car or not, have a right to the same amount of road space. Finally, public transport users contribute to society's well-being and should be prioritized much as possible, for example, by allowing them surface travel.

CHAPTER 7

The Car: A Trojan Horse

t's not just that cars inefficiently use road space; they also affect—and diminish—urban life in numerous subtler ways. The car made its appearance surreptitiously. Early models were light and slow, not so different in weight and speed from the horse-drawn carriages that preceded them, and indeed they were lighter than many of the heavier coaches. Nobody imagined that the car was a Trojan horse entering our cities. People assumed that the car's impact on the street environment would be similar to that of horse-drawn carriages. When cars became heavier, faster, and voracious usurpers of road space and began to kill thousands of citizens, some people attempted to react, but it was too late.[1] During the early decades of motorization, the minority who traveled in cars were those with the highest incomes and greatest influence, which made it even more difficult to limit cars' use in any way.

When cars appeared, we could have begun to make cities differently. But we continued to make them in the same way, only with more spacious roads, as if nothing had happened, even though everything had happened. And we only began to realize it decades after, as ownership of cars proliferated. We became accustomed to living under the threat of being killed in our own habitat. A caricature by Claes Tingvall strikes me as especially illuminating. He presents an image of urban streets with sidewalks, on which the space for cars is a deep abyss. It expresses clearly that once we step off the sidewalk onto the street, we are walking into mortal danger. We have made a habitat in which we have to be careful, and our children particularly so, to avoid losing our lives.

The wealthy, who until then had built their mansions along the city's main road, stopped doing so to avoid cars and migrated to low-traffic sectors or the outskirts of the city. Others went to the suburbs, where the most expensive lots are those with the least traffic. Historically, since ancient Rome and well into the twentieth century, the most valuable apartments had been those at street level: the higher the story, the less valuable. In Parisian bourgeois buildings, there were often marble stairways up to the second floor but beyond that they were wood. The old rooms for domestic servants, the *chambres de bonne*, where so many students now live, as I did, were in the attic, under the roof. Preference for lower floors persisted even after the invention of the modern elevator by Elisha Otis in 1852. This remained true until the appearance of cars in large numbers. Now the value of an apartment increases according to its height off the ground, and the top-floor apartment or penthouse is the most coveted and expensive. Urbanites went from wanting to live at street level to wanting to be as far away from it as possible.

Before cars arrived, there was no significant difference between house and street spaces. Both were safe, except for the busiest streets, and there was no more noise outside than inside. In some respects, one was an extension of the other. This situation changed with the arrival of the automobile: an abyss opened between the two environments; one was safe and welcoming, and the other was noisy and dangerous.

Silence is a precious natural resource, but we are so accustomed to the permanent noise of city car traffic that we don't notice that noise surrounds us all the time, makes us tense, reduces our creativity, and subtly tires us out. If we go outside at 3:00 A.M., we find a different city from the one at 7:00 P.M.—a city illuminated by streetlights and moonlight . . . and silent.[2]

When Bogotá started its quarantine for the Covid-19 pandemic and there were few motor vehicles on the roads, the noise of just one bus or truck passing sounded like thunder. One realized then the permanent wall of noise to which we have grown accustomed. It is enchanting to contemplate decreeing an hour each day with no motor vehicles to listen to the silence or only to the birds.

The Friendlier a City Is for Cars, the Less Friendly It Is for Citizens

Paradoxically, as I described in the last two chapters, the car has been the symbol of mobility *par excellence* in the last hundred years, but we have learned it's not a solution but in fact an obstacle to solving the urban mobility challenge. Furthermore, policies that cede more and more space to cars have dehumanized the city, making it bleak and dangerous for human beings, particularly those most vulnerable—children, the elderly, those with various disabilities.

We still talk of the Big Bad Wolf who terrorizes children because some hundreds of them were devoured by wolves in Europe over thousands of years. Today, however, in any given year, there are more children killed by cars than were eaten by wolves throughout all of history. The car today is the main cause of death for children and young adults aged five to twenty-nine.[3] According to the World Health Organization, 2.47 pedestrians are killed every minute around the world.[4]

The friendlier the city is for cars, the less so it is for human beings. If roads are wider, faster, and have fewer traffic lights, then they become more impassable obstacles, more dangerous, and more disagreeably noisy for humans.

Roads in old cities and towns are similar worldwide. In Babylonia, Siena, Rome, Toledo, Zanzibar, Venice, Cartagena, and Ahmedabad, they were wide enough for two horses to pass. They were roads for walking, and they formed networks whose centers were the plazas where citizens congregated. In country villages in the developing world, and even in low-income neighborhoods in those countries' cities, pedestrian environments similar to those of cities in the past still predominate. Children play on car-free streets without fear, citizens meet to chat there, and community ties are forged. The noise of motor vehicles does not pierce the silence, and when a car approaches, it can be heard well before it's seen. If the roads are not paved, then vehicles move slowly, which makes the space even safer for pedestrians.

When trams appeared in the nineteenth century, roads continued to be safe for pedestrians. We have photographs and the marvelous films of the Lumière brothers that depict urban scenes in which trams moved slowly along rails and posed little danger to pedestrians who continued to occupy road space. Photographs show that even in the early twentieth century, roads in the great world capitals such as Paris, Tokyo, New York, Berlin, and London were pedestrian-friendly environments. A letter Freud wrote from Rome in 1907 illustrates this: "Through the middle of it runs the Corso Umberto," he observed, "with its carriages and an electric tram, but they don't do any harm, for a Roman never moves out of a vehicle's way and the drivers don't seem to be aware of their right to run people over."[5] Naturally, the streets of the less advanced cities were even more pedestrian.

But only a short while ago, the car arrived and turned that essentially human environment, the city, into an extremely dangerous place. In 1900 nobody was run over and killed by a car in the United States. But in 1907 more than five hundred people were killed by them.[6] In his stupendous *Fighting Traffic*, Peter Norton describes the US city before 1920: "American pedestrians crossed streets wherever they wished, walked in them, and let their children play in them." He writes that "in 1914, the Chamber of Commerce, in Rome, New York, had to ask pedestrians not to 'visit in the street' and not to 'manicure your nails on the street car tracks,'"[7] a recommendation, he adds, that few heeded. But cars changed these environments forever: "In the 1920s, motor vehicle accidents in the United States killed more than 200,000 people,"[8] and "in 1925 in the United States, cars and trucks killed about 7,000 children—about one-third of the total motor death toll."[9] Today, pedestrians and bicyclists constitute the majority of those killed in traffic accidents in developing cities.[10] Even in developed countries, cars represent a real and enduring threat to human life and most especially to children who dare to venture outside their homes.[11]

When the car appeared, we could have restricted their use, for example, only to certain roads, keeping others exclusively for pedestrians. Had we done that we would have had cities with hundreds or even thousands of kilometers of roads exclusively for pedestrians and cyclists, without the noise and deadly danger of cars. Instead, we have built cities more for cars' mobility than for children's happiness.

Cars have damaged cities in a variety of ways obvious and subtle. When people are confined in a car, we cease to see them. They disappear behind hermetically sealed windows, and they don't see much either because they speed by quickly. Inside the car we isolate ourselves from what is heard, seen, and felt on the street. The city loses attractiveness, enchantment, and the capacity to fascinate when, instead of human beings, metal boxes on wheels pass alongside us. We lose the empathy and the solidarity that comes from seeing and being in contact with an eclectic assortment of other humans.

It is amazing how, sitting behind the wheel, people are frequently transformed—and not into better human beings. The peaceful, easygoing suburbanite becomes a fist-shaking hurler of insults. In developing cities some feel, like Cinderella in her coach, that as soon as they are seated behind the wheel of a car, they become part of a special elite, superior to the rest. Fired up, they barge their way aggressively through traffic, blaring their horns at any pedestrian or cyclist in their way. Many of those behind the wheel are not even the owners of the car but salaried drivers. They forget that their wives and children, and they themselves a little later when they go home, are pedestrians.

Road designs that favor driving speeds particularly dehumanize the environment, for example, corners that instead of being cut at a right angle are rounded to allow turning with the least reduction in speed. The nearer the corner is to a right angle, the better for pedestrians because it reduces both the distance the pedestrian must walk to cross the street and the speed at which cars can turn. But road design standards set by some engineers demand exactly the opposite.

Such design assumes that the only citizens in a hurry are those in motor vehicles. Pedestrians and cyclists are assumed to be on a recreational stroll. They can take their time and do not need to go in a straight line: they can be made to go the extra distance at each intersection so that they can cross at the narrowest point.

A roundabout is another road design that forces pedestrians and cyclists to waste time and endangers them, especially if there are no traffic lights or stop signs.[12] At the least they are a long way around to walk or pedal. These road designs, with pretensions of monumentality, are often used in developing cities, sacrificing the potentially recreational use of the inaccessible green space lost in the roundabout's center.

If roundabouts are an example of urban design that prioritizes motor vehicles to the detriment of pedestrians, a more flagrant feature still are underground pedestrian passages, found in cities such as Moscow, Harbin, Cape Town, Singapore, and Mumbai. So that cars will not be forced to stop at traffic lights, pedestrians are forced to walk downstairs into underground tunnels to cross the street. This is an impossible obstacle to someone in a wheelchair or an elderly person with limited mobility, and it's unpleasant for anyone to use such pedestrian tunnels, which are often malodorous and bleak. Some prefer to risk their lives crossing wide roads, dodging the traffic rather than using the tunnels.

Pedestrian bridges are also monuments to the primacy of the car over the pedestrian. They are less humiliating than tunnels, true, and more likely to have ramps with gentle gradients for those with limited mobility. However, a better city simply has more traffic lights or it has underpasses . . . for cars.

In all cities, hundreds or thousands of buildings are demolished to make room for new or wider roads. Very rarely is anything demolished to make room for parks, plazas, or other pedestrian spaces. Although it might sound counterintuitive, to the extent that these parks prevent the low-density expansion of the city, they could be more useful for mobility than roads. During my two terms in office, we did engage in demolition to build and widen roads; it gives me peace of mind that our major roads included the BRT and all of them included wide sidewalks and bikeways. We also engaged in major demolitions to create parks in central areas.

Today, we think it must have been difficult to live in early nineteenth-century London, with soot in the air that infiltrated buildings, clothing, and the skin and the pervasive, nauseating stench of sewage. Possibly at the beginning of the twenty-third century people will ask, "How could people have lived in those cities of the first half of the twenty-first century?" Naturally, we think that our cities are relatively fine. Londoners thought their nineteenth-century city, the world's most admired and imitated, was fine, too.

A Day Without Cars in Bogotá

Often, when individuals do something for their own benefit, such as study, care for their health, save, or invest, society benefits as well, but as we have seen, Adam Smith's principle that society benefits when individuals act in their self-interest is not always valid. What is rational and convenient from an individual's perspective is not necessarily so from society's perspective. Mobility is a right, but not necessarily mobility in an individual car. It is often necessary to limit or regulate individual behavior so that the community may function properly. For example, if each adult in a city decided to mobilize in a car to maximize their personal well-being, the result would be a colossal bottleneck. Car use must involve a spectrum of limitations, which go from the most basic, such as obeying traffic lights, to restrictions on car use at certain times or days or in some sectors of the city.

We began a novel experiment in Bogotá: a complete ban on private car use on a working day, the first Thursday of every February. We wanted to demonstrate that a large, dense city with abundant public transport, even if not of the best quality, could function without cars and invite public reflection on the best way to travel around and live in a city. Unlike "Car-Free Days" elsewhere that are held on a Sunday, Bogotá's occurs on a workday. However, in order to avoid simply creating another public holiday, buses, trucks, and taxis are allowed to work on that day. Also, and unlike "Car-Free Days" held in European cities, in which a few roads are closed to cars, in Bogotá, private cars are not permitted on any road on that day.

On "Car-Free Days," 99 percent of citizens go to work as usual, and most of them have shorter than normal travel times because buses are freer from traffic. The Car-Free Day makes it possible to glimpse a more sustainable and gentler way of life. Beyond its meaning in terms of mobility and environmental sustainability, it is also an exercise in social integration. On that day citizens of all income levels meet as equals, an exceptional occurrence in a developing city. They meet on public transport, bicycles, walking, or at least in the street while waiting for a taxi. On average, more than a million citizens mobilize on a bicycle on the Car-Free Day.

At first, the Car-Free Day seemed radical and even exotic. Yet in any developing city, only a minority use cars for their mobility; for the majority, every day is a Car-Free Day. Private car use negatively affects those who don't use one and doesn't benefit them in any way. They only gain—and lose nothing—with the ban on car use. There is less traffic and shorter travel time in their bus, jeepney, or other public transport; pedestrians face less danger; and they enjoy better air and less noise on the way.

Why are proposals as obvious as banning car use during a couple of peak morning and afternoon hours not made? Simply because, regardless of how small the minority that uses private cars, their numbers are concentrated among the most powerful elements of society. For example, owners of television channels and their journalists, leading businessmen and politicians and their friends, doctors, and even priests all use cars. But probably everyone, including those of us who have a car, would be better off if we learned to live without using it for our daily mobility.

We announced our first Car-Free Day weeks in advance. However, we only issued the decree implementing it the day before, a little before 5:00 P.M. We wanted to avoid the risk that the Constitutional Court might block its implementation on the grounds that it impinged on individual liberties or some other such thing. Relatives and friends of the justices of the court were generally high-income individuals who moved by car and were likely to oppose the exercise. After a successful Car-Free Day by decree, we promoted its implementation by a referendum, in which all citizens could vote. So approved, no authority, not even a president or Congress, could revoke it. The only way to do it would be through another referendum.

In the referendum held in October 2000, we sought the approval for an annual Car-Free Day, and something else: we asked citizens to vote on whether they wanted to ban car use during three peak hours in the morning and three peak hours in the afternoon, every working day of the year, beginning in 2015. Surveys indicated that we would win by a wide margin. So a group of businessmen financed a campaign against the proposal. Since they knew that they would lose, they didn't ask citizens to vote against it but rather to abstain so that the total vote wouldn't achieve the 33 percent participation of potential voters, the threshold required for the referendum to become a legal mandate.

Indeed, we did obtain a large majority; an annual Car-Free Day was approved by 63 percent, with a participation of 34 percent of the electoral census.[13] But on the question of the ban on car use during peak hours, the total number of voters was only 28 percent of the total potential number, according to the electoral census. Thus, Bogotá lost the opportunity to become a world example of a city that functions without private cars during peak hours. I still believe that any city would improve its mobility and quality of life by a ban on motor vehicles other than buses for one or two peak hours every morning and afternoon, so that those mobilizing on public transport, by bicycle, or on foot can do so faster, more safely, and more comfortably.

Car-Based Mobility Works Only If a Minority Uses Cars

As we conceptualize the future city, we must assume that everyone over sixteen will be able to afford a car. Sooner or later, even if it takes a long time, per capita income in today's developing countries will reach or even surpass that achieved by today's richest countries. Do we want a city in which everyone over sixteen mobilizes by car? Or do we believe that it will be necessary to restrict car use in some way, and, if we do, then why wait?

Imagine what would happen if three hundred individuals in a city decided to use a helicopter for their daily commutes. First, we'd hope that none of them was our neighbor: the deafening noise as its owner took off for the office or supermarket would disturb us. But the second point is that what functions well for the few does not necessarily work for the whole population. It's possible for three hundred, five hundred, or a thousand people to mobilize by helicopter every day but impossible for the entire population to do so because they would crash into each other. For example, in São Paulo, dozens of businessmen and senior executives use helicopters to travel and dodge traffic jams, but obviously this would not be a viable system if every adult in São Paulo were to do the same.[14]

The situation with the car in a major city is similar to that of the helicopter. It's possible, for example, that 30 percent of the population might use a car for mobility, but the city would simply collapse if everyone tried to move by car. It's just as technically impossible for everyone to mobilize by car as it is to have everyone mobilize by helicopter.

Would we vote to permit anyone who has a helicopter to be allowed to noisily land or take off next to our home? By the same logic, why would a low-income citizen in a developing city vote to allow others to use their cars without restriction? Probably because some lower-income citizens suppose aspirationally that in some not-distant future they too will travel in one. The fact is, however, that a majority of citizens in Ethiopia, India, or Colombia today will not have access to their own car in their lifetime.

Philosopher André Gorz wrote in 1973, "The worst thing about cars is that they are like castles or villas by the sea: luxury goods invented for the exclusive pleasure of a very rich minority, and which in conception and nature were never intended for the people. Unlike the vacuum cleaner, the radio, or the bicycle, which retain their use value when everyone has one, the car, like a villa by the sea, is only desirable and useful insofar as the masses don't have one."[15] Obviously, if cars are used only to go on outings to the countryside or on some evenings, it is conceivable that all adults could have one and enjoy it, despite the monumental investment and costs of parking and maintaining them. But if cars are to be used only for those kinds of excursions, then it would be more practical not to own but simply to rent one, which is already the trend among young people in major cities in advanced countries.

Statistics that show a high percentage of homes with a car may be misleading in analyses of urban mobility. That someone should have a car does not mean that he can use it, at least not to go to work. Often, limited parking spaces in office buildings and other workplaces are reserved for the highest-ranked executives or for those who have the capacity to pay for expensive parking. The use of the car to go to work therefore continues to be a privilege of the minority. This would further justify a prohibition on car use for a couple of peak hours in the morning and afternoon.

The car is also a status symbol. This is particularly true in backward countries, where car owners have a higher status and the more expensive the car, the higher the status. In fact, most ads for cars are appeals to status. Once more citizens own cars, they lose much of their allure of status—as has happened, for example, in northern Europe. In 1960, it was a status symbol to wash and wax your car in front of your home on a Saturday morning.

Today, that would be almost ridiculous as such. In poor neighborhoods of developing cities where there are few cars, a car parked on pedestrian space, even on a park, is still almost a welcome sight: it raises the social status of the neighborhood, as if a neighbor in a middle-class suburb in an advanced country were to arrive home in a helicopter. But in wealthier countries, the young are progressively less enthused by cars.[16]

Driven by computers that do not get distracted, text, or make mistakes, the car of the future won't crash. But of course, when cars drive themselves, they will lose much of their sex appeal, too. We'll no longer get a feeling of power as we accelerate. We'll simply be passengers driven by a robot.

Even those who mobilize in mass transport need or want to use a car from time to time—perhaps to go all dressed up to a party, take a parent to the doctor, bring home a large purchase, or take an outing to the countryside. As more and more individuals choose not to have a car, there will be a need for better taxi services, hired cars requested by phone apps, low-cost car rentals, and car-sharing schemes.

Urban Highways Are Poisonous Rivers

An urban highway is like a poisonous river: people cannot be close to it, walk beside it, or wade across it. They are noisy and reduce property values for hundreds of meters around. Unsurprisingly, the new highways aren't built by demolishing high-income residential sectors, only lower-income ones. And even where no demolition is needed, high-income groups are able to prevent it from passing through their neighborhoods.

In the mid-twentieth century there was a frantic rush in the United States to find space for the exploding number of cars. Hundreds of highways were built through urban zones, to the detriment of human quality of life. Peter Harnik writes, "Waterfronts were blockaded in Portland, Cincinnati, Hartford, Cleveland, Philadelphia, and San Francisco. Nooses of concrete were tightly wound around the downtowns of Dallas and Charlotte. Trenches of noise and smog cut through Boston, Detroit, Seattle, and Atlanta. Massive elevated structures threw shadows over Miami and New Orleans. And wide strips of land were taken from large iconic parks in Los Angeles (Griffith Park), St. Louis (Forest Park), Baltimore (Druid Hill Park), and San Diego (Balboa Park)."[17]

Highways are broad, and elevated ones darken whatever lies beneath them; their surroundings deteriorate, lowering property values. Even the best cities in the world have urban highways that no one is proud of. The M4 motorway links the center of London to Heathrow Airport, passing through urban sectors. It has elevated stretches under which pedestrians can cross the highway but that cast darkness below. When the M4 runs on the surface, railings in the median remind human beings that this is not their space. The value of buildings next to the motorway and near it are lower than those just a few blocks away.

I worked in a building next to one of the many road overpasses in Bogotá and experienced its unpleasant effects. With this one, thousands of TransMilenio passengers had to walk across the highway's exit ramp at great risk to their lives because there were no traffic lights and cars appeared at high speed without warning.[18] It is particularly dangerous for the elderly with mobility limitations. Thieves often cut power cables for street lighting to facilitate robberies. The stench of urine pervades the environment.

In the first half of the twentieth century on an island on the Nile in the middle of Cairo, called Zamalek, a part of the city was built, with four- to six-story buildings, good architecture, parks, and sidewalks. For decades authorities protected this charming island in the middle of the city, not even allowing cars to blow their horns there. But President Anwar Sadat, convinced that it meant progress, had an elevated road stretch constructed over 26 July Avenue, the very axis of Zamalek life. That elevated highway sliced through the sector like a saber, destroying its magic with one stroke, and the island has been deteriorating ever since. Despite the dust that covers poorly maintained buildings, the broken windows, and mansions carelessly converted to accommodate education centers, the sector has managed to conserve its beauty: there are cafés and the atmosphere is lively. The good architecture has proved resilient to deterioration. But the demolition of the elevated road would help the rebirth of Zamalek tremendously.

Unfortunately, in dense Cairo the opposite has happened. Overpasses have been constructed at many intersections, and buildings have been razed to make room for more and more and ever larger elevated highways, sometimes crisscrossing one another and often covering sidewalks and even going over parks and plazas. Not only have adjacent buildings and neighborhoods been affected but also some historical buildings.[19] Another example is in Buenos Aires, where at the end of 1980, during the military dictatorship of Jorge

Videla, the 25 de Mayo highway was built from the center to the international airport. It has a 9.5-kilometer elevated stretch around which the urban area has deteriorated and property values have fallen.[20]

The Costa e Silva in the center of São Paulo, commonly called Minhocão, is an elevated highway that diminished property values and security around it. Fortunately, for some years now, authorities have been closing it to cars every weekend and reserving it for cyclists and pedestrians. This is probably a first step toward its demolition, which would support a revival of São Paulo's beautiful center.

A number of elevated highways in advanced cities have been demolished and in several instances sent underground. In 1974 in Portland, 4.8 kilometers of the Harbor Drive Freeway, built in 1950 along the banks of the Willamette River, were demolished and replaced by Tom McCall Park. The result has been a reduction in crime and a steady increase in property values in the surrounding area.[21]

The Embarcadero viaduct in San Francisco was built in 1959, and 61,000 vehicles used it every day. In 1991, it was demolished and replaced by a 4.5-kilometer-long avenue, with 28 controlled intersections, flanked by 8-meter sidewalks. Property prices nearby increased 300 percent.[22] In 2005, also in San Francisco, the Central Freeway was demolished—another elevated highway with daily traffic of 93,000 vehicles a day. This and the construction of better pedestrian space increased property values by more than 100 percent. The 1989 earthquake, which seriously damaged the highways' structures, influenced the decision to demolish them. Initially, after the earthquake and the highway closures, traffic congestion increased. But soon after that, many who used to travel by car switched to BART, the San Francisco urban train, and traffic returned to normal.

In 1972 community pressure in Milwaukee led to the suspension of construction of the Park East Highway and the ring of highways around the urban center of which it was part. In land that was to be occupied by the highway, the 7.5-hectare East Point urban development was successfully created in the early 1990s. In 2000, Mayor John Norquist demolished the section of the Park East Highway that had already been built, which freed up another 11 hectares for well-located buildings.[23]

Between 2001 and 2003, Toronto demolished 18 kilometers of the Gardiner Highway, built between 1955 and 1966.[24] In 2001, Manhattan demolished 7.6-kilometer stretches of Manhattan's West Side Highway, built between 1927 and 1931, and replaced them with a boulevard with sidewalks and traffic lights. Alongside it they created the beautiful Hudson waterfront. In 2011, Seattle demolished the elevated Alaskan Way, built in 1953, and replaced it with an avenue and a tunnel.[25] Central to the 2014 Porto Maravilha urban regeneration project in Rio de Janeiro was the demolition of 5.5 kilometers of the Perimetral elevated highway, which was replaced by a tunnel. Mayor Eduardo Paes said at the time, "Getting rid of that monster we have in front of us, the city will reencounter with the sea."[26]

Naturally, not all elevated highways have been demolished, and many developing cities continue to build them. The minority of their citizens who move by car have inordinate economic and political power and pressure the government to build them. Few remind those in government of the flyover's futility as a solution to traffic jams or mobility.

Citizens Against Highways

Urban damage caused by highways at the ground level is not appreciably less than the damage caused by elevated ones. Civic protest against the dehumanization and destruction wrought by highways followed quickly after they began to be built. Some of the most powerful civic movements after World War II in the United States and England arose in opposition to the construction of urban highways, and they succeeded in stopping many of them. The triumphant opposition to major roads that Robert Moses wanted to build through Manhattan's Greenwich Village and Soho is legendary; among its leaders was Jane Jacobs, who would subsequently become a world-recognized urbanist.

In her classic book *The Life and Death of Great American Cities,* Jacobs referred to "expressways that eviscerate cities."[27] Later, while residing in Toronto, her leadership was instrumental in the cancellation of the Spadina Expressway and other projected highways there.

"Homes before roads"[28] was the name given to the London political movement against several peripheral roads, known as Ringways, proposed in the 1960s and, later, to similar campaigns elsewhere in Britain. Strong public opposition finally led to the cancellation of the Ringways project in 1973.

Highways built in Boston irreparably wounded and scarred the city. More were on the way, for which a good part of the properties had already been acquired and buildings demolished. Finally, public opposition became so strong that in 1970 Governor Francis W. Sargent, in a televised speech that became a milestone, announced the suspension of the construction of the urban highways in progress:

> You, your family, your neighbors have become caught in a system that's fouled our air, ravaged our cities, choked our economy, and frustrated every single one of us. To move ourselves, our goods, and our services, we built more and more and bigger and better superhighways and expressways. They seem the easiest, the more obvious answer to our multiplying needs. What we misunderstood was what those highways would create: massive traffic congestion. We found that we had defeated our own purpose and that we had been caught in a vicious cycle: more cars meant more highways which meant more traffic jams. More traffic jams meant the need for more highways, which meant more traffic jams and the need for superhighways.
>
> The result today: miles and miles of bumper to bumper traffic creeping along hopelessly crowded highways. The side effect, billions of dollars spent and more and more cities torn apart, more and more families uprooted and displaced. Worst of all, failure to solve the problem that started it off. How best to get from one place to another? Massachusetts, indeed America, confronts the same old problem, now complicated by a growing paralysis on our superhighways.
>
> The old system has imprisoned us. We've become the slaves and not the master of the method we chose to meet our needs. How do we break loose from a system that doesn't work? . . . Shall we build more expressways through cities? . . . No, we will not repeat history, we shall learn from it. We will not build the expressways, instead we will embark on a nearly 2 billion dollar program. . . . We shall build a transit and commuter rail system.[29]

Leaders of the opposition to new urban highways in Boston, which finally led to Governor Sargent's signal decision and speech were not radical environmentalists with a sentimental vision of the city; they included some of the most respected transport engineering professors at MIT, such as Frederick P. Salvucci and Kenneth Kruckemeyer.

One option for urban highways is to put them underground. It has been common to bury public transport and to hand over the surface, with its natural light and vistas of sky, trees, and architecture, to the car. It seems more democratic, as mentioned earlier, to put highways underground and give preference to public transport on the surface. The Costanera Norte highway, which runs 43.9 kilometers along the banks of the Mapocho River in Santiago, Chile, was built underground. An underground urban highway can support greenways above it: in the center of Madrid 7 kilometers of the M30 highway were buried and the beautiful Manzanares River Park was built above it. The A7 highway that had divided Hamburg for decades was buried, and parks were built on top of it, which instead of splitting the city knitted it together.

Shortly after I took office as mayor, I received a mobility study that the Japanese International Cooperation Agency (JICA) had prepared for Bogotá. One of its major recommendations was the construction of highways, several of them elevated.[30] I discarded the idea.[31] Given Bogotá's high density, the damage to its structure and human quality of life would have been significant. But I'm sure I would have received accolades from the minority had I built those elevated highways.

Curiously, some experts from advanced countries continue to recommend that developing cities construct elevated highways. As in the case of Bogotá, this is what mobility studies prepared by JICA usually seem to do. JICA has conducted dozens, perhaps hundreds, of urban mobility studies, and in all the ones I know of, they have proposed elevated highways.

Avenues Can Improve the City

Urban highways almost never have pedestrian or bicycle infrastructure. Amazingly, as is still the case in Mexico City, urban highways seldom have bus-only lanes and don't even allow public transport buses to operate on them, even though most of the city's population travels by road public transport. A jammed highway, with no bus-only lane, evinces technical problems and insufficient democracy.

Avenues, like highways, have several lanes for cars in both directions. However, while urban highways deteriorate and lower the value of property around them, avenues not only contribute to mobility but also make their surroundings more attractive and valuable. Nobody wants to walk along-side an urban highway. Instead, although the Champs-Élysées in Paris has eight motor-vehicle lanes, its pedestrian public space attracts those who live in Paris and tourists from around the world. Unlike a highway, an avenue has broad, tree-lined sidewalks and frequent intersections with traffic lights. Mayor Hidalgo's plan to reduce the Champs-Élysées' lanes from eight to four, to increase the green and pedestrian areas, will make it even more attractive.

With properly synchronized traffic lights, an avenue lane can mobilize 60 percent as many vehicles as a highway lane would. To the west of Man-hattan Island, alongside the Hudson River, there is 12th Avenue, Route 9A, or West Street, a large eight-lane road. But it has intersections with traffic lights so that vehicles and pedestrians can cross it at grade. And there is the beautiful greenway between it and the Hudson River, with a wonderful bike-way. Across the road are sidewalks and apartment buildings, with shops at street level, many of them exceptionally appealing architecturally.[32]

Parallel to 12th Avenue, but on the other side of Manhattan Island and against the East River, is a very different road: the Franklin D. Roosevelt East River Drive, or FDR Drive. Unlike 12th Avenue, it has no intersections with traffic lights and no sidewalks with buildings alongside it. Parking space often lies below the elevated sections. On the surface portions, for a pedestrian to reach the beautiful park that runs along East River for several kilometers in the southern part of the island, they must use pedestrian bridges that are enclosed with metal mesh, I would imagine to prevent sui-cides or people throwing things at vehicles below. The FDR Drive is a con-crete and noise obstacle to human beings, which damages what could otherwise be a magnificent waterfront.

As noted, with the same number of lanes, a highway can mobilize al-most twice the number of vehicles per hour as an avenue—provided there are no traffic jams. But almost all urban highways get jammed, and naturally, with traffic at a snail's pace, there is no difference between the number of ve-hicles per lane that an avenue and a highway can move. Such are the traffic jams in urban highways of developing cities that, as with Bogotá, there often are street vendors waving bags of sweets, cigarettes, or soft drinks as they walk between barely moving cars.

If highways are to be built, then it's best for them to resemble avenues as closely as possible. This means, for example, that they should have underpasses at intersections so that pedestrians can cross at grade, bus-only lanes, bikeways, and wide, tree-lined sidewalks that are well-lit and lined with buildings.

A challenge for the coming decades is to bury urban highways and build parks and plazas on top of them or transform them into avenues. I visited Tehran when its dynamic mayor, Mohammad Bagher Ghalibaf, was engaged in all kinds of public works, including major highways crossing the enormous city in several directions, for which he was acquiring and demolishing hundreds of buildings. As a complement to his highways, Mayor Ghalibaf demolished the buildings alongside them to create wide, green areas. In the future, those green spaces may become gardens along a major pedestrian way or elongated plazas, to be built over the highway once it is sent underground. Roads exclusively for BRT, bicyclists, and pedestrians can also be built above buried highways.

A Word on Motorcycles

The ban on motorcycles in Chinese cities is not democratic. It is classist. There is no justification for restricting motorcycles and not cars. But I must admit that the prohibition means less noise, more orderly traffic, and a tranquility that is not found on the streets of developing cities, especially in the tropics. It also means that crimes committed using motorcycles, such as stealing mobile phones, frequent in some developing countries, do not take place. Electric mopeds and bicycles used in China[33] are restricted to bikeways on arterial roads and are a world away from the swarms of noisy motorcycles in Ho Chi Minh City or Jakarta.

The relatively tropical climate of most developing cities and the ease of weaving through slow-moving or stalled cars in traffic has contributed to the proliferation of motorcycles over the last few decades. Motorcycles crowd the streets in Asia and Latin America and, increasingly, in Africa. When ridden and parked on sidewalks and other pedestrian spaces, as they often are, they harm the city. Many motorcyclists disregard traffic regulations, which is easy to do with their very flexible vehicles. In developing cities, motorcyclists, mainly young men, make up a rapidly growing share of traffic fatalities. In Bogotá half of all serious accidents involve a motorcyclist. On the other hand, motorcycles are a low-cost mobility solution for many individuals and families who live far from the center and even more so for those who live in small villages and rural areas. Motorcycle proliferation is a consequence of insufficient public transport coverage or its prohibitive cost principally where there are no integrated systems and citizens must pay every time they change vehicles. Sometimes, as is the case in Colombia, motorcyclists enjoy privileges, such as not having to comply with tag number–based car use restrictions, not paying tolls, and having subsidized insurance rates.

Most motorcyclists in developing cities are low-income earners. High-income earners are annoyed by motorcycles, which weave their way through any crack in the traffic. Of course, they are also annoyed by buses, taxis, bicycles, bicycle-taxis, jeepneys, and public transport buses—basically, by any vehicle on the street except their own cars and those of their friends. Their pressure has resulted in some restrictions on motorcycles. In some cases, motorcycle use has been banned one day a week; in others, motorcyclists are not allowed to carry a pillion passenger for crime prevention. In other cases, motorcycles are restricted from being used as taxis, regardless of the fact that low-income people can only afford a motorcycle-taxi and not an automobile-taxi. In Jakarta, where a majority of the population's mobility is motorcycle-based, motorcycles are not allowed on highways. Indonesia's Supreme Court is studying claims against this exclusion. And in Chinese cities, motorcycles are simply banned.

As motorcycles are evidently not going to disappear, motorcyclists need to be educated to behave well and observe traffic regulations. They need to be strictly forbidden to ride on or park in pedestrian spaces and punished for doing so, notwithstanding the regrettable Parisian tolerance of such parking. As the distribution of many products, from pizzas to legal documents, is made by motorcycle, perhaps there should be short-term parking facilities for them, both in streets and office buildings.

Several-story buildings rise up among the crops in Kathmandu's outskirts. On the edges of Kathmandu, Jogjakarta, and Dar es Salaam, urban tentacles creep into rural areas. Incipient urbanization surfaces among crops like islands or islets, large and small. Seen from the other side, agricultural fields encroach on the city: the green of crops enters neighborhoods or completely surrounds them. The same occurs in hundreds more Asian and African cities. Their perimetral neighborhoods teem with thousands of alleys impenetrable to cars, or there are simply houses in rural areas adjacent to cities where public transport is scarce or nonexistent. Motorcycles are a means of transport that adapt fluidly to such environments. Moreover, many neighborhoods have grown up in the last few decades based on the premise of motorcycle mobility.

*   *   *

Correcting the malformation of cities caused by cars in the past century is one of the great urban challenges of the twenty-first century. It is not an easy task, but at least we have more clarity now as to what is to be done. It is not simply a matter of urban design but of changing our way of life.

CHAPTER 8

The Right to Bike Without Risking One's Life

A well-made bikeway, physically protected from motor-vehicle traffic and with good signage, protects cyclists. But it also shows that someone on a $100 bicycle is equally as important as someone in a $100,000 car. In developing cities, where those who ride bicycles to work are often clustered in lower-income groups, bikeways are also important because they raise cyclists' social status and act as a symbol of respect. They include, construct citizenship, and express democracy.

On many occasions I've found bicycles even in houses with earth floors, no water, and malnourished children. The bicycle is a vehicle within reach for people of all income levels and ages. Bicycle use is good for the environment, health, and mobility[1] but perhaps even more beneficial for social integration. An extensive network of protected bikeways on urban and rural roads in a developing society is revolutionary in terms of equality construction.

As soon as we started to make bikeways in Bogotá, the humblest of citizens began to use the bicycle more and to wear helmets, not only because regulations required it but because they became proud of being cyclists. Between 1998 and 2000 we created over 250 kilometers of protected bikeways—before Paris, New York, or Madrid had them. At that time, bikeways only existed where they had always been: in the Netherlands, Denmark, and other northern European countries and in China. Indeed, we had to invent a name—*ciclorruta*—for the Bogotá bikeways because there were none before.

Bicycle use represents a major saving for lower-income citizens in a developing city because they no longer have to pay for public transport. The saving is between 10 percent and 30 percent of their income for those earning a minimum wage or less, who generally make up about half of all workers. In Bogotá, for example, transport costs consume 12 percent of the salary of someone earning minimum wage, which takes into account only expenses tied to their work commute. Savings in transport from bicycle use over twenty-five years for the typical couple in a developing city would allow them to purchase a house.

Hundreds of millions of people in the developing world walk several kilometers a day to work because they can't afford public transport. Many potential jobs are inaccessible to them because they are too far away. Although millions of poor people in the world still do not have enough money to buy a bicycle, many now have access to one. Quality bikeways open many possibilities to them.

Colombia has traditionally been the developing country with the most high-performance, internationally successful cyclists, and in Bogotá we already had the tradition of the "Sunday *Ciclovía*," during which dozens of kilometers of arterial roads were closed to cars so that cyclists and joggers could enjoy the roads for themselves. Yet in 1998, when I started my first term as mayor, no more than 0.1 percent of commuters rode bicycles to work. Cycling was dangerous, and riding a bicycle to work carried a stigma as well, of being among the poorest of the poor. It also involved shame: cyclists felt guilty for inconveniencing car drivers. Two decades later, bicycle commuters account for almost 10 percent of the population, the highest of any major city in the Americas. And although initially mostly low-income men rode bicycles to work, there are now riders of all income levels and a high percentage of women.

Build Bicycle Infrastructure and They Will Come

As cities adapted more and more to the car, highways were built, which stimulated urban expansion. For example, in the Netherlands, bicycles were widely used before World War II but were rather less popular after it, when the number of cars increased enormously. Average distances from home to work increased from 3.9 kilometers in 1957 to 23.2 kilometers in 1975.[2] This made it more difficult to use a bicycle as a means of transport. Infrastructure to allow cars to move at increasingly high speeds endangered cyclists. The number of cyclists run over and killed increased rapidly, to thousands a year. Many of them were children. In 1971 more than four hundred children on bicycles were killed by cars. Bicycle use fell drastically, and civic protests against the massacre of child cyclists multiplied.

The 1973 oil crisis, which brought fuel prices to previously unseen heights, provided the final push to change the model of mobility, the city, and life. The Dutch state took up the challenge of doing it, and further protests reinforced its decisions. Car Free Sundays were organized, in which important roads were closed to cars for several hours; historical center streets were pedestrianized; plazas were cleared of parked cars, and parking on many streets was progressively restricted; and, most important, high-quality, protected bikeways began to appear everywhere.

The citizen response was spectacular, with massive increases in bicycle use until the Netherlands became the worldwide example of bicycle mobility that it still is today. People ride a bicycle to study, work, shop, and enjoy clubs and cinema. The bicycle is now a transport system and a way of life. The Netherlands proved the adage "Build it and they will come."[3] In the Netherlands today there are more than 35,000 kilometers of bikeways. In tiny Amsterdam alone, there are more than 500 kilometers.

The egalitarian Dutch culture and the flatness of its geography create an especially fertile environment for bicycle use. But for citizens to opt for bicycling in substantial numbers, wide bikeways on which riding is not only safe but pleasurable are also required. Bicycle use remains marginal until governments provide the infrastructure to support large-scale use.

In other words, bicycle infrastructure comes before bicycle culture. This is exactly what happened in Bogotá. We built a 250-kilometer protected bikeway network at a time when almost no one used a bicycle for a daily commute. Little by little, that infrastructure encouraged people to bicycle. When some argue that no bikeways are needed because there are no cyclists, we might reply that there are no cyclists precisely because there are no bikeways. Here, there is no chicken-and-egg dilemma: bikeways come first.

In getting people to bicycle, as with any other behavioral change that makes individuals better citizens, I am skeptical about results simply derived from civic education. Before anything else, the city is a physical environment. If it shows respect and affection for its citizens, then they will respond in kind. It is difficult to convince someone who has to dodge cars parked on the sidewalk, or who is splashed when a car speeds through a puddle, or who needs to alight from the bus with children in the middle of the road to simply "love your city. Do not throw litter on the street." That same individual's reaction is completely different if the city provides wide, tree-lined sidewalks with benches and lighting or charming parks with games for children.

A city safe and friendly to bicyclists is also thus for vulnerable citizens—the elderly, children, people with disabilities, and those on skates, in wheelchairs, or even on tricycles. In terms of mobility, a civilized city is not one that has highways or a metro but one in which a child on a bicycle or a tricycle can ride around safely anywhere. For those who do not have a car or a motorcycle and for any child under sixteen, their only means of individual transport is a bicycle. In Lagos de Torca, the 400,000-inhabitant urban project in Bogotá we developed during my second mayoral term, there are bikeways on every street, large and small. And there are dozens of kilometers of greenways with bikeways as well.

Most of the world's urban population lives in cities of less than a million inhabitants, in which most journeys are short and can easily be made on foot or by bicycle. But even in the major cities of more than five million, it has been found that around half the population lives less than five kilometers from work. So a bicycle could be the main means of transport for many.

Someone in average physical condition can pedal ten kilometers to work over relatively flat ground, particularly if it is safe to do so on a protected bikeway. To manage the tropical heat, trees can be planted along bikeways for shade, which can reduce the temperature up to 6°C, or 11°F. At all events, even in the hottest weather, there are always people who work in the open air—not to mention golfers. It will be necessary to leave behind the suit and tie designed for London and its climate—and for the nineteenth century. There is always the option of electrically assisted bicycles, provided they do not reach such high speeds as to endanger other cyclists.

Citizens on bicycles can see each other up close and meet as equals, in solidarity against the threat of the car. Cyclists form almost a club of free spirits, together in the adventure of enjoying the city. When a high-income and a low-income cyclist meet at a traffic light, their relationship is totally different than if they meet with one in a luxury car and the other on a bus. At the traffic light, it is less relevant that one bicycle cost $3,000 and the other $30. Whereas cars are a means of social differentiation, bicycles are a means of social equalization.

The Bicycle as an Equality Indicator

It's unclear whether the wealthiest societies are more egalitarian because they are wealthier or if they are wealthier because they are more egalitarian. In the richest societies the greater relative scarcity of labor in relation to capital increases employees' remuneration, which improves income distribution and equality. Wealthier societies also provide greater educational opportunities and better health care, both of which contribute to equality. A more egalitarian society brings about more economic development because it better educates its lower-income citizens. And because it's an environment freer of privileges and more meritocratic, it makes better use of its citizens' ingenuity and creativity. A more egalitarian society is more fertile for creation because its citizens are freer to dream and undertake projects.

By this logic the bicycle helps unchain creativity and bring about progress. Given the abundance of bikeways in northern European cities with high household income and long, cold winters, how can we explain that in developing countries, where the only means of transport accessible to many is the bicycle and there are generally no cold winters, we don't have infrastructure that favors cyclists? The answer is that these are very unequal societies, in which higher-income citizens who directly or indirectly define political decisions do not use bicycles. In my two terms as mayor of Bogotá, more so in the first one, I received a lot of criticism and indeed insults from some who believed it was madness to take away a centimeter of road from cars to create protected bikeways.

It is no accident that in Europe, the Nordic countries use bicycles the most, even though the climate is milder in Greece, Italy, and Spain. Northern European societies have been more egalitarian than southern ones. While in the Netherlands a senior public servant or businessman never felt their status diminished for riding a bicycle to work, in southern Europe such attitudes are only beginning to crystallize. Naturally, in more backward and unequal developing world societies, fears of diminished status still hamper bicycle use; in Karachi, Lagos, or Dhaka, those with the means and wherewithal do everything possible to isolate themselves from the rest in air-conditioned cars. Even there, however, attitudes are changing among the young: bicycle use is almost always an indicator of social progress.

The main obstacle to bicycle use is not steep hills or the weather: it's inequality. Equality and bicycle use are both cause and effect. It is likelier that bicycles will be used in more egalitarian societies, and in turn bicycle use promotes more inclusive and egalitarian societies. In terms of infrastructure, the existence of bikeways reflects how egalitarian and democratic a society is, and the construction of high-quality infrastructure for pedestrians and cyclists produces a more inclusive and democratic society.

The Rite of the Bogotá "Ciclovía"

Bogotá's Sunday's "Ciclovía" (the Bikeway) allows us to enter the "prohibited" spaces otherwise occupied by cars and to enjoy that forbidden pleasure. Mayor Luis Prieto-Ocampo started this tradition in 1975. Ciclovía closes several arterial roads to cars for seven hours on Sundays so that people can enter that space on bicycles or foot.[4] Initially, the mayor closed a dozen kilometers, but the area has been gradually extended since then.[5] When Mayor Antanas Mockus came to office in 1995, the area had reached about 20 kilometers. He increased that to 81, and I subsequently extended it to 127. On any given Sunday, 1.5 million people of all ages and conditions, on bicycles, skates, and foot, walking or jogging, come out onto this great plaza of temporarily converted streets. On a sunny Sunday there are more than 2 million people out there enjoying the roads.

More than a sports scenario, Ciclovía is a ceremony of citizens reconquering their city, through which they had had to pass cornered and intimidated by motor vehicles and deafened by their noise. It is a ritual that remembers that the city is of and for human beings. During Ciclovía the normally dangerous and noisy road space becomes an oasis of human encounters and urban enjoyment. Walking in the middle of the vehicle-free road, we discover the architecture, invisible to us when we pass by the same places in a car in the midst of traffic. We can see trees and hear human voices.

More than any other public space in Bogotá, citizens of all income levels meet as equals during Ciclovía. Such integration as equals encourages solidarity. If on a given Sunday or holiday morning, those responsible for overseeing the Ciclovía are late in closing any part of it to traffic, people do it themselves by placing stones or other objects at hand to block off car access. In a city that suffers from crime problems, Ciclovía is a crime-free event.

During my first period as mayor, Colombia was going through one of its worst recessions ever. Unemployment was very high, and people were unhappy. At that time, we began to adorn the city's public spaces with especially beautiful Christmas lighting, which brought joy during otherwise difficult circumstances. Hundreds of thousands of people came out on the nights before Christmas to enjoy something new to the city. With the recession and unemployment, many families couldn't afford any other activity. But higher-income people also came out to drive along the illuminated streets—which, predictably, caused enormous traffic jams.

When we saw the droves of people coming out each night, as well as the traffic bottlenecks, we decided to organize the Ciclovía on a night close to Christmas. Millions of people came out onto the street on bicycles and on foot; indeed, on many stretches it was impossible to ride a bicycle because throngs of people were filling up the road. More than two million people came out to see the lights.

The Night Ciclovía has become an annual rite in Bogotá. Some years it takes place more than once. Crime was absent during the first and subsequent Night Ciclovías, and the event amounts to a collective conquest of the fear of going out at night.

Making Bikes Part of City Life

If bicycle use was more widespread, urban life would improve and cities would advance toward quality-of-life equality. A study published by the European Commission found that urban trips of less than five kilometers were faster on bicycle than by car.[6] The denser the city, the shorter the journeys, and therefore the easier to make them on a bicycle.

For bicycle use to become generalized, however, there must be bicycle parking facilities to complement protected bikeways. The train station in the Dutch university city of Groningen has an underground parking facility for more than 10,000 bicycles; Utrecht has one for 12,500; and Kasai station in Tokyo has one for 9,600. In Bogotá we built parking facilities in some Trans-Milenio stations that together add up to more than 5,000 bicycle spaces. The Metro now under construction includes 10,000 bicycle parking spaces at stations.

If dogs are allowed into buildings' elevators, then why not bicycles? Bicycles don't bark, or shake themselves and shower us with water when wet. Wouldn't it be convenient to require future buildings to have at least one lift fitted for bicycles?

And we'll begin our workday feeling better if we've pedaled for half an hour rather than arriving tense from sitting stuck in traffic. The Canadian government's statistical bureau found that journeys to work were the day's most pleasurable activity for 2 percent of those who drove cars but for 19 percent of those who went by bike.[7]

If the cyclist wears earphones, the bicycle becomes an almost magical vehicle, a flying carpet. One glides along like a bird, listening to music, flying low through the city. On many occasions I've felt an almost ecstatic joy on a bicycle in the crisp air of a luminous day with blue skies, watching people on the sidewalks, the young playing in the park, shop windows, architecture, people in open-air cafés, other cyclists, riding down any street, with no particular destination. Or cycling across a park, on a riverbank bikeway, watching parents with their children with a song on my lips, intensely enjoying the city.

Every person who rides a bicycle helps to reduce traffic, global warming, and health costs. The cyclist is a civic hero and should be treated as such. It seems an elementary act to provide safety and comfort to those who prefer that means of transport.

A city good for bicycle mobility is probably a good city. It evinces respect for human dignity and for those most vulnerable and shows that people feel safe in its public spaces. Late one night, at a café on the Spree riverbank in Berlin, I watched how women rode past on bicycles, alone. They came out of the darkness, passed me by, and vanished into darkness again. It seemed to me a very telling indication that Berlin is a good city.

A city in which many mobilize by bicycle is also more pleasant, fun, and sensual. Just as a bay is more beautiful when there are sailing boats on it, even if we are not sailing ourselves, the city is more beautiful with cyclists everywhere gliding past. Beyond being a means of transport, the bicycle is a toy. It's fun to use. A caricature by Jordan B. Gorfinkel posted on social networks shows a formal man in suit and tie, looking at an apparatus with puzzlement, and the person beside him, explains, "It's a bicycle. It makes you happier."

On several occasions, after a presentation in which I've referred to the importance of bicycles, someone in the audience, generally a higher-income person, has told me that there are no bicycles in their city and that it's impossible to bicycle there because roads are too steep, or because it is too cold or too hot, or for any other reason. But once I go out onto the street, and despite the lack of infrastructure to protect them, I find many cyclists, even if government officials and higher-income people don't notice them. On occasions those same people tell me, as if discovering some happy memory, "Really, when we were children and young, we bicycled a lot."

Cyclists are invisible to many, except when they are noticed as a nuisance by drivers on the road or as an obstacle to be eliminated through some restriction. And they do restrict them on many roads, particularly expressways, but also on roads in city centers, as is true in Shanghai.

Are Bikeways a Right Like Sidewalks?

For many, whether because of income level or age, the bicycle is the only means of individual transport. Mobility is a fundamental human right. The UN Universal Declaration of Human Rights says that "every person has the right to freedom of movement." That is an empty right if by exercising it a person puts their life at risk. In any democratic city today, it's obvious that sidewalks are a right and that if someone is run down by a car in a place where there is no sidewalk, they can sue the state and assuredly obtain a substantial indemnity. One day in the not-distant future the law will stipulate that those who bicycle are entitled to do so without an inordinate risk of losing their lives. And the courts will rule against the state if a cyclist is run over on a road without a bikeway.

A bikeway is not simply a painted line on the asphalt. It needs physical protection. Often when bikeways on main arteries reach an intersection, while cars have an underpass or an overpass to go across it, pedestrians and bicyclists are forced to make long detours. In a good city there is not one stretch, long or short, in which cars have a more direct, shorter way to go from one point to another than cyclists.

On the highway from Mexico City to Oaxaca, I saw signposts indicating that cyclists were banned. As occurs with similar signposts on roads in central Shanghai, cyclists irreverently sail right past them. More than traffic signs, they are classist messages. What those signs really express is that it will not be tolerated that the poor inconvenience the wealthier and more "important" citizens who travel in cars. Even without signs, the fact is that bicycles are not allowed on almost any highway's shoulders because highways were not designed to accommodate them. In a good city there can be no roads forbidden to pedestrians and cyclists.

Too many transport ministers, still unaware that their customers are human beings and not motor vehicles, ban bicycles on some roads, arguing that there is no proper infrastructure for them. This is like banning walking because there are no sidewalks. And forbidding walking is almost like forbidding eating or breathing.

If there is money to build motor-vehicle infrastructure, it seems there should be money as well to build humans' infrastructure. This is more valid still in developing societies, in which most citizens do not have cars.

It is well-known that public spaces are safer with people in them. In *The Life and Death of Great American Cities*,[8] Jane Jacobs emphasizes this. When there are many people on bicycles, cities are particularly safe because bicycles move quickly and silently and appear suddenly. An environment with bicycle traffic is not propitious for criminals.

Going to School by Bike

In Utrecht, Copenhagen, and Münster, the immense majority of children go to school by bike—even the smallest, on their parents' bicycles, fitted with a small seat, or sometimes two. At the start and end of the school day, children on bikes can be seen everywhere—alone, in twos, or in groups. The city is literally the children's space. It's not just a matter of biking to school but of moving through the neighborhood. In a city where children and adolescents can safely bike to a friend's home, the park, or a shop, they appropriate their environment as their own and grow up happier.

In the high-income New York suburb of Scarsdale, most high school students over sixteen drive their own cars to school. Many of those cars are luxurious, expensive status symbols. Hundreds of cars fill the school parking lot and spill over for several blocks around. The majority of those students live close by and could arrive on a bicycle in just a few minutes. Some of the children who live farther away, or who must climb hills, if they do not wish to use the school bus could use electric bikes. But they prefer their cars.

The atmosphere is different in the Netherlands, where children and adolescents bike to school. Consequently, they achieve freedom and mobility well before their Scarsdale peers because they've used a bicycle or public transport since they were eleven or twelve years old to move around their neighborhood and even some places beyond, unaccompanied by an adult. They don't identify freedom with the car but rather with bicycles and public transport, which allow them to go anywhere by themselves. Adolescents in Scarsdale identify the car as the supreme instrument of freedom and access to adult life. By contrast, children in the Netherlands never needed a car to be able to go wherever they wanted, and access to a car is not a milestone or anything particularly important.

For adolescents and youngsters in developing cities, driving to school is not an option, and most children in popular sectors go on foot. A minority use a bicycle, but many more could do so if there were safe bikeways on all streets and parking facilities for them at the school. In Bogotá we had a program that provided more than three thousand children under the age of twelve with bicycles to travel to school, accompanied by adult guides contracted by the city administration. Studies carried out by our Education Department found that, as in the United States and Europe, academic performance was better for children who arrived by bicycle.

A Boston program called "Bicycles not Bombs" offered a course in bicycle mechanics to adolescents in marginal neighborhoods. Those who attended classes for several weeks and graduated from the related modules were given a bicycle and a set of tools. Thus, they not only obtained a bicycle but also gained self-esteem and the possibility to earn some income.

Inspired and motivated by this program, during my second period as mayor of Bogotá, we built an attractive and functional building in a popular neighborhood and started up a project we called the "Bicycle School." It issues certificates in bicycle mechanics to those who study and graduate from a two-year technical program. It also offers courses in bicycle mechanics to adolescents in nearby schools. The program builds self-esteem and allow graduates to earn some money and even start microbusinesses.

The cities being built today have the latitude to incorporate ambitious radical concepts. Why not create networks of roads exclusively for pedestrians and bicycles? Better still if they run through green corridors, and better still if they do not run parallel to motor-vehicle roads. Or why not make roads in which at least half the space is exclusively for pedestrians and cyclists?

To promote even more bicycle use, Denmark has begun to build "bike highways." The first was eighteen kilometers long, from the Albertslund suburb to Copenhagen. To construct that one, and twenty-five more already planned, twenty-one local governments in the metropolitan region joined together to form an association.[9] There are two bicycle highways in London, both created by Boris Johnson when he was mayor, that cross the center of London: one runs north to south and the other east to west, with a combined length of twenty kilometers.

Our Bogotá Bicycle Highways

In 1998, flying on a helicopter over the southwest of Bogotá, which then was an enormous, compact conglomeration of informal settlements, expanding by the day over the green environs around the city, it occurred to me that we could make a major bicycle highway alongside the edge of the built city. It would separate the houses from the green spaces. I knew that with formalization processes and the infrastructure projects we would pursue, the city would expand farther to the west, leaving the bicycle highway in the middle of the urbanized area. In some segments the Alameda Porvenir, our name for the bicycle highway, would go through neighborhoods already constructed. With Andrés Camargo, the dynamic director of our urban road construction agency, IDU, and the young designers[10] we brought to the project, we walked many kilometers through pastures and informal neighborhoods and flew over the area, looking for space for the Alameda.

All told, we did many public works to improve these southwestern informal neighborhoods, including pumping stations to solve the problem of recurrent flooding, sewerage networks, schools, community centers, kindergartens, parks, and even a major library. But the most revolutionary of our works there was this bicycle highway, twenty-four kilometers long, ten to fifteen meters wide, lined with trees, and even buried cables for its lighting. Taking Alameda Porvenir, citizens can reach libraries, schools, parks, bicycle parking facilities at a TransMilenio mass-transport system terminal, and soon the first station of the metro line under construction.

Our objective was to exalt and dignify cyclists and pedestrians in neighborhoods where almost no one had a car. It was a potent symbol of new and different values because Alameda Porvenir, exclusively for pedestrians and cyclists, was the only paved road in the area. While motor vehicles slowly crawled along unpaved streets, full of potholes and mud in the rainy season, pedestrians and cyclists enjoyed an almost luxurious tree-lined path. In the area we only paved a few streets for bus access.

The citizens in these very poor neighborhoods welcomed Alameda Porvenir, initially with some surprise and soon afterward with pride. Alameda not only improves life but changes it. The pleasure derived from having a motor-vehicle road paved diminishes over time, while the pleasure of the Alameda does not.

Where the JICA transport study mentioned earlier proposed a highway, we built a greenway along the Juan Amarillo riverbanks instead. For decades, the contaminated waters from the stream had moved slowly, the stench was appalling, and the whole riverbed had become a breeding ground for rats, flies, and mosquitoes. We decontaminated it with a large box culvert that collected the wastewater previously discharged into the river. And the river, now channeled, became the backbone of the Juan Amarillo greenway, which stretches more than thirty kilometers, including its branches, across one of the world's densest cities. Tens of thousands of people use it daily to commute to work. This greenway connects some of city's poorest neighborhoods in the west to some of the richest in the east.[11] The improvement brought by the greenway was a catalyst for the construction of high-density housing developments on both sides of it.

Inevitably, we had to fight many battles to make the Juan Amarillo greenway a reality. We won the battle to remove illegal enclosures that had been erected by residential buildings and a club, essentially privatizing public land adjacent to the river. We fought another difficult battle to construct a branch of the greenway through a neighborhood called Niza. Some of its residents, who did not want poorer citizens from sectors west of theirs passing through their neighborhood, were able to get a court order in my first mayoral term to impede the greenway's construction on that stretch, arguing it would damage a wetland.

That group of residents had not previously expressed concerns about the environment. They had built a concrete tennis court just two meters from the water's edge. But their classist attitudes had already revealed themselves a few years earlier, when they removed the goalposts of a soccer field and planted trees in the field because lower-income citizens who came to play there on weekends annoyed them. The moment they found out about the greenway project, they hastily planted native trees around the wetland. Their pseudo-environmental argument was that a two-meter-wide bikeway that would run several meters away from the wetlands' edge would damage it. Ironically, in the same sector where they were able to block the greenway, three of the city's largest roads pass over the same wetland, on ugly pontoons less than one meter above the water's surface. Yet neighbors never complained about those roads or their widening.[12] Finally, in my second term as mayor, it was possible to undertake the construction of a pedestrian path alongside the wetland in Niza, though we had to make it explicit that bicycles would not use it.

Projects for human beings still have no powerful political support, especially in developing cities. Major roads, airports, or ports have the support of the most powerful members of society, and those who oppose such projects can do little to stop them. There is an unfortunate contrast between the success with which a few can block all pedestrian paths or bikeways for human beings and their lack of success when they try to stop projects for cars, aircraft, or ships.

During my two tenures as mayor, I managed to create or leave under construction more than 150 kilometers of bicycle highways like Alameda Porvenir and greenways such as Juan Amarillo.[13] Except for a few segments, there are no motor-vehicle roads alongside them, and where roads do exist, the pedestrian and bicycle space is more than fifteen meters wide and lined with trees. In addition to being attractive for walking, jogging, and playing, in an environment with trees and birds, these are high-quality roads for bicycle mobility, covering long stretches across a very dense city, free from the threat of the car. They are used daily by tens of thousands of cyclists.

In our Lagos de Torca housing project, for more than four hundred thousand inhabitants the main greenway is fifteen kilometers long and thirty meters wide, and every neighborhood's bike network incorporates a connection to it. On Caracas Avenue, underneath a five-kilometer segment of the elevated Metro line we left under construction in a central part of the city, we left only the TransMilenio BRT, while the rest of the road space was assigned exclusively to pedestrians and bicycles.

The Alameda Porvenir crosses another attractive and innovative project of ours, the Alameda del Canal de Bosa, a three-kilometer pedestrian walkway along a drainage canal. We built more than a hundred kilometers of greenways alongside drainage canals and on the banks of streams, rivers, and wetlands.

The hundreds of kilometers of rainwater drains in developing cities are usually barriers or obstacles for humans that frequently cause loss of property values to nearby sectors. With a small investment in infrastructure for pedestrians and bicycles alongside them, as well as trees and benches, they can become greenways that improve the neighborhood rather than the opposite. Unfortunately, in Bogotá, most of the more than one hundred streams that come down from the mountains to the east of the city have been buried in pipes. This is a preventable error for cities of the future.

* * *

Like a diving falcon or a horse at full gallop, a human being on a bicycle has thermodynamic beauty. As Rodney Tolley notes, "The natural form of loco-motion for a human being is walking. Humans on foot are thermodynami-cally more efficient than any motorized vehicle and most animals, yet humans on bicycles surpass them, able as they are to go three to four times faster and yet use five times less energy in the process. Equipped with a bicycle, man is more efficient than all machines and all animals too."[14]

Let us imagine for a moment a society in which almost all its members, without class distinction, walk, use a bicycle, and travel primarily in public transport. It's not too difficult to imagine. And yet that adjustment alone would make our lives completely different—and better.

There is nothing utopian about cities in which cars are not widely used. They already exist. Not only that: they are the planet's most successful. They attract more qualified professionals, investors, and tourists and the highest property values: London, Hong Kong, Manhattan, and Zurich, among others. But even they may come to assign much less road space to cars and more to pedestrians, cyclists, and buses or trams in exclusive lanes. I can foresee the moment when the design of roads for cars with no bus-only lanes or bike-ways will be seen as something incomprehensible, a relic of a thankfully past age. In terms of transport, an advanced city is not one in which the low-income citizens have cars but one in which even the high-income earners travel on public transport and bicycles.

CHAPTER 9

Pedestrian Public Space Is the Most Important Part of Our City

s societies become wealthier and households become smaller, social life takes place more and more outside our home. In dense cities, those small households, of one or two people, live in smaller homes in which they spend increasingly less waking time. At the same time wealthier societies enjoy a growing amount of leisure time, less and less of which will be spent at home. Given that progressively more work can be done anywhere, cities will need to attract people for reasons other than work, changing over from being places primarily for work to being places primarily for leisure. A great city is and will be more so one where people can most enjoy leisure time. And the first urban infrastructure for quality leisure is public pedestrian space.

At work, what we do is basically defined; not so, in our free time. Learning to live a better and more civilized life has to do mainly with what we do in our leisure time. In backward and unequal societies, leisure time activities depend on income levels. Access to sports facilities or music lessons is generally difficult for those with low incomes. In a good city, these activities are accessible to all. What one does during one's leisure time does not depend on income levels, but on what each of us enjoys. Citizens of all income levels can meet playing tennis, taking piano lessons, racing small sailing boats, hiking through the mountains, or sitting side-by-side on a park bench.

When we see images of Earth from space, the planet looks small and fragile, an oasis in the middle of nothingness, with an infinite dark space in the background. The image moves us, and we feel great solidarity with all our traveling companions, particularly with all human beings, with whom we share our destiny. That perspective makes national frontiers insignificant and underscores everything that unites us. But we have only to come down to Earth to realize we are not quite such close brothers and sisters as we had imagined.

We invented nations, and of all Earth we only have the right to be within the borders of our own country. To enter another one, we need authorization from its owners or the authorities that represent them. Especially if we come from less developed countries, there are dozens of countries we cannot easily enter. We need visas, which take time to process, are difficult and expensive to obtain, and are denied to many. Because of my Colombian passport, I have not been able to attend events in several countries because their visas took so long to process, and on two occasions, when I arrived in countries for which my visa had inadvertently expired, they have put me in a small room with police surveillance, like a criminal, and sent me back on the first available flight.[1]

Sadder still, our own country is not ours either. Almost all its land is apportioned into private property. If we enter the property of any farm, we can be driven out with guns: we even run the risk of getting shot. Most nations are well behind Scandinavia, where the *Allemansrätten*—literally, everyone's right (also referred to as the "right to roam")—is the law. Protected by that right, in those more democratic societies,[2] the entire territory of a country becomes almost a park. Anybody can enter and cross any rural property on foot, bicycle, or skis, as foxes or birds do, and even camp there for a couple of nights without asking permission. In Sweden, *Allemansrätten* connotes every human being's right to walk freely through nature.[3] It's even possible to enter properties with crops, provided that no damage is done to them. Enclosures designed to stop the passage of human beings are banned. In some other countries there is a right to pass through properties with pastures or woodland. The CROW law was passed in England in 2000, based on the same philosophy of giving the right of free passage regardless of whether property is private, although it does not apply to cropland.[4]

They say that when the English arrived in America, they asked Native Americans if they could buy the land. The Native Americans were initially surprised, but after reflecting for a while, they answered that, of course, they would sell it. Further, if the English wanted, they would also sell them the moon, rivers, and the air. It was incomprehensible to them that something that had been created by God for humanity to enjoy could be transformed into private property. When after the war of independence, Americans were settling the immense Northwest Territory, which would later contain the states of Ohio, Indiana, Illinois, Michigan, Wisconsin, and part of Minnesota, a Wyandot native called Turk said, "No one in particular can justify claim to this land; it belongs in common to us all; no earthly being has an exclusive right to it. The Great Spirit above is the true and only owner of this soil; and he has given us all an equal right to it."[5] But the Earth was sold. Today it is largely private and accessible only to its owners and those authorized by them to enter.

If we are not able to move around freely in our rural areas, the situation in cities is worse. We may be thrown into jail or even die if we enter the home or office of someone unknown. And if we venture onto the street, we may be killed by a car. Therefore, on our entire planet, the only space to which we have the full right of access is pedestrian public space. For that reason, among others, it is the most important space in our city and determines much of our quality of life.

One often hears that some cities are inhuman or aggressive concrete jungles. When a city elicits such feelings, it is because it doesn't have sufficient or sufficiently good pedestrian public spaces. What humanizes a city more than anything else is its pedestrian public space.

During Leisure Time, Income Differences Are Keenly Felt

At work, a high-level executive and the humblest worker may have similar levels of satisfaction or dissatisfaction. It's in their leisure time that the income difference manifests itself. High-income earners go to a large house, possibly with a garden. They attend concerts; go to restaurants, country clubs, and weekend homes; and take vacations far from home. Low-income employees live in a very small home with their children, sometimes with other relatives, occasionally in overcrowded conditions. The only leisure-time alternative to watching television or internet surfing is pedestrian public space. Therefore, to construct quality-of-life equality, a democratic society must do its utmost to improve its citizens' leisure time. At a minimum it should provide all its citizens with quality pedestrian public space. At any income level, public space makes life happier, but for lower-income citizens it is crucial.

The wider the sidewalk and the slower the traffic, the greater the human quality of a road. It's not possible to prove that a ten-meter-wide sidewalk is better than a three-meter-wide one. These decisions are closer to art than science. It's something we feel. The wider it is, the safer it will be for children, the greater our feeling of comfort, and probably the higher the value of properties around it. At minimum, a sidewalk should be wide enough for two people in wheelchairs to mobilize comfortably beside each other.

The mortal threat of cars is almost imperceptible but very real, and it slowly exhausts us. If we are walking on a sidewalk beside a large road with vehicles passing at high speeds, we are stressed, even if unconsciously; stress is increased if we have a five-year-old child holding our hand. We are relieved when we turn a corner onto a low-traffic, slow-speed road. And if in taking another turn we find ourselves on an exclusively pedestrian route, we draw a deep breath and feel great relief to be finally free from the latent threat of cars. Only then do we realize how much stress traffic was causing us. And we let go of the child's hand. The unconscious tension that the threat of cars generates is similar to the noise caused by air conditioning or a clothes dryer. We do not notice it, but when it suddenly ceases—what a relief!

When I was a student in Paris, my university was located in the Avenue de l'Observatoire, next to the Luxembourg Gardens. In the park I encountered high-income citizens, even occasionally media celebrities. The rich generally do everything possible to avoid places where poor people go. However, a good city has some public spaces so wonderful that not even the rich avoid them. In those exceptional public spaces, all citizens meet as equals. In New York's Central Park, the banks of the Thames or Hyde Park in London, the Bund in Shanghai, and El Retiro Park in Madrid, some of the wealthiest people on Earth and low-income people walk together.

In backward societies, high income-citizens and even middle-income ones avoid places where they would have to meet their fellow lower-income citizens as equals: they do not use public transport; they do not walk on sidewalks to reach shops with street fronts, as they prefer driving to exclusive shopping centers, which de facto exclude low-income citizens; they live in walled communities; they prefer clubs to parks. Although it might amuse someone from an advanced country, one indication that society is beginning to make progress toward development is that high-income citizens begin to go to parks and walk on the sidewalks.

The nature of pedestrian public space forges a way of life and defines a city's character. A good part of the memories we have of the cities of our childhood comes from what we experienced on its pedestrian public spaces.

The Quality of Pedestrian Public Spaces

We cannot ensure that all households have exceptional housing, but we can ensure that they all have quality pedestrian public spaces, especially if we are engaged in a new urban development.

A frequent discussion in developing countries is the minimum size for social housing. Idealists and demagogues propose that they should be large, at least a hundred square meters. The more pragmatic recall that since resources are scarce, if we truly wish to provide housing for the poorest majorities, we should construct smaller housing units of about forty square meters. I tend to agree with the latter, partly because people do not spend their entire lives in one home. Although they may not move to another city, they change homes several times, depending on their needs and possibilities.

Two matters are more important than the size of a home: first is location. How close is it to work, shops, recreation, public transport? Second is the quantity and quality of pedestrian public space in the area. How is the sidewalk? How many parks, sports fields, and plazas are nearby? In modern life, the home is principally a place to sleep or to work at a table. To live better, the size of our home is less important than having wide, tree-lined sidewalks, shops, cafés, public transport, parks, and sporting facilities, as well as proximity to our place of study or work.

Communities, architects, governments, and developers often spar over the height of buildings. Once again, more important than the building's height is the quantity and quality of pedestrian public space around it and especially in front of the building. The wonderful British architect Richard Rogers said that buildings do not end when they reach the ground. To the contrary, the most important thing about a building is what happens to the public space around it. Does the new building enhance its pedestrian public space? Does it make it more appealing to have a conversation there, walk alongside it, play or kiss there?

The iconic three towers of Marina Bay Sands in Singapore, connected at roof level by a platform with a swimming pool and designed by Moshe Safdie, are striking from a distance but disappointing on the ground. It is accessible only by car roads. There are no pedestrian spaces, to say nothing of cafés or other amenities. On the Hudson River side of Manhattan's 11th Avenue, the IAC building's opaque gray windows extend all the way down to a very narrow sidewalk. Designed by Frank Gehry, and sculptural as is all his work, it's not pleasant to walk alongside due to the opacity of its windows, the narrow space left for the sidewalk, and the absence of shops. In contrast there is the generous, attractive private space integrated into the sidewalk with a basin, benches, and trees, at the Seagram Building in Manhattan. Designed by Mies van der Rohe, it's located at Park Avenue and 52nd Street.

Condesa is a charming neighborhood in Mexico City with abundant parks and trees, attractive architecture, restaurants, and cafés. It is a pleasure to live, work, and walk in. But in recent decades small buildings have been steadily demolished to make way for larger ones without windows at the street level or even on the second floor. This is a serious problem in developing cities. Wishing to provide parking, and given the high cost of basement excavation, the buildings street-level floor and often several more have been given over to parking. The result is ugly and unpleasant to walk past; it even makes the public space unsafe, as the informal surveillance of public space from the building is lost.

We have the same problem in Bogotá. The urban development plan we presented to the city council did not allow parking and blind walls at ground level and included incentives to place apartments, offices, and, particularly, shops there.

In Bogotá, as in many other cities, many high-income citizens have not considered it aesthetically tolerable or distinctive to have shops in their buildings, or indeed on the same block. They prefer not to have them anywhere near where they live. This results in fewer people in public spaces, which is boring and even dangerous.

Local shops are a treasure. They make it possible for us to buy food on foot, walk to the bakery, the pharmacy, or a café. Ideally, any building with more than fifteen stories should have some sort of commercial activity at street level.

In contrast, motor-vehicle access to buildings across the sidewalk damages their quality. When buildings are tall, there is constant traffic entering and leaving parking garages across the sidewalk, which is both unpleasant and dangerous. Important world avenues don't have this kind of access: cars enter buildings through minor streets, perpendicular to the main road. Manhattan authorities are rarely persuaded to allow motor-vehicle access to buildings across sidewalks, even on these minor streets, but the opposite frequently holds true in developing cities. These luxury buildings have access ramps for cars with pretentious little roundabouts. Multistar hotels have access bays for cars on public space.

The first criterion to evaluate everything built in a city, not just buildings but also roads, drainage canals, or other projects, is the same: does it damage or improve the pedestrian quality of its surroundings?

Air Is Another Essential Public Space

High-rise buildings can damage some urban environments. Those who own buildings in valuable sectors and want to demolish and replace them with taller and more valuable ones to make a profit, pressure authorities to permit them the greater height. Invariably, some area residents will want the opposite. Withstanding pressures, governments in cities worldwide have enacted height restrictions to preserve many sectors' character and atmosphere. Contrary to what some businessmen demanded of New York's former planning commissioner, Amanda Burden severely restricted building heights on Manhattan's Lower East Side to preserve its character.

Edward Glaeser, in his fascinating book *Triumph of the City,* applies an economic criterion, arguing that height restrictions should be eliminated to reduce the cost of housing.[6] However, greater height would destroy much of the appeal of certain sectors. What is certain is that many of the world's cities' most attractive neighborhoods, which have best maintained and increased their value, have buildings less than ten stories high, and most of them less than six. With some exceptions, for example, if they face Central Park or some wonderful oceanfront view, low-rise buildings tend to better preserve their value.

Although it cannot be the only criterion to consider, residents of any sector almost never want buildings higher than those in which they themselves live, unless, of course, they are the owners of a house they want to sell or demolish to build a taller building. Usually building height follows a ratio to the width of the road, including sidewalks. But whatever the case, tall buildings obstruct more of the sky's view. They obstruct sunlight for more hours. The higher the building, the less neighbors know one another. Jan Gehl has pointed out that the farther from the ground someone lives or works, the less they venture into public space. Residents in the first four or five floors go out more frequently to the street, possibly because they have more visual and auditory contact with the public space below and their "journey" is not perceived as long or cumbersome.[7]

It's true that large towers can offer residents facilities that small buildings cannot, such as a gym, a swimming pool, communal rooms for meetings and parties, shared offices, or even facilities for pet grooming. Something that high-rise and low-rise buildings both can offer is a shared terrace to take in the sun, hold parties, or just read. In Bogotá, terraces had traditionally been reserved for the penthouse or for a few apartments on the higher floors. Our urban development plan presented to the City Council required these top-floor terraces not to be exclusive to one apartment but to be shared spaces for all building residents.

The Inexhaustible Capacity of Pedestrian Public Space to Produce Happiness

Roads, ports, power plants, warehouses, and other kinds of public and private infrastructure are essential for society to survive, function, produce, and achieve economic growth. They are necessary but by themselves do not produce happiness. Most public investments are necessary for society to achieve ulterior purposes. Pedestrian public space is peculiar. It is not a means to an end; it is the end in itself. It yields wellness, joy, tranquility, and inclusion: it produces happiness.

Unlike so many consumer purchases, pedestrian public space is a magical good, with an inexhaustible capacity to produce satisfaction. If we have a beautiful park or plaza opposite our home or office, we can see or enjoy it dozens of times a day, for months, years, decades. And it never ceases to elicit satisfaction. People demand roads in good condition, a good water supply, or a hospital. A new road has impact, and the community is grateful for it on the day it is inaugurated. A few weeks later, it seems something banal. It produces no satisfaction. Public pedestrian space is different. Although citizens rarely demand more or better pedestrian public space—especially in developing cities—when it appears they use it and enjoy it intensely without it ever losing its capacity to delight.

One might say that while roads are necessary to survive, parks and other pedestrian spaces are necessary to live. When we have very low per capita income, a significant income increase makes us much happier. As our per capita income grows, however, additional income increases yield progressively smaller increases in happiness until they become insignificant. The fact that depression is a massive and growing problem in rich countries and that pharmaceutical companies spend billions to develop antidepressants to deal with it are evidence of this diminishing happiness return on income. Access to a park or plaza close to one's home might not appear in income per capita statistics, but once a minimum level of income has been achieved, it can increase welfare more than higher levels of income.

Taxes paid to central governments can go to distant ends: national defense, a road in a remote area, the diplomatic corps, or the social security deficit. But local taxes pay for public works and services that directly improve citizens' quality of life: parks, sidewalks, sports facilities, plazas, public transport, libraries, cultural events, or improvements to cleaning or security. These are goods and services that not even high-income citizens can obtain individually. Citizens pay their local taxes if not with pleasure, then at least with less pain because they're paying for improvements in the quality of their daily lives.

That a good city is one that is good for human beings might sound like a truism. Unfortunately, all too many of the cities we have made in the last hundred years have sought more to accommodate motor vehicles than humans. Axiomatically, anything that makes the city more pleasant, safe, and comfortable to walk in is good; anything that makes it less so is not. A vital goal for those who are building cities today is to ensure that walking is not only safe but also an irresistible pleasure.

In 2010, I enjoyed several days in San Sebastián, an enchanting city in which, like in other Spanish cities, people enjoy life on the street, sidewalks, pedestrian walkways, beaches, and cafés. Here we see people of all ages and levels of mobility—grandmothers pushing baby strollers and children on bicycles. In the Old City's Bentaberri neighborhood, the Oihenart pedestrian street next to the plaza José Maria Sert was a meeting place for many preteen children on bikes. Near them, at street cafés, sat adults and some elderly people in wheelchairs. Boys and girls were buying sweets in the "*txuxes*" shop[8] next to a covered sidewalk. Children kept entering and exiting through large doors that connected the street to gardens inside the apartment buildings that lined the block. Public and private space were woven into a single whole. The city seemed to smile.

When I see Dutch cities with their ample pedestrian areas and cyclists everywhere, I wish that many developing world urban leaders would spend some time there. There are tens of thousands of small developing cities with pleasant climates where it would be easy to move on a bicycle, on foot, and on public transport.

Cartago, Colombia, lies in a fertile tropical region, luxuriant with all kinds of majestic trees, flowers, birds, butterflies, and the beautiful La Vieja River that runs alongside it. Year round, the temperature is between 20°C and 35°C (70°F and 95°F). The land is flat, which makes it easy to walk or use a bicycle, but there are few cyclists. In Amsterdam, which is cold and wet much of the time and has 2.4 million inhabitants and one of the world's highest income levels (almost every household can afford a car), the streets are teeming with bicycles.[9] Cartago has less than 150,000 inhabitants, of which only a minority has a car, but there is frequent traffic congestion. Drivers and thousands of motorcyclists blow their horns impulsively and often and show little respect for pedestrians and cyclists. Sidewalks are narrow, uneven, and discontinuous, and there are only a few kilometers of bikeway outside the urban area. Few people use bicycles for their mobility. Those who do not yet own a motorcycle want one, and those who have one want a car. An enclosed, air-conditioned shopping mall, recently built, was deemed major progress for the city.

There are thousands of cities like Cartago in developing countries. With urban designs structured around networks of walkways and bikeways, shaded by large tropical trees, and gardens with all kinds of birds and butterflies, quality of life could be more equal, better, and happier. This would also bring changes in dress. For example, in Cartago and dozens of other very warm Colombian cities, nobody wears short trousers. In the future it might seem incomprehensible that even children wore long trousers in tropical cities in the first half of the twenty-first century.

Public Space to See People and Be Seen

Any plaza, religious service, restaurant, or sidewalk is really a spontaneous, impromptu parade, in which people express themselves with clothing, hairstyle, and makeup. We go to mass concerts with hundreds of thousands of spectators, even though we could better see and listen to the singer on a screen at home, because the concert's experience is to be with others who share our enthusiasm. We could tan on our building terrace just as we do on the beach, but of course on the beach we come into contact with nature—and random other people! Full restaurants are more attractive than empty ones; a stadium is more attractive full than half empty; we like sharing sessions with others at the gym, a painting class, or a sport. We could pour ourselves a drink or make coffee at home, but we prefer to go to a bar or café because what we're seeking more than a beer or coffee is social contact, even if occasionally we feel the need to be alone. Sometimes we just want to see people and not to be seen ... to enjoy the city almost as if we were invisible, which is something the city allows as well.

Children are wise. They know that they are better off when they are with other children. I remember that in the New York suburb of Scarsdale, they much preferred a small public park to the private gardens of almost the same size of some of the large houses where some of them lived because they could meet up with other children there. We adults also enjoy seeing and being with other people, although, unlike children, we sometimes do not admit it.

A good pedestrian public space is one with people. But, as Jan Gehl writes, what we are looking for is not that people should walk in public space because they have to, but because they enjoy it, as they sit on a bench, a step, or in a café to see people. Gehl reminds us of an ancient saying in Scandinavia: "People come where people are."[10] William Whyte wrote that "a street that is open to the sky and filled with people and life is a splendid place to be."[11]

Some time ago, in an informal sector on the outskirts of Manila, walking along a large pond where tilapia and the popular Philippine milk fish were bred, I came across three radiant children on their way to school. It was past midday, and they were going to the afternoon shift: like so many cities in the developing world, the school had two shifts. I asked them where they lived through the social worker who accompanied us and served as an interpreter. They pointed to some houses on the other side of the pond, which were closer to the school than where we stood. They were taking a rather long walk to get there. I asked if there were no roads to the school from their neighborhood. "Yes," they said, "but we like going round this way because there is wind, it's nicer to walk." A walk in a pleasant environment with friends was a pleasure for these children. Their smiling faces were teaching me.

There persists an aspiration for grandiose monumental fountains or pools with majestic pretensions, where children are not allowed to bathe or play. In a Hong Kong plaza, I saw a shallow pool some fifty square meters, fenced by a railing to prevent children from going next to or into it to play. In the Luxembourg Gardens in Paris, they do not allow children in the water either, but at least they let them stand next to it and float model boats there. In Sydney, Chicago, Vancouver, and Medellín, among many other cities, there are fountains and pools designed precisely for the opposite: for children to get wet and play.

At the zenith of classical Athens, "the climate did not keep people in their houses, but brought them out into the company of their neighbors," historian Peter Hall puts it.[12] He also recalls the typical Athenian citizen, who says, in Xenophon's words, "I never spend my time indoors." Hall says that the Greeks' material austerity allowed them to spend many hours in the street talking. "So the Greek was able to spend his time sharpening his wits and improving his manners through constant intercourse with his fellow citizens." In this sense, social contact with eclectic and random fellow citizens on the street was an essential part of democracy itself. "It was in the streets and market-places and gymnasia and theatres that the Athenians educated each other, developing a ready set of social skills that made every place into an informal club."[13]

João do Rio likewise writes, "I love the street. That intimate feeling would not be revealed to you by me, if I did not judge, and I have reasons to judge so, that such absolute, exaggerated love is shared by all of you. We all are equal, we feel similar and equal, in cities, villages, towns . . . because we are united, leveled, unionized, by the love of the street."[14]

This writer understood, pedestrian public space is the great integrating element in a city and the place of encounters. This supports democracy and civil society. Before the arrival of the tram, people in western cities met in the street, the squares, and even under one roof, at church. Although the wealthy had fine horses and luxurious clothing, and all were aware of social distinctions, people of all stations met in the same spaces. When the tram arrived, cities expanded, and neighborhoods formed farther from the city center and became more sorted by socioeconomic level, each with its own public spaces and churches. Contact between people of different income levels diminished, but at least they continued to meet on the tram. Then, with the arrival of the car, the distance between neighborhoods sorted by income grew even greater, and these citizens no longer met on public transport.

One challenge for modern cities is to revive that eminently democratic encounter as equals, on public transport and in public spaces, across income levels. Without quality spaces that integrate society, urban life is impoverished; a vicious circle develops in which middle- and upper-class citizens don't venture into public spaces because they lack quality, and those spaces aren't improved because they aren't used by the more affluent and influential.

Thus, the absence of quality pedestrian public space worsens society's divisions and deepens feelings of inequality and exclusion.

Public pedestrian space convenes sectors of the city from different incomes and different cultures in ways that a highway or even public transport cannot do. My impression is that the discontent and revolts that erupted at the start of the twenty-first century in satellite towns around Stockholm and more recently in Paris, where immigrants concentrate, although they would be exemplary developments anywhere in the developing world, can at least partly be attributed to the lack of pedestrian connection with higher-income sectors. They are like islands that can be reached by train or by car on a highway, but not by walking or by bicycle, and are isolated from the central area of the city. Similar developments can be found in other European cities—and similar social unrest as well.

A massive study by Raj Chetty and others found that one important explanation of why some low-income youth are able to rise out of poverty is relationships with higher income youth. And proximity, living relatively close to each other, is one important reason why such relations take place. Chetty concludes that "Architecture and urban planning could have a role" in promoting the relationships that contribute to leave poverty behind. He writes: "Examples include social infrastructure, such as public libraries, to build social bonds across groups; the effects of public parks on social interactions; and the impacts of public transit on the interactions between people living in different neighbourhoods."[15]

In a dense city, sectors of different income levels are relatively close to each other. Many low-income citizens are able to walk or bike to higher-income sectors, pass through them, spend time in them. People of different incomes meet easily in public spaces. Such proximity constructs democratic inclusion and legitimacy.

Bogotá is a very dense city, and although it has some eight million inhabitants,[16] it would only take some seven hours to walk across it at its widest part. On a bicycle during the Ciclovía, when more than 120 kilometers of arterial roads are closed to motor-vehicle traffic, low-income citizens enjoy riding through wealthier areas. In a very unequal city, that is an exercise in social integration.

It is common in developing cities to see high-value apartment buildings with no sidewalks or very narrow ones flanked by high walls. Those are environments suitable only to spending one's time confined in private spaces.

Those are not apartments to live in but to take *refuge* in: they are homes without a city.

Slowly, developing countries are becoming aware that citizens who walk are as important as those in motor vehicles. In 2006 the government of India announced a national urban transport policy, and one of its priority objectives was "bringing about a more equitable allocation of road space with people, rather than vehicles, as its main focus."[17] But, although improvements have begun to be made with some sidewalks in many Indian cities, in general they are narrow and full of obstacles. As in other countries in the developing world, the democratic goal of the Indian government is still a long way off.

The quality of sidewalks tends to be proportional not only to a society's progress but also to its level of democracy. It is interesting that in German the words for *citizen* (*bürger*) and *sidewalk* (*bürgersteig*) are linked. The sidewalk is a space for the citizen, the space for citizenship.

It is a pleasure to walk on a broad sidewalk that is level and free of obstacles that would endanger a citizen using a cane or wearing high heels. The sidewalk should have low gradient ramps at corners to allow a wheelchair to go up or down effortlessly or, better still, continue at the sidewalk level at the intersection; it should be well lit and ideally lined with trees. A good sidewalk has another ingredient: destinations. It takes people to places they want to go and is flanked by attractive features such as shops, mass-transport stations, bakeries, and cafés.

A street that is pleasant to walk is short. With that, we feel freer, we can change our direction at the corner near us or simply look far away through the open-walled corridor to the sky when crossing an intersection. Jane Jacobs underscored the inconvenience of excessively long city blocks, which give the impression of an endless journey.[18] And she noted that shopkeepers of New York, like their fellows in Bogotá's popular neighborhoods, preferred corner locations. Corners are few when blocks are long. Joan Clos, former mayor of Barcelona and former secretary general of UN-Habitat, observes that a good city has between 80 and 150 road intersections per square kilometer, whereas some Chinese cities, for example, have only 30, which makes them not particularly pleasant to stroll through.

If someone does not believe that the widening of sidewalks and the removal of cars parked on them is a revolutionary measure, I would invite them to try it.

Even the best cities, which already have wide, well-built sidewalks, can benefit from widening them even further and have been doing so. To widen sidewalks, thousands of street parking spaces have been eliminated in Madrid and replaced by underground parking built by private investors, who operate the garages for several years. In marvelous Vitoria-Gasteiz, in the Basque country, the number of lanes on one of the main roads was reduced from eight to four in order to widen sidewalks, forming a kind of linear plaza with trees, benches, a bikeway, and a tram. In Tokyo, where there had been many roads with no sidewalks for decades after the hasty postwar reconstruction, they have halted the practice of parking where there should be sidewalks and have built sidewalks instead. At the beginning of the twenty-first century, Paris's mayor Bertrand Delanoë eliminated thousands of parking spaces to widen sidewalks and to locate stations for the public bicycle system, Vélib. In the center of Melbourne, sidewalks have been widened, eliminating parking spaces and indeed additional car lanes, thus generating more than eighty hectares of new pedestrian public space, which notably increased the number of people who enjoy walking there.[19]

Informal Vendors in Pedestrian Spaces

When lower-income citizens want to enjoy a walk through the center of their city, they often find some of those heavily trafficked sectors invaded by street vendors, which diminishes the quality of their experience and everyone else's as well. Higher-income citizens who can avoid such disorder do so. Those who have no other option resign themselves to using public space, vendors and all.

Informal vendor invasion deteriorates any sector, particularly historical centers, not only affecting those who live there but also driving away tourists, which causes unemployment. When the public space of office tower sectors is overrun by vendors, the area loses value, which also means fewer property-tax dollars and loss of investor confidence in the city.

Some people, genuinely concerned about the poorest in society, suppose that informal street vendors are among them and say that they should be allowed to set up their stalls on the sidewalks. Street vendors who set themselves up at strategic points of the city are far from being among the poorest citizens. On one occasion, when I was mayor, I saw a recent-model sport utility vehicle parked on a wide road median, next to an informal vendor's stall, around which stood some customers. I was annoyed, so I got out of my car and asked whose vehicle it was. It turned out it belonged to the vendor whose stall was invading this public space. Vendors occupying strategic points on sidewalks have higher incomes than many of the passersby inconvenienced by them. During my first term as mayor, we recovered the San Victorino square in the center of Bogotá, paying indemnities to the vendors who were occupying it. We were surprised to find from the socioeconomic studies we conducted for this process that they were among the top 30 percent of earners in the city. Many of the vending stalls' owners didn't even serve the public themselves but had employees do so.

Vendors' concentration at any busy corner downtown in any city does not occur because they are ambitious early risers but because they are supported by mafias who control public space and charge them for the privilege of selling their wares there. The disorder caused by the occupation of pedestrian public space also brings with it theft and other forms of crime. Again, the problem doesn't arise because street vendors are accomplices to crime, although sometimes they are, but because disorder signals an absence of authority and, worse, that those who break the law are in control.

As mayor, I was able to recover a great deal of public space from vendor invasion, often paying them or providing them a place to carry out their activities. In some cases, we were able to help them by awarding them kiosks or tricycles to sell their wares in more amenable and less disruptive public spaces: indeed, if properly sited, vendors can improve public space without obstructing pedestrian traffic.

For example, nonagglomerated sellers of fruit, juices, coffee, herbal tea, and candy adapt well to public space, in places where they do not negatively affect it. And an umbrella seller is always a welcome sight when it starts to rain. Some of them, like flower vendors, make public space more attractive. But the sale of handbags, glasses, clothing, and shoes does not make public space better; rather, the opposite. Vendors who cook with boiling oil or generate smoke should also be prohibited from occupying public spaces.

Well-organized farmers' markets that are set up, for example, one day a week or once every couple of weeks for a few hours in a well-located public space also construct community and belonging. We organized dozens of these. They are traditional in Europe, Rio de Janeiro, New York, and many other places. The stalls full of colorful fresh fruit, fish, and seafood, cheeses and home-baked bread, and the life bustling around them, brighten the atmosphere. But behind their apparent spontaneity are strictly observed rules. Assigned spaces are respected. Vendors must keep their space clean, and nobody can set up a stall without authorization. This is very different from the permanent occupation of sidewalks with high pedestrian traffic in central locations to sell clothing or handbags manufactured in Asia.

The courts often make it difficult to recover public pedestrian space invaded by street vendors, arguing a constitutional right to work. Now, if the informal vendor sets up his wares in the lobby of a building where a judge lives or in the judge's garden, that judge finds a means to get the police to swiftly come and remove the vendor. When the judge's private property is involved, the vendor's "right to work" is forgotten, but not when public space is being occupied. Differential treatment by courts toward the illegal occupation of private and public property evinces that for them what is private is more sacred than what is public.

Moreover, some judges think that public space for cars is more sacred than public space for human beings. If a vendor sets up in the middle of a main road, obstructing a full lane, the judge will immediately order the police to remove him. Once again, in this case, the concern for the right to work disappears. His position is very different when the street vendor sets up his stall on a sidewalk.

In developing countries, high-income citizens or senior officers of the state do not spend much time walking on sidewalks and do so even less in places invaded by street vendors. Those most affected by public space deterioration occasioned by vendors are lower-income citizens.

A large number of informal vendors occupy space on the sidewalks in New York, frequently inconveniencing pedestrians at busy points. Today, however, there are places in New York with no street vendors. In recent decades, pedestrian public space has been created or improved there, including the greenway along the Hudson riverfront, Bryant Park, the new parks of Brooklyn, and the High Line, a greenway built on an abandoned elevated metro structure. They are impeccably maintained along with others that have traditionally been used by high-income earners, such as Central Park and Riverside Park. And there are no informal street vendors on the sidewalks of high-income residential sectors such as the Upper East Side or on those of luxury shopping streets, such as Madison Avenue. New York authorities have allowed them in other parts of Manhattan, harming lower-income residents and weekend visitors.

Sidewalks for People or for Cars?

In developing cities, sidewalk invasion by cars is a much more serious problem than informal street vendors. Moreover, given that less than half of households have a car, cars on sidewalks are a classist symbol of lack of respect for others. Children in school uniforms surrounding cars parked on sidewalks is an archetypal picture of underdevelopment. Although I made efforts to recover and construct sidewalks during my periods as mayor of Bogotá, I must admit that on nine out of ten streets there, it's still not possible for a wheelchair to go from one corner to the next.

When I became mayor in 1998, people had been parking for decades in bays illegally carved out of the sidewalk or simply directly on the sidewalk. All major roads made after 1950 had been built without sidewalks, perhaps supposing that these would be built later or that the owners of adjacent properties would construct them. Of course, this didn't happen.[20]

On roads that had sidewalks, they were in a disastrous state, especially around shops, because drivers believed they had a natural right to park there. Although in theory it was illegal, decades of this behavior had transformed it into a tolerated "right." No authority had ever questioned such a "right"; no police officer had issued a fine for parking on a sidewalk. It was a problem that hadn't even been identified as such.

Shopkeepers and their customers were enraged when we began to remove cars from sidewalks and to build wide sidewalks with high curbs, inaccessible to cars. But the process of constructing or reconstructing sidewalks was expensive and slow. We needed something massive and fast to create awareness and to do away with the habit of parking there. Therefore, where budget limitations did not allow us to build sidewalks, we installed thousands of bollards, short vertical posts to prevent cars from parking on sidewalks.

I can remember no more unified or massive reaction by the establishment against anything. Owners of businesses that operated based on illegal parking on sidewalks collected funds to support my impeachment. The entire media—print, radio, and television—attacked me ferociously, first for leaving cars with no place to park and then for any other reason. Bollards had never been seen nor had the word been used before, but now they became the main topic of conversation. The media seemed to have nothing else to talk about. The power of the media was so enormous in that age before social networks that soon even the poorest citizens, who were far from being able to own a car and had important needs, considered bollards to be society's greatest problem. This was particularly ironic and contradictory, seeing as how they walked the most and thus were the main beneficiaries of having decent sidewalks. I became Public Enemy No. 1, even worse than the guerrilla commanders who at the time were inflicting severe damage to our country.

A frequent criticism leveled against me was that I was a "city decorator." That didn't offend me. I believe that order, good architecture, design, and beauty do not cost more, or not much more, and promote well-being and dignity. As Stendhal put it, "Beauty is the promise of happiness."[21]

In reality, something deeper lay beneath the ferocity of the war against me. In 1998, only 12 percent of Bogotá's households had a car.[22] Acquiring a car was the ticket to enter the ruling class, a distinct and superior elite, apart from the rest of the citizenry. It was unimaginable for those who belonged to that select group, many of whom had only recently joined it and with much effort, that someone would challenge them—and worse yet had the audacity to restrict the use of precisely the symbol that certified their membership in a superior social class. So, they not only felt that curbs or bollards inconvenienced them but that by removing their parking we were more grievously degrading their status.

The construction of equality requires difficult battles. Increasing taxes to upper-income citizens to finance subsidies to lower-income residents may bother them less than the removal of sidewalk parking. It seems that the more equality is generated, the greater the discomfort of the privileged. This is invariably the case, for example, when space is taken away from cars and given to public transport, bicycles, or pedestrians. The louder the howls of protest, the higher the certainty that we have touched on a point of great inequality. It is akin to when a doctor touches the point where we feel pain: that's precisely where the problem is.

In Bogotá nobody had previously thought of making the pedestrian respected. It was implicitly assumed that the pedestrian was relatively insignificant and that really important people were those who traveled in cars. While we were fighting the difficult war to recover sidewalks for pedestrians, nobody dared to defend me, not even one important architect or school of architecture. The battle reached a climax when we intervened on three kilometers of Carrera 15, emblematic of the high-income sectors of Bogotá at the time. It had once been an exclusive residential neighborhood, but in recent decades houses had been turned into shops and the gardens and sidewalks in front of them into parking spaces.

An editorial in Colombia's most widely read and influential newspaper, *El Tiempo*, reflected the classist attitudes of its owners and of the upper classes in general, when it opined about the removal of cars from the sidewalks on Carrera 15 for rebuilding and widening: "In an almost arbitrary act, without consultation, the city administration has begun some works which make no sense, which have produced very serious losses to shop owners in the area. . . . The only ones who are going to benefit from this are the street children and beggars, who will now have wider sidewalks to sleep on."[23] The entire editorial was classist, including the use of the term "*gamines*," the upper classes' pejorative for street children. (Today, less than three decades onward, it is difficult even to imagine that at that time there were still hundreds of groups of homeless children who lived in the street and slept on sidewalks.)

Though almost forgotten, there was a precedent for the reclamation of sidewalks and the rights of pedestrians in Bogotá. Álvaro Gómez Hurtado, a political leader assassinated a few years earlier, wrote in the 1970s about the invasion of sidewalks by cars.

> The sidewalks of Bogotá . . . have ceased to be public domain, and their function is now . . . private instead of urban. . . . They do not belong to the passer-by. Would it suffice to fine the cars that destroy the sidewalks and obstruct pedestrians by parking on the sidewalk? Because the sidewalks in better-developed cities are a physical continuation of parks . . . spaces for recreation, for contemplative and philosophical leisure, a platform from which to watch the rest of humanity. The uncontrolled growth of the private car . . . is sentencing the width of those spaces. . . . The sidewalk is the intimate and vital nucleus of all that is urban. It is through their sidewalks that cities die or are revitalized for man.[24]

Nobody listened to him then, but I found comfort when his son sent me that document as I was waging this difficult bollard battle as mayor.

Decades before, in 1936, when there were only some six thousand cars in Bogotá,[25] the prescient Colombian historian Germán Arciniegas wrote, "Pedestrians—drivers will say—should walk against the walls. . . . I cannot see, for us pedestrians, any other remedy, but patience, and as the saying goes, 'cursing under our breath.' Until, that is, some old maid, or 'civic-minded' person creates an organization to protect us, as dogs and horses are protected today. May the fairies wish that such a redemptor is not far off."[26]

Unsurprisingly, even the most ferocious defenders of parking on the sidewalks couldn't bring themselves to confess that what they wanted was precisely and only that—to park on sidewalks. The hundreds of young people hired to go all over the city collecting signatures to revoke the mayor's mandate told those whose signatures they were canvassing that my brothers and I owned a bollard factory! There was never any formal accusation of such a ridiculous statement, and nowhere in the media was there even a mention of it. It was a well-financed rumor, systematically and persistently transmitted, that became an urban legend, like many others of which I have been victim. The bollards subject came up in all my later political campaigns, and there are still many citizens who believe that I had some kind of bollard business.

The media attacks were effective. I became a public enemy for recovering the sidewalks for pedestrians. The realities the media created were even more real than reality itself, including the reality that only 12 percent of households had a car.

During a visit we made to one of the poorest sectors of Bogotá, a long way from the nearest paved road, one of my colleagues asked a ten-year-old girl, "Do you like the mayor?" She replied forcefully, "No!" "Why?" they asked her. And the girl exclaimed, "Because of the bollards!" She probably didn't know what a bollard was. Almost certainly, she had never gotten into a private car in her life. The removal of cars from the sidewalks benefited her, her entire family, and everyone she knew. The fact that many low-income citizens who did not have cars were passionately opposed to the recovery of the sidewalk space with bollards illustrates the power of the media when aligned to high-income citizens' interests.

It is a constant that efforts to benefit lower-income citizens are turned upside down to make those same citizens believe they will be worse off for them. The elites affected do not have to make much effort. Self-declared populist politicians see no problem deploying brain-scrambling somersaults of logic and will use any pretext to attack any project pursued by an administration they oppose. They did it with our sidewalks' recovery, the construction of bikeways, the BRT, greenways that linked low- and high-income sectors, the improvement of public education in the lowest-income sectors through the administration of schools by the best private schools and universities, and even the conversion of the polo field of the most exclusive club in the country into a public park. They even managed to attack the investment in public infrastructure essential for the progress of popular sectors, such as roads, sewerage networks, sports facilities, schools, and hospitals, as mere "cement"; or said that the synthetic turf in nearly two hundreds soccer fields we built (natural turf quickly becomes gravel or mud) was carcinogenic. In short, they opposed any public work we did in lieu of limiting ourselves to what they did when in government: shell out subsidies, in all possible forms.

Simultaneously with the battles to get cars off the sidewalks, we had other fronts in our battles—thousands of semi-informal bus owners who opposed the creation of TransMilenio and whose strikes brought the city to a halt; street vendors who had occupied sidewalks and important plazas; residents of exclusive neighborhoods who had illegally enclosed parks in their sectors; members of the most exclusive club in the country who opposed the conversion of their polo field into a park; and so on.

The situation was unpleasant for me but more difficult for my family. My wife and I decided to send our daughter, Renata, twelve years old, to live with my brother in Canada for a year. For my team members it was also difficult, as they were my "accomplices." My positive approval rating, which had been 49 percent in January 1998 when I took office, was 18 percent in April 1999.[27] At a staff meeting at the nadir of the crisis, when the process of revoking my mandate seemed to be moving forward inexorably, almost all the members of the team told me, "Why get into so many fights at the same time? Let's not take any more cars off the sidewalks, let's not install any more bollards. Let's concentrate only on a few short segments where we can build some pretty sidewalks, which can have a demonstrable effect."

I had spent decades thinking about and studying what to do to put the city on the right track and ten years trying to get elected to implement the projects I had dreamed of for the city. I'd lost two elections before this one. And I had only one three-year period, without the option of reelection. I couldn't hope for a second or third term to realize all that we aspired to accomplish. Being mayor, for me, was not an end but only a means to an end—to take steps that I was convinced would make the city better. I was not interested in *being* mayor but in what I could *do* as mayor. If I was not going to be able to do that, it didn't matter to me if they revoked my mandate. So, I said to members of my team that instead of holding back efforts to make sidewalks, bikeways, and the BRT, we should work even harder to do more of them.

Almost always, when things are wrong in a city, it's not because we don't know what should be done. It's because there are powerful groups interested in maintaining the status quo. There are those who reap benefits, or think they do, from keeping things unchanged. And there are political adversaries who will always ally with whoever opposes us, whatever the project or program. Whenever private interest prevails over the public good in the long term, it's because it has economic and political power, power over the press, influence in some powerful national government institution, or over some judges. Whatever the case, to achieve change is difficult, politically costly, and painful.

Naturally, Bogotá's traffic regulations had always banned parking on sidewalks. A characteristic of underdevelopment is laxity in adherence to rules. People often think that it's democratic to be able to negotiate the law, but this can lead to concessions that are contrary to the common good in favor of organized minorities capable of exerting pressure. Of course, there must be negotiations when regulations are going to be made. Everyone, majorities and minorities, should be listened to, but once a rule is approved, what is democratic is to enforce it. In Latin America many believe that strict enforcement of the law is authoritarian and undemocratic. I believe the contrary, that when the law is strictly observed, the most vulnerable are protected. Laxity in the observance of the law favors opportunists and bullies. Nobody would suggest that in Switzerland there is no democracy because it isn't possible there to negotiate with a representative of authority about obeying a regulation.

Shop owners argued that I was irrational and stubborn when I removed cars from the sidewalks because sidewalks had adequate space for both parked cars and pedestrians. In any city, those who drive cars will use the same argument against the widening of sidewalks if it means fewer parking spaces on the roads. They will say that existing sidewalk space is adequate. The width of a sidewalk, like the size of a park, is never "enough." I wrote some television commercials to explain why parking on the sidewalks was not only illegal but also damaging to quality of life in the city. One said, "We think that the sidewalks are related to roads, because they live together. But the purpose of the sidewalks, unlike roads, is not so that people can go from one place to another; even if they can be used to do so. Sidewalks are for conversation, play, doing business, and contemplating the city. In fact, sidewalks are much closer relatives to parks and plazas than of roads and streets. It is therefore as mistaken to say that the sidewalk has enough space for cars to park, as well as for people to walk, as it would to be to say that we can convert a park or the main square of a city into an open-air parking lot, so long as enough room is left between cars for people to pass."

Another television advertisement depicted a group of people sitting in a circle in the middle of a wide and congested road, playing cards, while car drivers who are jammed up because of them furiously blow their horns. Then the voiceover says, "Just as people cannot be in the space of cars . . ." And the image changes to some cars parked on a sidewalk while pedestrians must walk around them in order to avoid them. And the voiceover continues, ". . . cars cannot be in the space of people." The commercials closed with the same phrase: "Sidewalks for people, for a city that respects human dignity."

We did convince a few people, but I continued to poll badly. The battles for sidewalks without cars no doubt hastened my hair turning grey. However, as time passed and after we built broad sidewalks with buried cables and trees, along with many other improvements to the city, the majority opinion turned in my favor. My opponents failed to collect the necessary signatures to revoke my mandate, and the people of Bogotá increasingly appreciated the importance of pedestrian space. Places where we built sidewalks significantly increased in value. From then on, private developers began to build quality sidewalks with no parking bays in front of their buildings.

Everywhere in the world people enjoy tables set out on sidewalks or on a pedestrian street. In Copenhagen it is so pleasant to be out there that they prolong the "summer" with heaters on the outdoor terraces and blankets so that people can sit outside ten months a year. However, certain precautions are necessary so that pedestrian movement is not unduly obstructed. Care must also be taken to avoid what has happened before in too many sectors in Bogotá. First, a restaurant puts some tables out on the sidewalk; later, it sets up some potted plants surrounding the outdoor dining area; then, they put up an awning to keep the sun and rain off, followed by stretching canvas walls from the awning down to the ground; finally, the plants and the canvas walls are replaced by a brick wall and the awning by a permanent roof. In this way they complete their gradual and incremental theft of public space. It seems that something of the kind happens elsewhere in the world because restaurants on the sidewalks of the world-famous Via Veneto and Champs-Élysées seem to have come into being in the same way. In order to avoid this, we issued regulations that require each element installed on the sidewalk, whether tables or plants, to be stowed inside the restaurant for several hours a day.[28]

Mass Pedestrian Transport: Hong Kong's
Elevated Walkways

In Hong Kong there are some "sidewalks" that have positive elements: they are perfectly flat, with no obstacles, and they pass alongside many cafés, restaurants, and shops, or rather though them, because they are not sidewalks but kilometers of elevated walkways at the level of the fifth floor, running alongside buildings, crossing streets, and even going through the buildings. They are to be found along Admiralty, Central, and other sectors of the city center constructed mostly on land generated by sea infills. They are interesting due to the number of people who walk there, with their gamut of expressions and their different forms of dress; the interior and external architecture, which is monumental; the abundant mechanical stairways; and even because of the frequent climate changes as one passes from the tropical heat outside to the refreshing air-conditioned spaces as the walkways go through a building. Personally, however, I'm not keen on the feeling of being channeled or funneled on a kind of industrial conveyor belt.

In some way, the elevated walkways in Hong Kong are similar to the eleven kilometers of subterranean walkways in Toronto, built presumably to avoid the winter cold. Like a gigantic vacuum cleaner, they suck the life out of the street. But unlike the street, poor citizens or young people on skateboards are not welcome. Like their elevated counterparts in Hong Kong, they come to life during working hours, not at night or on weekends. But what they take away from the street still depletes it's commercial potential.

It's sad to see the street in these Hong Kong sectors ceded over to motor vehicles. In these sectors the fronts of the buildings at street level do not have the allure that they do in other parts of Hong Kong; generally, they have windowless walls and entrances only for cars and distribution trucks. Streets are not made for walking, and indeed it is difficult for pedestrians to cross them. Elevated walkways are efficient for moving people, reaching the metro stations or the office buildings. They are a sort of "human metro" to move people but not to enjoy a walk. The feeling is that there are no *flâneurs*—people who walk just for the enjoyment of it.

* * *

Although pedestrian public spaces enhance integration, belonging, inclusion, democracy, and quality-of-life equality, and make cities more enjoyable, developing cities tend to measure their progress by roads for cars instead. And this needs change. In terms of infrastructure, what differentiates an advanced city from a backward one is not its highways or metro systems but its sidewalks. There are highways in some African cities in which almost half the population lacks drinking water, but the minority who have cars and power ensured that highways got built. Likewise, there are very infrastructure-deficient cities that have metros. What developing cities never seem to have is quality sidewalks. The most prominent characteristic of an underdeveloped and unequal city is roads without sidewalks, or uneven sidewalks, or other kinds of obstacles on sidewalks, for example, cars parked on sidewalks, or empty spaces where there *should have been* sidewalks. This is the quintessential emblem of underdevelopment.

CHAPTER 10

Malls, Commerce, and Safety

When shopping centers replace public spaces as meeting places, it's a symptom that a city is ill. Victor Gruen, the creator of the first "mall," or major enclosed shopping center, built the South-dale Center in Edina, Minnesota, in 1956. He was an urbanist who dreamed of making an ideal city. He designed dozens of shopping centers, and his creation was so successful that only fourteen years later, in 1970, people in the United States would spend more time at a mall than anywhere else other than their home or workplace. At the end of his life, however, Gruen rejected what shopping centers had become.

Designed to be reached by car, initially malls were a complement to the suburbs, which lacked Main Street shopping and thus a place to see people. There are practically no shopping centers in good cities such as Paris, Madrid, or Manhattan. The shops in such cities usually have windows on the street. Because sidewalks are wide with no obstacles, well-lit, and safe, citizens do not feel the need to take refuge in a shopping center.

Malls Are Not Public Squares or Large Stores

Shopping centers differ from large stores. We go to shopping centers to walk, have a coffee, lunch, or an ice cream, or to go bowling, get a haircut, see a film, let the children play, and even attend a religious service. With the advent of internet shopping, the trend around the world has been for shopping malls to have fewer shops and more places of recreation. Regardless, we go there to see and be with people. The shopping center effectively replaces the city's public space.

In the case of US suburbanization, James Howard Kunstler says that "by the 1970s, when malls started to multiply across the land, the public realm had been pretty much eliminated from the American scene. Yet the hunger for public space remained. . . . What had existed before in an organic state as Main Street, downtown shopping districts, town squares, hotel lobbies, public gardens, saloons, museums, churches, was now standardized, simplified, sanitized, packaged, and relocated on the suburban fringe in the form of a mall."[1]

Revolutions often start on a square. No revolution has ever begun in a shopping center. If in some sense "public space" in shopping centers can be compared to an ideal urban public space, there is a radical difference when it comes to facilitating democracy. In several of my political campaigns, the police kicked me out of shopping centers, not because I had set up a platform and a microphone or even because I had been speaking to the public. They drove me out simply because I was distributing some printed material and on one occasion not even that. They removed me and those who accompanied me because we were wearing campaign T-shirts. Now, on many occasions, shopping center managers kindly allowed me to go in and to distribute campaign material. But that was a favor on their part and not a right on mine. Shopping centers are a far cry from the Greek *agora*.

Aware that shopping centers have become "public space," some US state laws require that certain political activities be permitted, such as the collection of signatures to support petitions or indeed the registration of candidates but not outright campaigning for a candidate.[2]

On a Saturday afternoon or a Sunday, you will see few people on the street in the center of Manila, which is rare for a great city. But when you enter one of the mega-shopping centers you get the impression that the entire population is there. Couples, groups of young people, families—the hallways teem with thousands of people who fill dozens of restaurants, some of which occupy huge interior plazas, and establishments with electronic games for children and the young, which are always full. The dearth of parks and the deficiency of sidewalks in most of the city are at least partly responsible for this massive migration to shopping centers.[3] It may seem the city is resigned to defeat from the shopping center.

In developing cities, to a greater or lesser extent, shopping centers have progressively replaced public space. Citizens spend a good part of their leisure time there. Residents of sectors where these centers are built consider them a blessing, and in cities of less than one million inhabitants, they are welcomed as a powerful indication of progress. But the damage that the shopping center can do to these smaller cities may be even more serious. Higher-income citizens with cars, and others, stop going to street-front shops downtown, which in turn begin to weaken, languish, and often simply die. Previously, the presence of higher-income and powerful citizens downtown exerted pressure to keep the area clean and safe, with well-tended parks and gardens and sidewalks in good condition without parked cars and street vendors. Now indifference toward the traditional center hastens its decay.

It is true, however, that in some cases of severely deteriorated urban areas, shopping centers can actually contribute to the rebirth of the sector, particularly if they're installed in abandoned or very deteriorated but iconic buildings. The book *Downtown, Inc.* by Lynne Sagalyn and Bernard Frieden presents examples of this.[4] In those sectors with crime problems, the shopping center became a safe place for the young to meet or for the elderly to spend time with friends or take exercise walking.[5]

But overall, shopping centers are more a symptom of urban failure than a cure for it. Developing cities are home to large numbers of microbusinesses that produce clothing, shoes, and other local goods. Frequently they sell their products in their own shops or some neighborhood outlet. But they rarely have access to shopping centers, dominated by international chains, whose products are mostly made in Asia. Consequently, the domination of the shopping center indirectly makes multinational brands more predominant and weakens local producers.

If children ask their parents to take them to the shopping center rather than anywhere else, if the shopping center is the venue for young people to meet, if it's the destination for the family walk with the baby carriage or the grandfather's wheelchair, then that's an indication that the city, and principally its pedestrian spaces, have a problem. Those who defend the occupation of sidewalks by cars or street vendors are doing a favor to shopping centers: the more that public space deteriorates, the more people will visit malls.

In a healthy city there are very few shopping centers, malls where people take refuge from the city and isolate themselves from the open air, the weather, daylight, and darkness of night, or from mountains, clouds, and trees. Shopping centers are less free than a public square, a park, or a sidewalk. There is no possibility that people in Spain, Italy, or France, who spend a great part of their leisure time in pedestrian spaces of their cities, in all seasons, will shut themselves away in a shopping center. Pedestrian spaces are the essence of a city.

In principle, anyone may enter any shopping center. However, because shopping centers have a keen sense of social class, they tend to be geared toward one class. Some, more expensive and antiseptic, are designed to make those without a high income feel uncomfortable. Prices at shopping centers designed for high-income citizens intimidate and discourage lower-income ones. A cup of coffee there can cost up to a third of many workers' daily wage. From the way that security guards at the mall's entrance look at those whose physiognomy or dress betrays them as lower-income citizens to the cultivated arrogance of the stores' staff, the message is clear: they are not welcome. In the exclusive Andino mall in Bogotá, security guards do not permit construction workers to enter wearing their work clothes. This deters them even from cashing their paychecks in the center's banks, and they must go to another bank branch nearby.

The White Tiger, a novel by Aravind Adiga, describes how a humble citizen is denied admission to a shopping center in Delhi. He says that the headlines on the newspapers used to ask, "Is there nowhere for the poor in India's shopping centers?" Later, the narrator observes, "The glass doors had opened, but the man who wanted to go into them could not do so. The guard at the door had stopped him. He pointed his stick at the man's feet and shook his head—the man had sandals on his feet. All of us drivers too had sandals on our feet. But everyone who was allowed into the mall had shoes on their feet."[6] On another occasion, when the character goes to the shopping center, he says, "I was sure the guard in front of the door would challenge me and say, No, you're not allowed in, even with a pair of black shoes and a T-shirt that is mostly white with just one English word on it. I was sure, until the last moment, that I would be caught, and called back, and slapped and humiliated there. Even as I was walking inside the mall, I was sure someone would say, Hey! That man is a paid driver! What's he doing in here? There were guards in gray uniforms on every floor—all of them seemed to be watching me."[7] I identify with citizens intimidated by expensive shopping centers. I've felt likewise when I glimpse inside a shop where the least expensive shirt costs $500.

Obviously, shopping centers are also built in some popular sectors, where high-income citizens naturally do not go. What is clear, regardless, is that shopping centers don't facilitate the mingling of people with different levels of income, which does indeed take place in well-functioning pedestrian public spaces.

The discomfort and rejection low-income citizens feel in an expensive shopping center are absent when they are on a sidewalk next to luxury stores. There they belong to the space and the space belongs to them. When they stroll down the sidewalk alongside some of the most expensive shops in the world, on Madison Avenue in New York, Madero in Madrid, the Faubourg Saint Honoré in Paris, or Ginza in Tokyo, they feel totally at ease. They have the same right to be there as someone who gets out of a limousine to buy thousands of dollars' worth of clothes or jewelry. In a good city, even the most luxurious and exclusive shops are on the street, and on the sidewalks alongside them pass by citizens from all walks of life. In public space we are all equal.

In Manila, Singapore, or Culiacán, they say the shopping center is necessary because the weather is often too hot and humid. But in Bogotá, where the temperature is usually ideal, or in Dalat in Vietnam or Kunming in China, both with exceptionally pleasant climates, citizens also go to shopping centers. But in Madrid, Rome, or Manhattan, where summer temperatures can be extremely hot and winters uncomfortably cold, there are almost no shopping centers.

In Latin America, the argument goes that shopping centers are indispensable for people to walk around without fear of crime, but in Asian cities, where crime is practically nonexistent, shopping centers abound. The explanation for shopping centers' success in the developing world is related to two problems: first, lack of urbanistic quality, especially deficiencies in sidewalks and other pedestrian spaces; and second, inequality, which leads higher-income citizens to seek spaces that exclude those different from them.

Although shopping centers tend to disappear in cities of advanced countries, they prosper and proliferate in developing cities. The phenomenon of the shopping center as a substitute for the traditional "Main Street" is now a Third World phenomenon, one that takes place in dysfunctional cities and societies.

Shopping malls imitate the real city or, rather, the ideal city: they have broad pedestrian corridors free of cars, and with their perfectly flat floors and no obstacles, they are totally accessible to the elderly, children, wheelchairs, and baby carriages; shop windows on those corridors are attractive, and there are even cafés with tables, ice cream stands, and some "informal" vendors.

We can let go of a small child's hand without fear that they'll get run over by a car. Lighting is optimal, signboards discreet, never perpendicular to the wall, or blaring in neon. Shopping center design experts know well how wide shop façades ought to be and the ideal mix of shops along the internal corridors to maintain interest and optimize the pleasure of walking past them. They are spaces entirely covered by security cameras, where we can walk without fear. And these spaces are impeccable. Citizens go to shopping centers because they offer what the city is not providing. However, benches are usually not abundant as mall owners are uninterested in providing a meeting place for old people to come and read a newspaper or chat. If somebody wants to sit down, let them go to a café and pay for the privilege.

Those who govern developing cities have much to learn from the pedestrian quality of shopping centers. They could use them as models to make irresistible sidewalks and walkways that would provide other attractions that shopping centers lack, such as trees, sky, interesting architecture, and a wider variety of people.

The owners of shops facing the street often suppose that their customers, or former customers, prefer the shopping center because it provides abundant parking. On several occasions I've seen the fierce opposition mounted against City Hall projects to widen sidewalks or to pedestrianize shopping streets, reducing or eliminating parking space.[8] Shopkeepers argue that without parking in front of the shop, they will go out of business. At times it seems they want cars to be able to park inside the shop! In reality, customers don't park next to the door of the shop in a shopping center; on the contrary, they have to walk long distances, sometimes kilometers, inside it. What attracts customers to the shopping center isn't parking close to shops but the space's pedestrian quality.

To compete with shopping centers, traditional shops need to improve the pedestrian quality around them, in a way to become themselves an open-air "shopping center." Parking is not allowed on many of the most valuable shopping streets of the world, and many have been pedestrianized completely. In 1962, Strøget Street in Copenhagen was pedestrianized against heavy opposition from shopkeepers. The result was so successful for them that shop owners in nearby streets also requested that their streets be pedestrianized. Today, there is an extensive pedestrian network in the heart of that city.

If streets need to be more like shopping center corridors, then shopping centers, conversely, need to be more like a city and do a better job of integrating themselves into it. For example, the large areas of open-air parking space around shopping centers damage the urban fabric as they create unpleasant adjacent areas for strolling. And in dense cities such as Bogotá, where there is no such parking, the windowless, doorless walls that surround shopping centers do damage as well.

Shopping centers are less harmful if they aren't surrounded by surface parking, which kills pedestrian life in the environs. They are less damaging if their façades aren't blank walls but have shop windows and cafés that open onto broad sidewalks. They are better when, instead of being large, enclosed boxes, they have some internal corridors open to the sky, entering the shopping center from the public space outside, as walkways integrated into the city. And they are better if they have abundant benches. If, additionally, shops occupy two or three stories of a building while upper floors have housing and offices, then this could be a well-achieved city piece.

In some ways, Venice functions as one large, well-made shopping center. There are shops, restaurants, and, cafés at street level in most buildings and on the upper floors are workshops, housing, and offices. Although in the United States, there are still many enclosed malls, hundreds have gone out of business. The new version of the shopping center in the United States is integrated into the city and includes housing and offices.

Increasingly, shopping is done online. However, there are many products shoppers still like to see at close range, to touch, smell, and try on, even if a product viewed is later bought online. Entering a store is not simply a functional, practical task. It's a sensory experience. It's an exploration of a product's or a brand's character. And, of course, the experience in a café, a bar, or a restaurant cannot be had online. The experience of going shopping is also social. It is an urban experience that, if it takes place in a city's public space, can be more enriching.

If someone blindfolded us and then put us on a plane for a few hours, landed, and then took us, still blindfolded, to a shopping center in our destination city, we wouldn't know what city or country we were in: all shopping centers are maintained at the same temperature, regardless of whether we are in a Moscow winter or tropical Barranquilla. With globalization, almost all the shops in shopping centers worldwide are the same. Shopping center interiors are usually bereft of vegetation, geographical features, or distinctive architecture.

When I come to a city I do not yet know, I often ask the hotel doorman for a pleasant place to walk and see people. I feel disappointed if he tells me that I should go to a shopping center. And if effectively that is the only place where it's pleasant to walk and see people, I will not be much interested in returning to that city.

Tourists visit museums and other emblematic places, shop, and dine at restaurants, but above all they walk! Therefore, urban tourists prefer places where it is pleasant to walk, such as Prague, Kyoto, London, Paris, or Venice.

I don't recall ever visiting a city where its people did not believe that tourism would be an important source of revenue and employment in the future. Even in small villages in rural areas of Colombia or Indonesia, leaders believe that tourism will be an important activity. And they're right: it's an enormous business in many countries that generates employment that cannot be replaced by robots and artificial intelligence. More than thirty million tourists visit London every year; one in seven jobs in that city depends on tourism. A fraction of those visitors could transform the economy of many developing cities. And if developing cities can attract tourists, some of them will become purchasers of local exports or even investors.

A city attractive to tourists has character and identity. In addition to monuments and museums, it has unique and interesting architecture in its grand old houses and its formerly informal neighborhoods; vegetation, waterfronts, and mountains; local music and dance; local fashion labels; restaurants that are not part of a chain; local dishes and fruit; unique rites and customs; and perhaps the unique aural landscape of church bells or calls to worship at the mosque. The context for all of that is pedestrian spaces.

Those who work to make their city attractive to tourists generally suppose that they achieve it with some monument, some buildings of exceptional architecture, quality restaurants, or a cultural event. Those things are indeed important. But often the most important thing is disregarded, which is improvement of the city's pedestrian infrastructure: sidewalks, promenades, piers, plazas, and parks. The beautiful Navona Square in Rome attracts many tourists that congregate around Bernini's fountain. Although most of them appreciate the beauty of the fountain and the architecture of the buildings that frame the Piazza, the exclusively pedestrian surroundings and the people there are almost equally important attractions. The atmosphere would be quite different if the Piazza were a parking area or if roads with roaring traffic surrounded it. One of the reasons why extensive areas in all European cities and villages have been pedestrianized in the last fifty years is to make them more attractive for tourists.

Before anything else, Disney World is a pedestrian city. It has hundreds of hectares of parking, where those who visit leave their car to continue by monorail, on little trains, by boat, or on foot. It has been estimated that visitors to Disney spend less than 3 percent of their time on rides or at shows; the rest of the time they enjoy a pedestrian city, where they walk in the street, see people, a place in which the child can let go of a parent's hand without danger of being hit by a car.[9]

Our ideal vision of a tourist attraction does not include cars. Photographs in tourism magazines show a wide variety of means of transport: boats, horses, dromedaries, bicycles, cablecars—but rarely a car. A couple of cars in a photograph apparently lessen a site's appeal. Even when it is a picture of a place that normally has traffic, the photographer must have gotten up early on a Sunday morning because there is not a single car in the picture.

There are countries whose natural wealth attracts millions of tourists. However, those tourists do not visit their cities, and indeed they make a point of avoiding them. Tourists go to Costa Rica to see humid tropical jungles, birds, butterflies, and beaches on the Pacific; if they stay overnight in San José, it's because their travel logistics require it but not because the city is an attraction for them. Something of the same happens in Kenya and Tanzania, where there are parks such as the Masai Mara, the Ngorongoro, and the Serengeti, visited by millions who go to be awed by lions, giraffes, elephants, and rhinoceroses. But Dar es Salaam or Nairobi are not part of the itinerary for most of them. If San José, Dar es Salaam, and Nairobi are to become tourist attractions, they need to become friendlier to pedestrians.

Hoteliers ought to be the most interested of all businesspeople in making the city better; they ought to be the most radical defenders and promoters of pedestrian space. But, ironically, too often they are the first to destroy sidewalks with access ramps and illegally carved parking bays.

Sidewalks Are for Walking, Not Parking

High-income citizens in developing cities have traditionally kept commerce away from their residential areas. That is because they have had unfortunate experiences with shops arriving in residential areas and bringing severe deterioration. This experience tends toward a pattern: initially, in one house on an important street in an attractive sector with high-value residences, someone opens a sophisticated shop that sells expensive clothes or a delicatessen with imported goods, as befits the area. If from the start they do not cover the front garden with concrete, they do so shortly afterward—and also turn the sidewalk into a parking bay.

Being an elegant business, geared to a high-income clientele, neighbors initially do not reject it. There may be zoning laws that prohibit commerce in that sector, but laxity surrounds those rules. Then comes another similar business and then another and another. Some neighbors who have an interest in making a profit from the increased values of their homes view this process favorably. Little by little, other shops are set up on the street until it becomes a completely commercial area.

Then, almost imperceptibly, things begin to change. Any sidewalks that were there become colonized by parking spaces. Less-sophisticated businesses begin to arrive, such as fast-food restaurants with their luminous plastic signboards. Street vendors set up stalls on the sidewalk in the middle of the disorder caused by the cars parked there. Often, too, there are noisy bars and shops selling alcoholic drinks that are then consumed in public spaces. The sector increasingly deteriorates, and property loses value. High-income residents leave, along with the businesses that were originally intended for them. In more dramatic cases there are also problems of prostitution and drug-dealing, and a once-valuable sector becomes a site of urban deterioration.

The exclusive shops that began the process, and similar ones, then spot another valuable residential area and move their businesses there, with the cycle beginning again. To prevent this, middle- and upper-class citizens mobilize to prohibit city authorities from authorizing commerce in their neighborhoods. They also oppose the construction of office buildings, cafés, and even gyms. They identify commerce as the cause of urban deterioration, but their diagnosis is wrong. The world's most valuable shopping streets have been prestigious and valuable for decades or even hundreds of years and neither lose value nor deteriorate. In those streets, shops are often in buildings where there are high-value apartments, whose residents do not find that having shops on the ground floor is a problem. What corrodes the sector where shops are established are not the shops themselves but the corrosion of the pedestrian public spaces in front of them—especially turning sidewalks into parking bays and having signboards that are too large or bright.

Parking on sidewalks marks the beginning of the end of a quality urban sector. The owners of shops and restaurants are myopic when they turn the sidewalks in front of their businesses into parking bays. They are sowing the seeds of their own destruction, depressing values in the sector, and setting their own businesses on the road to bankruptcy. Parking bays on sidewalks, or where there should be sidewalks, are one of the distinctive characteristics of backward and unequal cities.

Signs, Billboards, and Encroachment on Public Airspace

Space in the air as well as on the ground belongs to us all. When authorizing building height, authorities effectively allow the occupation of public airspace. In so doing, they tacitly permit the builder to take a piece of a sky view away from citizens. Therefore, authorities should do it judiciously.

A city's public space includes everything a citizen can see from the street. What can be seen on the façade or the roof of a building is public space. Any notice or signboard there occupies public space. As such, it can be interdicted by the state or be subjected to detailed regulation, which may charge for a sign's use of that space. What gives value to a sign is not the property where it is installed but the possibility of seeing it from public spaces and through public airspace.

Perpendicular signs on façades or excessively large or bright ones tend to make sectors deteriorate and lose value. The definition of the type of signs permitted in a city or sector is subjective. Whatever the case, ownership of a building does not grant the right to install signs on it that can be seen from public space.

Enormous signs from businesses such as McDonald's and their kin that invade public airspace over motorways in the United States and in other countries that have copied the model deface the sky and the city. Even in dense areas like Manhattan, McDonald's and others set up canopies and signage that damage architecture and the urban environment. In historical pedestrian areas of European cities, there are also McDonald's restaurants, but there the signage is discreet, set into the building's façade. And they most probably sell as many hamburgers as their counterparts that use protruding, invasive signage.

Another characteristic almost as endemic to developing cities as poor-quality sidewalks are large billboards along roads and on buildings, usually above the height permitted to buildings. However, it is not easy to regulate billboards and make their owners pay municipalities a fair price to erect them. Billboard businesses lend space to some campaigning politicians and donate money to them as well. I confess that I rented some billboards in my first political campaigns, but I soon stopped doing it when I became aware of the damage they inflict on the city and the environment. Although we removed dozens of illegal billboards and thousands of items of illegal outdoor advertising, and fined those who installed them, I did not succeed very well in implementing more restrictive regulations.

Do citizens have a right to ad-free views of their city and their countryside? Do they have a right to darkness at night, without the glow of luminous signs from their apartment windows? I believe so—at least after 9:00 or 10:00 P.M. Hopefully one day this goal will materialize.

The huge city of São Paulo achieved an incredible feat in 2006. Mayor Gilberto Kassab had all billboards, oversized or protruding shop signs, and advertising screens taken down. Then he issued very restrictive regulations for signs on shop and business façades, and perpendicular signs were prohibited. Those permitted were classified into small, medium, or large, and what could be installed in each case depended on the area of the building's façade. If the façade had a surface less than 10 meters long, then the sign's maximum size was 1.5 square meters; if the façade was between 10 and 100 meters, the sign's maximum size was 4 square meters; if the façade was longer than 100 meters, two signs were allowed, with a total of 10 square meters. No sign is permitted above 5 meters over the street level. In 2011, some years after this regulation, known as "Cidade Limpa" (Clean City), was implemented, 70 percent of São Paulo's inhabitants said they believed the ban had been beneficial for the city.[10]

If there are no rules, and if every business can look out for its own benefit, someone may decide to install a large, perpendicular, luminous sign on the façade of their shop. Soon, neighbors would do likewise, until they arrive at a situation in which all signs across the street, all at the same height and of similar size, end up blocking each other in an exuberant competition of self-destructive selfishness.[11]

The above behavior has reached an advanced and almost comical expression on some Hong Kong streets, where illuminated shop signs actually traverse the narrow streets. As they are very close to each other, each sign blocks the view of the next one and can only be seen almost from underneath. This has the benefit of illuminating the street and does have a peculiar charm, no doubt, on a few streets, but probably most people would not want it on all their city streets. Another example is Times Square in Manhattan, which has an identity, character, and attraction based on its enormous, illuminated signs. There, urban regulations not only allow illuminated signs but also require that they have a minimum of lumens.[12] The case of street signage is another in which Adam Smith's principle of allowing each person to seek their own profit fails to generate benefits for society.

At the other end of the spectrum, Paris, London, and most European cities have strict regulations regarding shop signs. They must be small, set into the façade, horizontal, and not neon, with only a couple of bulbs for discreet illumination. And shopkeepers sell no less for that.

The Return of Main Streets

Shops respectful of pedestrian space with discreet signboards do not mar their surroundings. On the contrary, they improve them. Offices and other nonhousing spaces coexist in harmony with housing, provided that public pedestrian space is held sacred. For Rob Adams, who led the campaign to revitalize the center of Melbourne, the number of cafés and restaurants that opened facing public space—and sometimes partially using it—was one of the main measures of his success.

In many local shops, neighbors can pin up offers of products and services they offer for sale. People venture onto the streets more when there is local commerce. Neighbors and acquaintances meet in shops or on the way there. Since they attract people to public spaces, shops improve security. A delicatessen or a pharmacy on our block improves our lives. And if it's open twenty-four hours, then it almost deserves a medal from municipal authorities.

In neighborhoods of developing world cities, there are shopping streets or areas that concentrate a wide variety of shops, almost all owned by neighbors or small businessmen and not by large chains. There are fruit and vegetable shops, the butcher, the baker, the restaurateur, shops for dairy products, the pharmacy, the small hardware store, a stationers, the shoe shop, the boutique, the beauty parlor, the bank, and so on. These commercial areas are meeting places for the community and part of its identity. Jobs are generated there, and many of those who work there live nearby. Neighbors and young people meet, local information is passed by word of mouth, and civic or political campaigns occur. Shopkeepers know many of their customers by name.

To strengthen those traditional shopping sectors in Bogotá, we started a program called "Main Streets." The program selected a traditional shopping street and helped it become more dynamic, protecting it against deterioration with an extensive series of public works: expansion and improvement of sidewalks; the burial of overhead cables; the installation of improved lighting, security cameras, benches, waste bins, and other urban furniture; the regulation of signage, the planting of trees, the reclamation of pedestrian space occupied by street vendors or cars; and the strengthening of shopowners' organizations, even authorizing them to generate income through rental of public space for exhibitions or other events. I would have liked to do that in hundreds of sectors pulsing with commercial activity and life, but limited funding meant we could only do twenty of them.[13]

Large supermarkets can put many small grocers, bakeries, or local shops out of business. As a result, the community may suffer. Typically, relationships aren't established in these supermarkets between customer and employee or neighbors. Aware of the benefits of small shops for a community, many cities have issued regulations that prohibit or restrict large supermarkets in some neighborhoods. Adjusting to or anticipating such regulations, some supermarket chains have structured programs to team up with neighborhood shopkeepers to combine economies of scale and the technologies of the major chain with the social and community benefits of the traditional corner shop.[14]

In US-styled suburbs, there is no commerce in walking distance, but there is plenty of green. In dense cities such as Manhattan, there is relatively little green but plenty of commerce close to home. The regulations that restrict commerce in residential zones of developing world cities sometimes produce the worst of both worlds: sectors with no green and no commerce. Although some exclusively residential streets feel more tranquil, neighborhoods function better and are safer if shops, a café, or a bakery with tables to sit and have breakfast are in short walking distance.

The polluting industries of previous centuries brought zoning regulations to keep industry far away from housing. Modern industry, however, does not contaminate. Although some large-scale manufacturing plants, with a heavy flow of freight vehicles, need to be in specialized industrial zones, some smaller ones can be located next to residential areas and even inside them without doing any damage and rather the contrary. To live close to where something is produced, whether furniture, lamps, or anything else, constructs identity and a sense of belonging.

The Right to Enjoy Public Space Without Fear

Security is the most important ingredient of a public space. In a good city we live without fear; women and children can go out alone into public space at any time. The fundamental right to live without fear was somehow forgotten in the United Nations Declaration of Human Rights and in the national constitutions that I know. It is essential for us not to prefer to stay barricaded at home but instead to want to go out to enjoy our city's public spaces. Assuming security is indispensable for public space to be attractive, then a public space that is attractive—due to its design, lighting, and maintenance—in turn also constructs security. It brings people out into public space, and having people there is what is most important to achieve security.

Security is the top priority of all citizens, and democracies should tend to the priorities of their citizens. But some governments in developing countries, particularly in Latin America and Africa, seem to have resigned themselves to coexistence with crime. That tolerance for or low priority accorded to security stems in part from the fact that politicians know that people are more grateful for a road or a hospital than for a new prison.

Lack of security results when a society lacks legitimacy, which makes us feel that we don't have the moral authority to punish what are ostensibly minor crimes. But these are crimes that prevent us from being able to enjoy our public space and that prevent public space from fulfilling its function of social integration, inclusion, and the construction of equality. The lack of legitimacy also means that citizens do not engage in the necessary collaboration with authorities in the battle against crime. Everything that constructs equality and inclusion strengthens legitimacy and thus helps to reduce crime. Improvement of informal settlements; the building of schools, cultural and sports centers, bikeways, and parks; and BRTs that not only expand opportunities for employment, education, and recreation but also give priority to public transport over private cars all construct legitimacy.

I was living in New York when the September 11 terrorist attack happened. It was a sad time. However, one positive aspect was the deeply enhanced sense of community that the tragedy brought out. The community feeling lingered for weeks. Tragedy brings us together, beyond everything that separates us in everyday life: differences in income, educational level, age, cultural preferences, religion, and political leanings.

Likewise, in poor societies, when informal neighborhoods are forming, residents rely essentially on mutual support for their survival. Material progress leads us to believe, wrongly, that we no longer need to belong to a community or participate in one. And precisely when we start to believe that we do not even need to know our neighbor's name, something may occur that brutally reminds us of the contrary—if not a terrorist attack, then an earthquake or a pandemic. When these tragedies occur, our feeling of community is strengthened, and we realize how much we miss when we isolate ourselves.

The more people in the public space, particularly neighbors, the better the security. The most important thing for security is that neighbors should know each other. Studies cited by Robert Putnam found that social capital is a more important predictor of the murder rate than education level, the rate of single-parent households, or income inequality.[15] Criminality studies in Colombia have not found that poverty in itself is a cause of crime,[16] but they have identified a correlation between areas of colonization and crime.[17] In small, recently built towns, usually in jungle areas to which people have migrated because there is a legal or illegal boom in oil, bananas, gold, or coca, there is no consolidated social fabric. There are neither grandparents and grandchildren nor cousins, and friendships are recent. Most of the residents have no intention of staying there for the rest of their lives; they aspire to make money and leave. Many men have no family, or their families do not live with them. Bars and prostitution abound.[18] Such environments are breeding grounds for crime.

Something similar happens in some neighborhoods whose residents are resigned to live there but would prefer to leave, where there are not enough relationships, friendships, or common aims to build a better future.[19] It is possible to build infrastructure and carry out activities to change this. A good public pedestrian space dignifies human life and helps people to meet and integrate, which reduces crime.

Although cowboy films and TV series are much less common today, when I was a child there were many. They romanticized crime and violence during the colonization of the US West. But the West at that time experienced real violence, which had to do with the absence of the state and the lack of a tightly woven social fabric.

A splendid custom persists in small cities in the Colombian tropic and in many popular neighborhoods in major cities. People, mainly the elderly and sometimes accompanied by relatives, sit for hours in front of their homes on a kind of small porch or balcony at street level or on the sidewalk in the shade of a small tree. They chat and watch the world go by. Neighbors and friends who pass by greet them, sometimes stopping to chat for a few minutes. In the all but traffic-free streets, children play. Those are neighborhoods where everyone knows everyone, and it would be difficult for any felon to commit a crime there.

In those neighborhoods, houses have no air conditioning, so windows and even doors tend to remain open to allow the breeze to circulate. I am not convinced that installing air conditioning, locking up the house, and buying a car to drive to a shopping center for a Saturday afternoon outing would represent progress over these rituals. A majority of single-family homes in the United States have a porch. They may not be as intensely used as those quasi-porches in Colombian low-income neighborhoods, but the philosophy is the same: to watch people go by and to say hello to the rare neighbor who passes on foot in those mostly low-density environments. Inspired by the small terrace at street level in the popular houses of our tropical cities, as well as the traditional porches, ground floors in modern high-rise residential buildings could include similar spaces, perhaps with a small café, for residents to be able to sit and enjoy life on the street as it passes them.

In contrast, dirt and disorder in public space creates a sensation that there is nobody in charge, which encourages crime. The "broken window theory" has received ample space in many publications.[20] The theory holds that if someone breaks a window in a building and it isn't repaired at once, more windows will be broken; next, people will start to throw trash outside the building. The lack of authority and control attracts people who engage in illegal activities and eventually commit crimes. I am partly in agreement with this theory. However, I believe that disorder, dirt, and broken windows above all betray an absence of community rather than a lack of authority. Community is at least as important to security as authority. Where there is no community, good citizens do not act in unity to help someone being attacked by criminals, and the police attention and response tend not to be so effective. By the same token, the fact that a public space is clean and orderly is the result of efficiency in the waste collection company but, perhaps even more important, of the presence of an engaged community with self-esteem.

Bogotá is a long way from being as secure as it should be. The Colombian state has not enacted the required laws or allocated adequate funds; nevertheless, Bogotá's security has steadily improved, even though Colombia has been affected by international criminal organizations engaged in drug trafficking. The murder rate in 1993 was 87.87 per 100,000 people,[21] and it has been steadily decreasing since then. The year before my second term of office began, it had dropped to 17.1 per 100,000. We managed to reduce that to 13.9 by the time I left office at the end of 2019, significantly lower rates than the other two major Colombian cities, Medellín with 21.96 and Cali with 43.39,[22] and indeed, lower than Washington, DC, which reported 23.52 per 100,000 in that year.[23]

Cities at War, edited by Saskia Sassen and Mary Kaldor, emphasizes how progress in security in Bogotá has not been based on policies of repression but on efforts to ensure that people will go out into public space and travel democratically, thus taking advantage of their city.[24]

The City Design Can Improve or Decrease Security

Primitive human beings organized, obeyed chiefs, and observed rules in exchange for security. Security was so crucial that for thousands of years, societies charged their best young men with providing it. Only members of the elite contributed to armies in Greece and Rome or to the Japanese samurai.

Insecurity not only affects societies at any given moment but deforms the city for many years to come. It encourages shopping centers and walled housing developments and makes it difficult for high-income citizens to leave their cars and take public transport or use a bicycle, which in turn means that public transport and infrastructure for bicycles do not receive the funding or support they deserve.

The shape of the city can encourage or reduce security. Jane Jacobs described how security in public space was intricately tied to the relationship between public and private space; for example, sidewalks are safer if they can be seen from adjacent buildings, particularly the first two or three floors. Naturally, this is impossible if those floors are used for parking cars and have windowless walls or if there are walls that isolate gardens and buildings from the sidewalk.

A walk on a sidewalk along blind walls is dull as well as dangerous. Those walls are abundant in developing world cities, from the suburbs in South Africa to the high-rise apartment buildings in Medellín, Colombia. If a building is not to damage the city, its parking spaces should be underground, or, if it has a large base area, they could be placed at street level but at the back of the building. But to have cars parked at sidewalk level or with walls built to conceal them damages public space. Jacobs also observed that the presence of people on the street encourages those in buildings to look out the windows. It's not interesting to look through a window at a deserted street because what people want to see is, precisely, other people.[25]

The urban environment is more pleasant and safer when there are no enclosures and when façades come down to the sidewalk or a public garden, when there are apartments, gyms, offices, or shops with windows on the ground floor against the street. There are thieves in most cities in the world, but in good cities there are no blind walls at street level. There are windows with bars or safety glass. Thieves in China must be especially agile, because I have seen a number of buildings that have bars over their windows and balconies right up to the tenth or twentieth floors.

Where there are ample gardens between a building and the sidewalk, and if in any event there is to be an enclosure, it's better that it should be a transparent one such as a wrought-iron fence rather than a wall. This improves security in all spaces because it allows those on the private side to see happenings on the public side and vice versa. If there is a wall, and a criminal manages to climb over it, he won't be seen from the public space, but that's not so with a transparent enclosure. Alternatively, a criminal in the street feels observed from the private space if there is a transparent enclosure, while a wall hides him from those in the private space. We have found that in neighborhoods with crime problems, security was better in schools with fences that allowed visibility than in schools with walls.

Raul Juste Lores describes how buildings in the Conjunto Nacional development on Avenida Paulista, São Paulo's central artery, have been successful and resilient:

Conjunto Nacional proves that São Paulo once knew how to build intelligent buildings. On its 33 floors, divided into three blocks, there are offices and apartments with separate entrances. The wide sidewalks outside the building are made of the same material as the floors inside, thus obliterating the boundaries between public and private. The ground floor hosts cinemas, shops, banks, pharmacies and restaurants. This varied use demonstrates how to inject modernity and new life in a 1950s building without damaging it. The result is that the block of the Conjunto Nacional is the liveliest on Avenida

Paulista. Continuous streams of people walk the area, weekdays and weekends. In a city that is prisoner to paranoia about safety the generous and welcoming architecture of Conjunto Nacional offers coexistence and safety for thousands of people. Criminals, who prefer dark and abandoned places where they can be left alone, are unwelcome there.[26]

CHAPTER 11

Waterfronts for People's Enjoyment

Waterfronts wield particular magic. One can walk, jog, or ride a bicycle along a riverbank; look far to the sea horizon or at a river from a bridge at night while some buildings' lights are reflected on its tranquil waters; listen to the murmur of a stream running between ferns and flowers. Waterfronts that are well integrated into the urban design are a treasure: just the sight of them elicits peace, inspires us, and makes us feel good. London has a large number of parks that are quite beautiful, yet the paths and squares of the Thames embankment are teeming with people on weekends. Cochin, the capital of the state of Kerala in the extreme south of India, built a promenade of more than 1.5 kilometers[1] along the seashore as part of the Marine Drive project.[2] When I visited it, the stink of sewage was still strong; nonetheless, the magic of water attracted tens of thousands of people who enjoyed walking along the promenade.

Waterfronts create such beautiful and charming public spaces that even the wealthiest citizens cannot resist them. They are spaces where we meet as equals, regardless of income level or status. In this way they help create that city we seek, in which no one feels inferior or excluded.

There are obstacles that prevent waterfronts from contributing to integration and happiness. One is that they may be contaminated by wastewater or industrial residues. Another is that they are sometimes private and reserved only for the few. Sometimes roads for cars are built alongside them, bringing noise and danger or simply spoiling their beauty. Or they may lack the infrastructure to facilitate pedestrians' and cyclists' access to and enjoyment of them.

From Sewers to Destinations

For thousands of years the banks of bodies of water were the least attractive part of cities for people to live in or stroll along. It was where the poorest citizens lived, in overcrowded and unsanitary conditions. Sewage arrived there through numerous surface canals or simply draining down the streets by gravity. Waterfronts flooded regularly, and homes near the water were left partly or completely underwater. Malodorous puddles on the waterfront were breeding grounds for mosquitoes and rats. For much of the year there was mud everywhere. This was the case in Paris, London, and Tokyo. Part of Central Park's charm in New York was that it was a long way from the foul-smelling Hudson and East River waterfronts.

Friedrich Engels wrote of the Manchester waterfront in the 1840s, "Everywhere one sees heaps of refuse, garbage and filth . . . one walks along a very rough path on the riverbank . . . to reach a chaotic group of little, one storeyed, one-room cabins. Most of them have earth floors and working, living and sleeping all takes place in one room."[3] In Chicago toward 1870 "along the banks of the dirty river were 'patches'—shanty towns that housed the city's outcasts and recently arrived migrants in wooden shacks. The majority of the tens of thousands recently arrived had to live in . . . temporary shacks built on marshland."[4]

Many waterfronts in developing cities in which millions of people live continue to be like that. In some cities, such as Lagos, Nigeria, or Buenaventura in Colombia, many low-income citizens live over the water on houses built on stilts. More frequently. citizens have filled swamps and bogs to build their homes. In Manila, Jakarta, and hundreds of cities around the developing world, informal neighborhoods in low-lying areas flood during the rainy season.

When I took office in Bogotá for the first time in 1998, that was the case in most of the western border of the city, which had been illegally built below the Bogotá River level. Using precarious piping systems and small pumps, rainwater and sewage were brought up over the embankment and discharged into the river. But during the rainy seasons, the river level rose, and when those little pumps broke down, which was frequently, the pipes, instead of evacuating water, sent it back into the houses through the toilets and flooded them, not only with rainwater but also with the sewage. Families would lose a good part of their possessions and were left homeless. We built sewerage networks and a large pumping station to finally resolve the flooding issue.

While in wealthy societies, any stream or river is appreciated and taken advantage of by the public and private infrastructure in its banks, still today in developing country's villages, towns, and many cities, rivers and streams are sewers and garbage dumps that abut houses whose unfortunate owners have not been able to get a home far from the water. Pigs are the only creatures who enjoy these waterfronts. In some developing cities, this sort of situation persists, even in middle- and high-income sectors of high-rise buildings.

Historically, many of Paris's poor homes also clung to the riverbanks, which frequently flooded. In 1851 one-third of the population still lived on the right bank of the Seine in a space smaller than twice the size of Central Park, an "almost impenetrable hive" of shops of all kinds and miserably overcrowded tenements. The density was higher than that of the Lower East Side in New York in the 1930s, which was greater than two thousand inhabitants per hectare.[5] And of course all the wastewater from those settlements and from the rest of Paris flowed to the Seine.

Notwithstanding Georges-Eugène Haussmann's titanic reconstruction of Paris that began in the mid-1850s, perhaps his most important work was the transformation of its sewerage system, which included the building of huge collectors that carried the water downstream and drained into the river in Asnières and Clichy.[6] It was only in the second half of the nineteenth century, after scientific discoveries established the relationship between epidemics like cholera and contaminated water, that advanced cities such as Hamburg, London, and New York built sophisticated sewerage systems and progressively decontaminated their waterfronts. The decontamination of rivers, lakes, and seas next to cities, even in the most developed countries, was only completed at the end of the twentieth century. Waterfronts as beautiful and attractive urban sites are a recent development.

In addition to sewage, large industrial plants that used rivers' waters in their processes or required docks located on their banks and shores made waterfronts unattractive. Ports bring commercial activity and prosperity to cities, but in the past their surroundings were places for activities that made them unsafe, and, in any case, port areas are not particularly attractive pedestrian environments. But in recent decades many waterfront industries and ports have left urban centers, owing to changes in technology and economic considerations, as well as the increase in the size of ships.

On many sites of old industrial plants and ports, there have been urban redevelopment projects, known as "brownfield developments," which in addition to bringing housing and offices to central areas have generated beautiful public pedestrian spaces on waterfronts that improve the life of the city. Among the best known of these are the Inner Harbor in Baltimore and Canary Wharf in London. And old ports for great sailing ships in the center of cities such as those on both sides of Manhattan and in Nyhavn in Copenhagen, Puerto Madero in Buenos Aires, and Port Jackson in Sydney have become iconic pedestrian spaces.

Hundreds of cities over the last fifty years have recovered their waterfronts for human enjoyment. They have achieved this through processes of decontamination and the construction of pedestrian infrastructure or its reconstruction and improvement. This has occurred also along streams and even canals. Marvelous opportunities exist in places that have not yet turned their waterfronts into attractive public spaces, and these locales now have many examples to draw from.

In London there are more than fifty kilometers of pedestrian infrastructure on both sides of the Thames. Beyond those, almost three hundred kilometers of paths alongside the water continue through rural areas and villages outside the capital. The transformation of Guayaquil was led by the promenade along the Guayas River, which became a meeting place for citizens of all income levels and rejuvenated citizens' self-esteem. Melbourne has a beautiful greenway as well as plazas along the Yarra River; on the banks of the Spree in Berlin, people drink beer and kiss. In the plazas, steps, and gardens around Lake Zurich, grandfathers and their grandchildren play and watch the geese.

Waterfronts delight and provide peace to citizens. They generate value not only for buildings along the water but also for those at a distance from where it can easily be reached on foot. They attract tourists and generate jobs. They construct inclusion, attracting the wealthy, famous, and powerful alike who meet in a context of equality.

In contrast, private waterfronts are incompatible with democracy. Waterfronts, like a blue sky or the wind, are one of the gifts of our planet for human enjoyment. It seems not only cruel but almost sacrilegious or immoral to deprive some citizens of that enjoyment. If democracy implies more than anything that all citizens are equal before the law and therefore that the public good should prevail, then waterfronts should be public spaces, or they should function as such with free access to all. Many battles have been fought to achieve this, mostly successfully. But unfortunately, there are still thousands of kilometers of waterfronts around the world, including in or around cities, that are still private and out of reach for the majority. This is not something a democracy can be proud of.

Americans have always believed that their democracy is exemplary. And in many ways, it is, but not in this one way. Although most beaches on oceans in the United States are public, there are thousands of kilometers of other waterfronts that are private and exclusive. Millions of people who live north of Manhattan in the states of New York, Connecticut, and Rhode Island live close to the beautiful Long Island Sound. But in terms of enjoying it, they might as well be three thousand miles away because all of the coastline, except for a few small parks where all citizens can access the water, belongs to private owners. Beautiful houses, generally luxurious, line the Long Island Sound waterfront, leaving no public access. If democracy implies the prevalence of the public good, then the lives of millions would be happier if the Long Island Sound waterfront was a public greenway, with paths and bikeways hundreds of kilometers long. I suspect that even the residents of the exclusive mansions that today prevent access to water would enjoy it. Even with capitalism, there may be this sort of quality-of-life equality.

Ocean waterfronts in the United States were not always accessible to all citizens—and some still aren't today. The legendary Robert Moses, who effectively governed New York for roughly twenty years, had to threaten several tycoons with expropriation so that they would sell their extensive beach properties to the state to create the Jones Beach public park.

In Manhattan, Moses expropriated the buildings of the aristocratic Columbia Yacht Club on the Hudson to demolish them and incorporate the property into Riverside Park. The club was so luxurious and exclusive that its members had become the "semi-official city hosts to visiting royalty (the club's proudest boast was that the Prince of Wales had made it his headquarters on not one but two visits aboard his yacht, the *Renown*)."[7] The club occupied public land, paying rent for its use. In March 1934, three months after becoming parks commissioner, Moses informed them that it was necessary to remove the Columbia Yacht Club from the site to make way for Riverside Park. In the ensuing legal battle, Moses was attacked for the haste with which he'd demolished the club because Riverside Park was more than nine kilometers long and it would take several years to complete it. Unfazed, Moses didn't budge from his position, managed to win the legal battle, and four months later had demolished the clubhouse. Moses always reminded people that "the whole question is whether private interest should yield to public interest."[8] He created a park that has been, is, and will be enjoyed by many generations. When I visit the park and see children playing, bicyclists riding by, elderly people sitting on a bench looking at the river, or perhaps a couple strolling, I suspect few of them know of Moses and the battles he waged so that they could enjoy that park.

Upper-crust members who sought to delay the expropriation of the Columbia Yacht Club knew that procrastination was a good tactic, particularly when dealing with people in government, who tend to turn over with each election. Unfortunately for the elites, there were judges who, complying with democratic principles, ruled in favor of the club's expropriation. Further, the de facto government of Moses in New York lasted for many more years. I was less effective than Moses: I didn't manage to make irrevocable the creation of two parks around reservoirs close to Bogotá, for which we'd worked hard.[9]

For the Riverside Park expansion, Moses also buried a substantial segment of the railroad line coming into Manhattan from the north along the Hudson. Railway lines along waterfronts were quite common some time ago before their aesthetic value for cities was properly appreciated. For Riverside Park, as for other projects, Moses made infills to enlarge the riverbank. Writes his biographer Robert Caro, "For mile after mile, the earth and rock that constitute the shoreline of Brooklyn and Queens, and of Manhattan's Hudson shore, are his, the cement and steel that hold them in place are his, the grass and shrubs and trees that adorn them are his—as are the concrete and steel of the marinas, the shoreline overlooks, the parking fields, the bicycle paths. . . . Not nature but he put them there."[10]

Amazingly, in a country as democratic as the United Kingdom, almost all watercourses, including rivers and canals, are private. The owners of the banks also own the river to its midpoint. Scotland is more democratic: here prevails "the right to roam" of the 2003 Land Reform Act, similar to the Scandinavian "Allemansrätten," which gives all citizens the right to walk, bike, or canoe through private land and watercourses because "the public's right to nature supersedes the landowners' right to exclude them."[11] The United Kingdom Parliament is studying similar regulations.

Waterfront Access in Bogotá

Citizens of Bogotá have no access to any regional parks relatively close to the city where they can enjoy contact with nature, to say nothing of a park with a lake. A large proportion of city inhabitants has never even seen the surface of a lake or reservoir, much less a sea. We organized a program to take low-income schoolchildren to camp along the shores of reservoirs in nearby mountains, and they enjoyed it enormously.

About forty kilometers outside Bogotá lies the Tominé Reservoir, seventy-two square kilometers of water surrounded by mountains. It belongs to the Bogotá Energy Company that for decades was fully owned by Bogotá's City Hall, which today still owns most of its shares. Although the Tominé Reservoir was the citizens' property, they were never able to access its banks. But the company did allow some influential families to build holiday homes there, paying an absurdly low rent. It also handed over some properties for free to sailing clubs whose members, unlike those of the Columbia Yacht Club, were not acquaintances of the British royal family, although some had similar pretensions to aristocracy and were influential locally.

During my second term as mayor, we were able to put an end to the occupation by private homes of lots on the energy company's land next to the reservoir. Furthermore, we designed a park with a bikeway and a pedestrian path on the reservoir's shores. The minority private shareholders of the energy company allowed for its construction, and indeed they even agreed that the company should provide some funds for the park's construction. At City Hall we secured additional funds for it. But some owners of the country homes around the reservoir, naturally high-income citizens who didn't want a park with crowds of plebeians in their surroundings, managed to have the environmental authorities procrastinate, delaying the project. Unlike the prolonged period of power that Moses enjoyed in New York, my four-year term in Bogotá ended, and I was not able to leave with the contract for the park signed. Among the first things the new mayor said after her election was that she would not do the project. I maintain hope that it will become a reality at some future time.

San Rafael was another park around a reservoir for which we managed to have complete designs and funding was located on property belonging to the city's water company, on the other side of the mountains that line Bogotá to the east. We designed a six-kilometer cable car over wooded mountains, which started from a TransMilenio station of a line that we had designed and funded. On this occasion a politicized judge stopped the park and the cable projects, issuing a ruling to delay it, not based on the violation of any law but as a "precautionary principle." And once again the mayor who succeeded me canceled the project. The judge who facilitated the project's dismantling probably will realize in the future that neither he nor his children or grandchildren will have access to any space like the one the park would have provided them.

Another example of democracy at work in the United States, similar to Moses's expropriation of the Columbia Yacht Club, was the 2003 conversion in Chicago of an airport used mainly for private aircraft into a park. Meigs Field Airport was situated opposite Chicago on the Lake Michigan waterfront, a place where executive jets of the powerful and wealthy would land. At first glance it would even seem that since the park on the lake was already so large, it was not particularly important to expand it into the land occupied by the airport. However, Mayor Richard Daley considered the park so important for the quality of life in the city that he decided to acquire the airport to expand the park. He obtained a favorable decision to expropriate it on Friday, March 28, 2003. To prevent the airport owners from appealing on the following Monday, Mayor Daley informed plane owners that the runway would be torn up on Sunday afternoon. The owners therefore had to remove their aircraft during the weekend if they wanted to fly them out. And on Sunday night, March 30, the bulldozers arrived and demolished the runway, leaving a dozen aircraft stranded that had to be trucked out.

The prominent architect Daniel Burnham, who designed the famous Flatiron Building in Manhattan and the train station in Washington, DC, among many more, wrote in his 1909 Plan of Chicago, "The Lakefront by right belongs to the people. Not a foot of its shores should be appropriated to the exclusion of the people." Resentment by some local Chicago politicians and businessmen have thwarted the full development of the Northerly Island Park, where Meigs Field used to be. But petty, local political resentments wane, and the park will someday realize its potential.

Given its recent history of extreme racial inequality and exclusion, it is especially incongruous that South Africa should have private beaches, such as the Radisson Hotel's in the center of Cape Town. I doubt that Nelson Mandela would have approved. By contrast, one valuable legacy of the Mexican revolution is that all beaches are public as a sacrosanct principle, despite pressure by the powerful tourist industry to change this.

Most shores of lakes in Argentina, Chile, Canada, and the United States and of most rivers and streams around the world are still private property, inaccessible to most citizens. Almost always, countries in northern Europe have democratically attempted to make waterfronts public: the Bavarian lakes are a recent example of these efforts. Albeit slowly, the world advances toward more democratic access to waterfronts. In 2005 the State of Michigan's

Supreme Court unanimously ruled that everybody has a right to free access to the more than five thousand kilometers of Great Lakes' beaches in Michigan, even if owners of waterfronts plots don't like it. The court sided with Joan M. Glass who had sued her neighbors to get access to the Lake Huron waterfront. Around 70 percent of Michigan's shoreline plots on Lake Michigan, Huron, and Erie are privately owned. But the court's ruling opened the waterfront to all citizens.[12]

Access for Public Waterfronts

The right to education or health are empty promises if there are no schools or hospitals to make them effective. So, too, if public waterfronts are to be enjoyed, it's also essential that they should be accessible, that no walls or buildings bar access, and that there are paths and other infrastructure to make their enjoyment possible. In many cities and tourist regions, houses, hotels, and apartment buildings are built on the beach, preventing access to it. One after the other, buildings and their enclosures merge to form an impassable barrier. Although in theory beaches might be public, there is no way to access them. As buildings for those who go for vacations are built in a coastal city or town, the locals without access to expensive hotels and apartments cannot go to their own beaches and have fewer places even to watch the sea.

Although Colombian law says that all beaches are public, crafty builders and incompetent or complicit local authorities have allowed many stretches of beach in the coastal cities of Cartagena and Santa Marta to be effectively closed to the local population who have lived there and enjoyed them for generations. And on these cities' outskirts, houses, clubs, and hotels sit on de facto privatized beaches. Many of them have jetties built out over the beaches and into the water, which is also public. So all of that is public space, and in a democratic society the consistent policy would be to allow anyone to tie up a boat at those jetties and to access the adjoining beaches. Even more so, any citizen would have the right to swim or paddle a canoe to any beach.

There may be private ports for passengers, freight, and some industrial terminals. There may even be marinas for luxury yachts, where the piers are closed to the public, and for that privilege, boat owners pay substantial fees to the state. But the democratic thing to do is to ensure that waterfronts where these piers meet dry land should be public spaces accessible to all. This is the case in hundreds of cities where anyone can walk along quays next to large yachts or on walkways perpendicular to the piers. It's unsurprising that in developing cities with more unequal and less democratic societies, the land of these docked waterfronts is private and enclosed.

Regulations in democratic cities require any building erected on a waterfront to leave ample space with pedestrian infrastructure to allow any citizen access to the water. That is valid, even in the case of a small river. Chicago mandates new buildings on the Chicago River to leave at least ten meters between them and the water.

Ideally, waterfronts not only allow access to everyone but do not intimidate their potential visitors and, on the contrary, make them feel welcome. Amanda Burden, New York's planning commissioner for twelve years under Mayor Mike Bloomberg, said of the Brooklyn redevelopments along the East River that the regulations had required the projects' architecture "to clearly express that waterfronts are public" and, moreover, that access roads to the waterfront parks should "invite" people to go there and that everything should feel "very open and public."[13]

In the United States, which has some of the worst examples of privatized waterfronts on seas and lakes, there are good examples in relation to ocean shores. At the beginning of the twenty-first century, Miami built many kilometers of paths along the beach in front of hotels and apartments. Even the most exclusive hotels have public beaches. Puerto Rico has a beautifully democratic rule: if there is no comfortable access to the beach, then the citizen is entitled to reach it through the private spaces of hotels and other waterfront buildings. There is little point to public waterfronts if there is no way for the public to access them.

Recovering Waterfronts from Cars for People

When cities made progress on the decontamination of rivers, lakes, and seas in the twentieth century, a problem just as destructive as contamination emerged: roads for motor vehicles on waterfronts. In frenzied efforts to make more space available to cars and to accommodate the growing volumes of traffic, engineers found that waterfronts were ideal sites for major roads—frequently highways. If that required building demolition, then the costs were low because waterfront buildings typically were not attractive. If yet more space was required, it was also possible to widen the banks with infill. Better still, routes along waterfronts were irresistible for road engineers because they were the only urban routes without intersections to reduce vehicle speed.

But a road on the waterfront destroys it for human enjoyment. It became progressively evident that one of the most serious mistakes was to desecrate waterfronts with major roads for cars. Nevertheless, even after 1950, the construction of roads for cars along waterfronts continued, even in advanced cities. Most of the Franklin Delano Roosevelt Drive along the East River in Manhattan was built between 1948 and 1966. Today, there is no doubt that it would be better to have a large pedestrian public space between buildings and the water. But for the time being, what is in place is the ugly, noisy, and impassable barrier of the FDR Drive. French president Georges Pompidou built the disastrous highway across Paris along the Seine in 1967. And even today many developing cities continue to build roads along the shores of seas and lakes and the banks of rivers and canals.

Although it might take hundreds of years to repair the damage done by roads to urban waterfronts, there have been important projects to recover them from cars and return them to people. Madrid's relationship to its Manzanares River illustrates both the past and the future: the park the city built along its banks is an example of what even a small stream can mean for the life of a city, when it's conceived as a setting for human enjoyment. For hundreds of years Madrid stayed away from its riverbanks, as sewage drained to the river from multiple quarters and its surroundings reeked. The river was not only polluted but also recurrently flooded the land around it. In the second half of the nineteenth century, Madrid began to build sewers, but wastewater continued to be discharged into the Manzanares River and two smaller ones. Toward 1914 the river began to be channeled through the construction of retaining walls, principally to avoid flooding. That work continued until the mid-twentieth century, and in the final phases it included underground interceptors to decontaminate the river's water as well as the widening of the riverbed and the construction of seven dams upstream to control floods. As a result of these adaptations, in the 1950s new buildings approached the right bank of the river in Madrid's center.

What happened next has occurred in many cities: just as the river, now decontaminated and channeled, was becoming attractive to citizens and improving the city's quality of life, the government decided to prioritize motor vehicle traffic. Authorities found the Manzanares banks ideally suited to build a major segment of the first Madrid Ring Road. And in the 1970s, the M30 motorway was built on both sides of the river, staving off any possibility for citizens to have contact with their river and making it impossible to access some existing pedestrian bridges.

But a few decades later, beginning in the twenty-first century, the Madrid authorities did something extraordinary: they buried the M30 in a seven-kilometer tunnel and created a ten-kilometer-long park on top of it and on some adjacent sectors, covering ninety-five hectares of the riverbank. Less inspiring is that the initial justification of the project, led by Mayor Ruiz Gallardón, was not so much the park or the redevelopment of more than six hundred hectares around it in the center of Madrid but the desire to optimize traffic management. Over time, however, it became clear that the main benefit of the project for the city would be the park. The Río Manzanares Park has children's playgrounds, sports facilities, and dozens of kilometers of paths and bikeways.

In Santiago, Chile, the Mapocho River waterfront, with streets on a good portion of its banks, did not hold much charm or appeal for pedestrians. The situation only worsened with the construction of the Costanera Norte Highway, much of it on those banks. However, pressure from citizen groups achieved the positive result of putting the highway underground. Above it, the creation of a large park is under way, which will enhance citizens' enjoyment of the river's waterfront. In Utrecht, Netherlands, the road alongside the Cathariajnesingel Canal was pedestrianized, and the ground floors of buildings along that road were turned into flourishing shops, restaurants, and cafés. In Dusseldorf, a major road along the Rhine in the city center was put underground and the pedestrian waterfront is today the city's most important meeting place and tourist attraction.

The mayors of Paris Bertrand Delanoë and especially Anne Hidalgo turned the motorway along the banks of the Seine that President Pompidou had built though the middle of Paris into a marvelous waterfront walkway. For this project and others designed to make Paris a city more for pedestrians and cyclists and less for cars, Mayor Hidalgo was violently attacked, and her popularity sank. In February 2018 the opposition managed to take her to court, arguing that the closure of the motorway had been based on inaccurate data of pollution and traffic reduction, but the administrative tribunal of Paris ruled to maintain the pedestrianization of the road along the river. And the verdict of the citizens of Paris was also clear because they reelected Mayor Hidalgo in 2020.

In Lyon the roads along the left bank of the Rhône were transformed in 2008 into public pedestrian spaces with a beautiful architectural design, thus converting its waterfronts into the city's most attractive place for residents and tourists alike. The project also included the creation of parks in large lots previously used for parking spaces.

Jan Gehl says that areas around the river in Aarhus, Denmark, are the most popular public spaces in the city. This river, buried to build roads above it in the 1930s, was brought back to the surface in 1998 with pedestrian spaces along its banks.[14]

At the beginning of the 1990s, more than thirty kilometers of the elevated highways and railway lines that ran along and above the Platte River were demolished in Denver, Colorado. Work was also done to end the recurring flooding of land close to the river, and infrastructure was built to facilitate human enjoyment of the waterfront. Since that time Denver's center has become increasingly attractive as a place to live, work, and recreate. In Oregon a motorway that ran along the waterfront of the Willamette River through the center of Portland was removed and replaced by Tom McCall Park.[15] The center of Seattle was improved by the demolition of the Alaskan Way elevated highway, which robbed the city of the beauty of its waterfront on the sea. The highway was replaced by a tunnel.

In Seoul only a small stream ran under the elevated highway. Since the 1950s the stream had been piped underground across a central area of the city. Yet at the beginning of the twenty-first century, 9.4 kilometers of a four-lane elevated highway built in 1976 were demolished. Once the highway was demolished and the stream brought back to the surface, an 11-kilometer greenway was created around it, with roads on both sides. The Cheonggyecheon project's popularity significantly contributed to the election of Mayor Lee Myung-bak as president of South Korea in 2007.

Boston invested more than $20 billion in the so-called "Big Dig," a major excavation to bury the highways along the seashore in the center of the city and create attractive pedestrian public spaces. Unfortunately, this portentous work was largely a missed opportunity because instead of devoting the space created over the buried roads to wonderful parks and pedestrian spaces, it was ceded to local roads and unexciting pedestrian spaces.

We enjoy waterfronts more if there are no roads for cars between them and the buildings that face them. That is the case in the center of Melbourne, Battery Park in Manhattan, Harbour Green in Vancouver, and sections along the Thames in London and the Spree in Berlin, among others. San Sebastián, capital of the Basque country in Spain and one of the most humane cities I've ever visited, removed cars from the street alongside buildings that face La

Concha beach, and now the area between buildings and the sea is exclusively pedestrian.

While advanced cities make major investments to repair the damage done by roads along urban waterfronts, many developing cities continue to build them. And in the developed world, there are still many roads that damage waterfronts. In the first half of the twentieth century, one of the most frequented and liveliest public spaces in Boston was a path along the Charles River. Then in 1951 the Storrow Drive highway was built along the river waterfront, destroying that enchanting human space and isolating the city from the river, most painfully and acutely the buildings facing it, including those of Boston University. Across the river, site of the renowned universities Harvard and MIT, the situation is not any better: the multilane motorway Memorial Drive, noisy and dangerous for humans, runs along the waterfront. To jog looking at the river, students use a narrow path running alongside the traffic. Likewise, Zurich has promenades and parks along the edge of its lake, but many private buildings on the waterfront force cyclists and pedestrians to go around the back of them, depriving them of the water view.

In New York a large park on the banks of the Hudson River was to be located in spaces created by moving the West Side Highway underground and expanding the waterfront on spaces between dozens of docks dating from the nineteenth century. The Westway project, as it was known, was conceived in 1973 when a flyover over the riverbank partially collapsed. The project was going to generate 280 hectares for waterfront parks and housing. But some civic groups objected to the project for a number of reasons: gas emissions from tunnel traffic, the covering of water between the docks, and the profits of private developers involved in the project. Short-term political squabbles impeded the project. Finally, in 1985, a judge ruled that the project could not be implemented because the shadow over the water that would be covered, in addition to the area already covered by the existing docks, might affect the fish. Consequently, the city lost an opportunity to bury a major motorway, build thousands of homes, and create a beautiful park on the river in the south of Manhattan. After a few decades, instead of that great park without roads between the buildings and the water, a much narrower and more modest, yet still beautiful park was built between the eight-lane 12th Avenue and the river.

Bogotá, high up in the Andes, is hundreds of kilometers from the sea and has neither lakes nor major rivers. So I especially appreciate the view of any large expanse of water, and I'm surprised when those who do have such a view don't value or properly protect it. Between Santo Domingo, capital of the Dominican Republic, and its airport, there is a translucent blue sea, and waves crash against rocks and small cliffs along the shore. A beautiful promenade with tropical trees could have been made fronting the sea without a road for motor vehicles scarring it. Instead, in the space between buildings and the sea, a large road connects the city to the airport, isolating buildings from the waterfront. The road could have easily been built behind the buildings, particularly because it was built before urban development really began.

In Perth, Australia, with dozens of kilometers of splendid beaches, the beachside areas have roads as well as parking lots. The story is similar in Lake Como in northern Italy. I had been told how beautiful it was, but I have to confess that when I finally saw it, I found it breathtakingly beautiful but I was also rather disappointed. Most of the waterfront is privatized by expensive mansions. The narrow ring road has no bikeways or even sidewalks. And in the picturesque villages around the lake, almost invariably the best waterfront view is not from an enchanting pedestrian space with a balcony but from a parking lot.

There are some successful waterfronts, even in cases where motor-vehicle roads separate the water from the city. Rio de Janeiro is one example. The famous Bund, the river Huangpu promenade in the center of Shanghai, has a road alongside it. But the promenade is isolated from it because it sits at a higher level and vegetation separates it from the road. In the middle of this intense city, the river flows quietly along, and despite the high volume of river traffic, it's a relaxing sight. On the other side of the river is the new city of Pudong, which built a broad waterfront park along the river with small plazas and cafés, away from the traffic of the road alongside it.

Environmentalist Concerns or Classism?

Earlier I described how some residents of the Niza neighborhood in Bogotá, deploying pseudo-environmental arguments, managed to secure a court order to prevent the construction of a bikeway along a wetland, which was a segment of the Juan Amarillo Greenway. What those Niza neighbors really wanted was to keep citizens from lower-income sectors to the west, like Colsubsidio, from passing next to their neighborhood. Ironically, some of these "undesirable" Colsubsidio residents tried to do the same thing toward others from even lower-income sectors farther west. They did everything possible to prevent the construction of a bike path that would allow citizens from popular neighborhoods that had been informal settlements to cross a canal and a small river and access the metropolitan park, with numerous recreation and sports facilities, that we built next to Colsubsidio.

Like the inhabitants of Niza, they used allegedly environmental arguments to radically oppose the construction of an elevated bikeway, 3 meters aboveground, 5 meters wide, 1.2 kilometers long, supported by piers spaced 25 meters apart.[16] According to them, the bikeway would severely damage the Juan Amarillo wetland, as it would go near its banks. In this case the Colombian courts dismissed the supposedly environmental criteria of those who sued to stop the project and approved it.[17]

In so many cases, I have confronted ferocious opposition to projects that might bring lower-income citizens near a higher-income neighborhood, and I've become convinced that such projects are effective and necessary to construct equality of quality of life and inclusion. Of course, they are not easy to accomplish. It is even possible that they arouse more passionate opposition than do tax increases to achieve greater equity.

The influential members of social clubs that occupy large areas of well-located land had been able to pass legislation to pay little in property tax for their clubs because they are "of environmental interest." Given the favorable tax status they enjoy, we worked to prevent a club from raising a wall the club's directors wanted to build to prevent pedestrians and cyclists passing through the Juan Amarillo Greenway from seeing them as they played golf. We at City Hall believed that in exchange for their preferential tax treatment, they should at least allow the public to enjoy the view over the golf courses. Finally, we convinced the courts to order that the enclosure of that club and all others be 90 percent transparent. In the case of the Juan Amarillo Greenway, the enclosure remained transparent enough to allow views of the golf courses, but unfortunately the cunning and influential members of other clubs have managed to dodge the rule.

Classist attitudes can become almost delirious in backward societies. For example, we built some kiosks for women who had traditionally sold flowers in a high-income sector of the Juan Amarillo Greenway,[18] and near them we began construction of children's playgrounds. Then, some women from the association that presumably represented local residents angrily objected that "the flower vendors would bring their children, and the sector would deteriorate."

The creation of pedestrian public space faces myriad difficulties. To open up space for a bikeway next to a canal on another section of the Juan Amarillo Greenway, we needed to move the wall of the Colombian Army's officer cadet school a couple of meters. We only managed to settle these difficult discussions when the minister of defense intervened.

As part of the greenway, we enlarged the eastern section of the wetland that gives the greenway its name, dredging a lake of dozens of hectares. For that we acquired land and even houses in the neighborhood. On the northern side of this new man-made lake, we built a concrete promenade along the water's edge and a retaining wall that descends vertically down to the water so that citizens from popular neighborhoods nearby could enjoy walking next to the water—something almost impossible to do in Bogotá at the time. On the south side of the new lake we left a soft border: this was more natural, but the vegetation that grows there blocks the view of the water. It is difficult to collect refuse along the banks there, which are marshy due to fluctuating water levels. Some alleged environmentalists attacked me for making the hard northern border. If instead of having built the new lake, we had done nothing and left the houses and the privately owned grassland lots untouched where subsequently buildings would have been erected, I could have saved myself from those attacks.

In developing cities there are self-proclaimed environmentalists who oppose the adaptation of waterfronts for human enjoyment. They do not intervene when multilane interurban roads are built along riverbanks or the shores of lakes or sea, or, if they do, they are powerless to impede them. But they tend to be effective when blocking human infrastructure along urban waterfronts. We need some minimum infrastructure to be able to enjoy waterfronts, be it in a canoe, on foot, or by bicycle: in other words, piers, paths, and bikeways. London, Paris, New York, Shanghai, Toronto, and Melbourne all have these things. Frequently, objections of some to these light civil works, although disguised as environmental concerns, conceal classist attitudes and the desire to keep lower-income citizens from going near their neighborhoods. But on other occasions, sincere radical environmental positions, albeit generally derived from positions of intellectual and moral superiority, justify the opposition to the construction of infrastructure for human enjoyment of urban waterfronts.

Those most harmed by the lack of infrastructure to enjoy waterfronts are lower-income citizens, for whom it is most difficult to go to the countryside to have contact with water and nature generally, and in the city as well, their leisure-time options are scarcer. Upper-income citizens who have access to country houses, country clubs, beach vacations, and a myriad of possibilities for their leisure, often argue that waterfronts should be left "natural" and untouched. However, most waterfronts, particularly those of rivers, have long ceased to be "natural," particularly as they go through urban areas. Dams, embankments, and dredging have long made rivers into very different waterways than they were in their pristine state.

During my second term of office, we came up against opposition and lawsuits when we built paths around the wetlands in the midst of dense urban areas. A previous mayor had regulations that prohibited bikeways around wetlands, because riding a bicycle was "active recreation." He was trying to discredit pedestrian infrastructure we had created around waterfronts in my first term. Allegedly such recreation harmed the environment. It must make those who mobilize on bicycles or jog along the edge of the waters in Stanley Park in Vancouver, the Yarra River in Melbourne, or Garda Lake in Italy, and many others around the world, wonder why "active recreation" would be damaging to the environment. Indeed, some activists in Bogotá managed to secure court orders for the installation of chain-link fencing to prevent citizens from approaching the wetlands, allegedly to protect them. I believe those wetlands are better protected if it is possible for people to walk alongside them or ride a bicycle along the edges, discover and enjoy their fauna and flora and come to love them.

In both my first and second term as mayor, we made the largest investments Bogotá had ever made in the recovery of wetlands: removal of residues, removal of invasive plants, and especially the elimination of wastewater discharges by the installation of sewage pipes. But we also wanted people to enjoy the wetlands. Therefore, we made some three-meter-wide permeable concrete paths around them. The paths not only allow citizens to enjoy the wetlands but also protect them.

Hundreds of wetlands in urban zones have been filled over, reduced, or completely eliminated due to the absence of paths around them. When such paths do exist, citizens can walk or ride a bicycle around the water's edge, which prevents owners or occupants of waterfront lots or houses from surreptitiously making infills into the water to expand their land.

In Cartagena, in the Colombian Caribbean, I had visited the Ciénaga de la Virgen informal settlements many times. For decades, poor citizens had been filling in the Ciénaga, a large mangrove swamp, to build homes. Originally the Ciénaga had been much larger and lined by mangroves. Since the water is shallow, it's easy to make enclosures in the water with tightly bound, thin wooden rods, which can then gradually be filled with earth and refuse until firm ground is created and a home can be built on it. Once that home is built, occupants proceed to make another enclosure out into the water, and thus the process continues. In this ad hoc fashion, they have extended hundreds of meters of land over the water for several kilometers.

The national government was going to build a peripheral road around the Ciénaga in 2004 for mobility and to stop the advance of these neighborhoods into the water. To make the road, they were going to fill in several additional meters of swamp. I thought that that road, which did not even include sidewalks, would suit drivers from other parts of the city who would go through there next to the informal settlements, but do little for the poor residents of the sector, who at the time did not even own motorcycles. As the project was the responsibility of Minister Maria Consuelo Araújo, who had been my director of the Botanical Gardens in Bogotá, I managed to persuade the national government to make some adjustments. The infill was made much wider in order to create land for public infrastructure such as schools, kindergartens, and parks in addition to the road and to make a broad promenade for pedestrians and cyclists for several kilometers along the water's edge. Had such pedestrian infrastructure existed from the beginning, the infill of hundreds of hectares of mangrove swamp would have probably been averted.

Although the extended part of the Juan Amarillo wetlands is an artificial lake we created with bulldozers, I could not obtain authorization from the environmental authorities to allow people to use canoes on it, which was a pity, for this would have been a special and enjoyable experience for low-income citizens, many of them living in neighborhoods adjacent to the wetland. This is particularly perverse because only eighty meters to the east of the wetland is the lake of the Los Lagartos Country Club, which is part of the same large wetland, as is evident from any aerial photograph or a map. Alleged "environmentalists" prevented the use of canoes on the Juan Amarillo wetland lake, which is surrounded by popular neighborhoods. But they have never dared question that a few meters away, on a lake that is part of the very same wetland, a private country club uses motorboats and holds water-ski championships.

The History of Civilization Is Largely the History
of Drying up Marshes

Civilizations arose simultaneously with the construction of cities. One was
not possible without the other. And the emergence of both required highly
productive alluvial valley agriculture in drained swamps. Civilizations have
risen and prospered principally in fertile alluvial valleys, slowly traversed by
a meandering river. For thousands of years, in rainy seasons or with the
thaw of snow, those rivers flooded the valleys around them, which is precisely what made the areas fertile. A large part of those alluvial valleys
were unhealthy marshes, or wetlands, to use contemporary terminology,
particularly during the summer months. The history of civilization is in an
important measure the history of the drying up of marshland around rivers
in alluvial valleys.

The drying up of the swamps was almost synonymous with the rise of the
Mesopotamian cities of Uruk, Ur, Eridú, and Babylon; Rome; Tenochtitlan,
where Mexico City is located today; and hundreds of other cities. Edo, the
old Tokyo, was built on what was a large marsh that was dried out under Sho-
gun Tokugawa. Later, beginning in the nineteenth century, 25,000 hectares of
the bay were filled to extend the city. The same was true of Paris: in 52 B.C. the
Romans settled around the Cité island and called it Lutetia Parisiorum, or
"the place close to the marsh" of the Parisii tribe.[19] One of the most central
and traditional sectors of Paris today is still called "Le Marais," or the marsh.

There were once marshes where London, Paris, Cairo, Berlin, and Tokyo
are now located. As French historian Fernand Braudel writes in his splendid
book *The Mediterranean and the Mediterranean World in the Reign of
Philip II*, it took centuries of human work to dry out the marshes where
civilizations arose. Those marshes, unhealthy for humans, with stagnant
water and mosquitoes, were the source of malaria and other diseases. Early
organized societies prospered in the mountains because "plains were originally a land of stagnant waters and malaria, or zones through which the
unstable riverbeds passed. The thickly populated plains which today are the
image of prosperity were the culmination of centuries of painful collective
effort. . . . Human habitation only gradually progressed from the highlands
down to the fever-ridden flats with their stagnant pools."[20]

For example, human occupation of what was to become the very rich
lower Rhône valley began in the higher regions. "It was not until thousands
of years later that work began on the draining of the Rhône marshes in the

fifteenth century."[21] The Etruscans, the oldest inhabitants of the Toscana in Italy, settled on the higher parts of the hills. Even much later, when the valleys were drained and cultivated "around Florence, the marshes remained a threat for a long time to come."[22] Fevers extended and increased, defeating all the efforts of the Medici to develop wheat crops for export.[23]

Braudel says that those stagnant waters were the source of "the terrible swamp fevers, the scourge of the plains in the hot season."[24] Before quinine arrived in Europe with the colonization of South America, malaria was often a deadly disease, but even in its less lethal forms, it terribly weakens its victims. Braudel describes several Mediterranean towns abandoned by their inhabitants to escape the fevers that emanated from marshy areas.[25]

Contrary to what we initially suppose, most cities were built next to rivers not because of opportunities for fishing or navigation but because that was fertile land created by recurrent flooding over thousands of years. In other words, cities were built near or on wetlands. Had they not been dried out to develop highly productive agriculture, civilizations or cities would never have emerged. With the drying of swamps thus came civilization—and inequality: societies with the assets and technology to create inheritable wealth.

Western civilization comes fundamentally from the Mediterranean. Braudel describes how over centuries the valley's marshes around the Mediterranean were drained and water channeled for irrigation, transport, and urban life.[26] "Mediterranean man has always had to fight against the swamps." He describes how the drying up of marshland in lower Andalusia by the Romans was a dazzling triumph of human progress. In the early years of the Roman Empire, the entire valley of the Guadalquivir River was marshland. The success was phenomenal, and Andalusia became the heart of Roman Spain, "a garden of cities."[27] Centuries before, drained swamps around the Nile, converted into fertile land, formed the base of Egyptian civilization. That fertile Egyptian land and the land created by draining the Andalusia marshes in Spain were the mainstay of the Roman Empire, and thus largely the backbone of the rise of Western civilization.

Peter the Great built St. Petersburg in the eighteenth century on the marshes of the Neva River in the Gulf of Finland, off the Baltic Sea. Since 1703, when the city was being built, it has endured hundreds of floods. Its canals, like those in Amsterdam, Hamburg, and Bruges, were built mainly for drainage and to avoid flooding, but today they are enchanting waterfronts enjoyed by residents and tourists alike.

In the United States a good part of contemporary Manhattan, Chicago, Washington, Boston, New Orleans, and Denver was once marshland. A great part of the territory that Bogotá occupies today also flooded. For this reason the Spaniards founded the city against the foothills of the mountains, one of the few places free of the risk of flooding.

In recent times, cities or infrastructure have continued to be built over water. Between 1965, when Singapore was created, and 2015, it increased its territory from 58,000 to 71,000 hectares by importing sand from Malaysia, Cambodia, Vietnam, and Myanmar.[28] Much of Hong Kong is built on ocean infill, some quite recent. Infill islands were built for its airport and a Disney park, and several more islands are under construction. The city of Incheon and its namesake airport in South Korea were both built on coastal marshlands. In China, Pudong across the Huangpu River in Shanghai was built on marshland; 13,000 hectares were filled to build Nanhui, near Shanghai; and the huge port of Shanghai was built twenty kilometers offshore.

In contrast, in other places it has become progressively more difficult even to make a pedestrian path along the waterfront. With today's more extreme environmentalism, many of our great cities in western civilization would not have been allowed to be built.

When I discovered the rivers of Europe, I was impressed by the uniformity of their width and, in the case of larger ones, their year-round navigability. I was also surprised to learn that although they were navigable, the flow was relatively small. In Colombia, with the exception of a few that pass through cities, rivers are irregular in depth and width, and in many cases their courses divide into two or more branches, which creates islands; frequently, those branches change course. The majority of rivers overflow during rainy seasons and flood large swaths of land.

Rivers in Europe seem like roads: they have a uniform width and, although unseen, a uniform depth. They have been modified by humans for hundreds of years with dredging, dams, and embankments. In urban stretches the interventions are even more radical: some rivers have been widened, others have been narrowed. All have retaining walls in urban areas to prevent the erosion of its borders and pedestrian infrastructure in their banks to facilitate human enjoyment and to make life happier.

And almost none of those interventions would have been tolerated by today's environmental extremists in developing countries. These self-inflicted restrictions prevent our cities from being as fertile for equality and happiness as they could be.

The adaptation for human enjoyment of riverbanks in urban areas and the construction of housing and other buildings alongside the waterfront—leaving ample pedestrian space between the buildings and the water and adding green and trees as well—does not affect the water quality or damage the environment in any way. It is compatible with our respect for nature. When citizens have access to watercourses, they can appreciate them and love them, and they become activists in their defense—demanding, for example, their complete decontamination.

The billions of human beings who live in cities would have more contact with nature, would appreciate it more, enjoy it more, and look after it more with infrastructure that makes it possible for them to access their waterfronts. And to the extent that waterfronts make it attractive to live in dense cities, they help reduce energy consumption and thus global warming. Moreover, urban waterfronts are a very small fraction of rivers, lakes, and seas. In Colombia, for example, less than one-thousandth of rivers and wetlands are in urban areas. Today, urban areas do not make up even one-thousandth of the surface of the Earth.[29]

In some situations it seems that "environmental correctness" means that a city should not even be allowed to approach a waterfront, leaving wide areas of woodland or grassy fields adjacent to the waterways. Some small or even mid-size parks on waterfronts have charm and can succeed, but large ones tend to be rarely used, and even less so if they're forested. We cannot go from making cities for cars to making cities for fauna and flora more than for human beings. Cities are human habitats, and the extent to which they nurture human happiness is, before all else, the measure of their success and sustainability. If a butterfly comes to rest on a tropical anthill, voracious ants will devour it. This does not mean that the anthill is not a sustainable habitat: it means that it is a habitat for ants. A city is a habitat for humans and must be crafted for human happiness. Only 3 percent of the world's land surface is occupied by urban areas; only 0.5 percent of Colombia is occupied by urban areas. In those small bits of our planet where we humans live, human happiness should be the preeminent design criteria. Probably the best thing for nature would be for us humans not to exist. But we do exist. It would seem that one objective of urban design should be to seek the free happiness and quality-of-life equality that waterfronts afford.

Bogotá has no navigable canals like those of London, only some for rainwater drainage, but during my two terms as mayor, we decontaminated hundreds of kilometers of those canals and constructed greenways along thirty-nine kilometers. We built another forty-seven kilometers of greenways along riverbanks and wetlands.

The citizens of Bogotá have been living as far away as possible from the evil-smelling Bogotá River, which sporadically overflows its banks. Only a few low-income neighborhoods, initiated as informal settlements, were built on those banks. During my second term as mayor, we not only undertook major works to decontaminate the river; we also left designs and the funds to support a large treatment plant, the final major investment needed to clean up the river.

My purpose, however, was also to change the image citizens had of the river, from an open sewer to the axis of city life. For that, we preliminarily designed development along the meandering river's edge and a seventy-kilometer park along its banks. We managed to change the regulations that banned construction less than three hundred meters from the river. We designed a financial scheme for the riverbank urban development to pay for the work. We left detailed architectural and engineering designs for the first seven kilometers of Bogotá River City, as we called it. The scheme includes a widening of the river to make it navigable for restaurant-ships, the construction of a retaining wall, and a riverbank park with a promenade, small plazas, bikeways, and cafés, along which could be built housing with a view of the river. Bogota's River City would have buildings overlooking the river, without car roads between the buildings and the river. Unfortunately, the mayor who succeeded me blocked Bogota River City on pseudo environmental arguments, killing the possibility that its 10 million citizens and many more in the future enjoy the waterfront. Given that in Colombia urban areas occupy less than one half of 1 percent of the territory, it is sad that urban designs are not made for citizens to have as happy a life as possible. I hope that this project will be resurrected and materialize over the next decades and extend onto the other bank of the river that belongs to other municipalities, as well as to the north and south, also belonging to other municipalities. In this way the river, which people avoided in the past, will becomes a source of quality of life, value, and social integration and inclusion—a backbone of Bogotá's future.

*   *   *

Waterfronts with human infrastructure are one of those public spaces of exceptional beauty and charm, capable of attracting even high-income citizens. Hence they help create the essence of a good city: the meeting as equals of citizens of all conditions. They help construct inclusion and equity. Not to take advantage of them is to miss an opportunity to create a more egalitarian and happier city.

Cities such as New York, Paris, and Melbourne take advantage of waterfronts for human enjoyment, with promenades, paths, and bikeways. In many cases they have complementary attractions, such as the sports facilities along the Hudson and East Rivers in New York; swimming pools on the rocky coast in Sydney; and the large chessboard on the ground in the Corniche promenade in Beirut.

Lagos in Nigeria, Jakarta in Indonesia, Tumaco in Colombia, and many other cities in Asia, Africa, and Latin America are home to millions of low-income citizens who live in overcrowded conditions along the banks and shores of contaminated rivers, lakes, and seas, in precarious housing, much of which floods recurrently. These are dense urban agglomerations, usually illegal, furrowed by narrow streets or alleys and sometimes canals. They almost always lack one or more essential public services, such as electricity, drinking water, or sewerage. With time, the settlements will be formalized, the works required to prevent them from flooding will be undertaken, and the infrastructure and public services missing today will be provided. Therefore, we have opportunities to build quality waterfront pedestrian infrastructure in those settlements, even in the early stages of their improvement. Although such infrastructure is not as essential as other needs, it can build self-esteem, a sense of belonging, and quality of life. It may even attract visitors from other parts of the city, generating business and pride.

CHAPTER 12

Parks Are Critical for a Democratic City

"What you are doing in Japón Park is terrible!" a young man yelled at me when we were inaugurating a new building for his school in one of the poorest neighborhoods of Bogotá. I was surprised that he was more interested in a small park of half a hectare in a high-income neighborhood at the other end of the city than in the impressive new buildings of his school.

That this young man should have been aware of a problem, which was not a problem, and that he should have taken up the position of a group of wealthy, classist people, was ironic and almost tragic. Because what some influential neighbors of the Japón Park wanted when they opposed our intervention there was precisely to keep low-income people like him away from the neighborhood.

Frequently, upper-class citizens and politicians with opportunistic motivations in tacit alliances, aided by a media often controlled by them, are able to persuade lower-income citizens to support positions against their own self-interest. With the proliferation of social networks and the lies they often and systematically spread, the possibility to mislead large numbers of citizens has grown exponentially.

When I decided to put a small soccer field with synthetic grass, a playground, paths, and some gym equipment in a park in a sector where some of the wealthiest and most powerful people in the country live, I knew that I'd come up against powerful opposition. But I wanted to make it a model for many similar parks in high-income neighborhoods. Higher-income citizens never like the idea of lower-income citizens passing through their neighborhoods, much less going to their neighborhood park. And they're afraid that a park with recreational infrastructure might attract such citizens.

Therefore, practically the only design criterion for parks in higher-income sectors in the north of Bogotá has been to do everything possible to prevent low-income citizens from visiting them. In some cases these citizens have installed railings and other illegal enclosures. They have removed the occasional goalpost when they see with horror that it attracts low-income soccer players, such as workers from nearby construction sites. On several occasions they have brought in truckloads of earth to create mounds of grass that make playing soccer impossible. But more than anything, they have planted trees in every available space. This has prevented soccer playing and spaces that the sun might reach, both of which might attract those they wish to keep away.

They have not considered, apparently, that these dark, cold parks they have created, where the shade of trees does not allow even grass to grow, not only discourage low-income people from enjoying them but also hampers their own enjoyment. Therefore, such parks do not contribute either to the integration of neighbors or the construction of community. For this reason, and because they are so dark, they often foster crime.

Japón Park became a national issue. It quickly acquired notoriety, and everything related to this little park illustrates the unequal and class-ridden problems of our society in Bogotá and Colombia, and the degree to which powerful elements in society can exert pressure and influence some of our institutions.

When we began to make it known that we intended to improve the park, which up to that time only had a couple of narrow paths in poor condition and some precarious night lighting, I received a note or, rather, an order from a feature writer, a member of the elite, saying that we should in no way intervene in that park. His family had owned the all-powerful *El Tiempo* newspaper, which had for generations, even after the arrival of television, unmade ministers and made presidents as well as a nice profit. One of his great-uncles and his brother had been presidents of Colombia. Ironically, his columns always reflected a left-wing attitude, and indeed, when his brother was president, he helped him advance peace with FARC guerrillas who had laid waste to Colombian rural areas for decades. But he found intolerable a small soccer field in his own neighborhood that might attract workers from nearby construction projects and employees from nearby businesses.

Before I became mayor of Bogotá, I lived near the park and worked in an office with a window that overlooked it. I noticed that almost nobody went there, even though it was sited in a dense residential area. It was dark and cold due to the excessive number of trees and conveyed a feeling of insecurity, although there was a police post there.

As often happens with classist attitudes that seek to exclude others with lower incomes, enemies of our Japón Park project appealed to faux "environmental" arguments. The project called for the felling of six of the ninety-eight trees and the replanting of three more. None of the trees was particularly large or beautiful, but objectors called this "tree homicide." It didn't matter that we were going to plant ten new native trees. At meetings about the project, neighbors kept repeating, with great generosity, that the park money would be better spent in poorer sectors of the city, which needed it more. One well-known woman even said on one occasion, expressing the feelings of the others, "We don't need parks; we go to our country club."

The influential neighbors in opposition managed to have the media—owned by their friends and staffed by journalist friends of theirs—to foment a relentless, months-long, nationwide scandal around the park. Institutions of the Colombian state, which one would have thought might have had more important things to do, began investigations. Among other things, they alleged that "there has not been adequate management of the birds, mammals, insects and reptiles, in a way that they should find new and better conditions of habitat."[1] In that small park in the middle of the city, there were neither mammals (except dogs that neighbors took out for a walk) nor, as far as I know, reptiles. We didn't understand either what the lofty institution meant by "adequate management," required so that insects affected by the cutting down of six trees would find "new and better conditions of habitat." When work began, a court issued an order with no justification that trees should not be cut down, which delayed the project.

Simultaneously, some three thousand trees were being cut down in the median of a major road to widen it. None of the "environmentalists," journalists, politicians, or institutions that were so consternated about the six trees to be felled in Japón Park said a word about that. The institution that was so concerned about the insects kept silent as well.

I love trees, and I know a bit about those in the region around Bogotá. From my mother, who had a nursery and designed gardens, I learned to love plants and trees. I planted more trees in Bogotá than any other mayor. When I arrived for my first term of office, there was not even an entity responsible for the planting and upkeep of trees in the city. I assigned the task to the Botanical Gardens and strengthened it for the task so that it could do it effectively.

That said, trees in public space must be well selected and well located so that they attract birds and insects and also make the park beautiful and attractive to humans. Extreme defenders of any and all trees, regardless of their size, species, or state of health, probably forget that the building where they live, the place where they work, and the streets on which they move were once all woodland. And their home furniture probably contains some illegally logged tropical hardwood. In the city and even in its parks, it's sometimes necessary to cut down some trees to build schools, roads, homes, playgrounds, sports facilities, or a path. And naturally, just as we fell some trees, we plant others.

In the case of the Japón Park and other projects so passionately opposed, once the park was finished, the consensus was that the result notably improved the sector and its residents' lives. Most of those who had objected admitted as much. One well-known journalist who had radically opposed the Japón Park said afterward, "I am now happy to take my niece to the park."

Parks were born in Liverpool. In 1843 the Council of Birkenhead in metropolitan Liverpool was concerned about urban expansion and the lack of space for people to engage in leisure activities, and so, for the first time in history, they decided to buy land to make a public park. The land was partially marshy, with a small house on it where beer was sold, dogfights held, and illegal gambling occurred. It was on the outskirts of the town but sufficiently close to be walkable. The land was bought cheaply because it was not very productive, and the Birkenhead Council did exactly what governments of many growing developing cities could do today. They made fifty of the seventy-four hectares into a park and sold the other twenty-four for development. With that, they recovered both the cost of the land and of the park's construction.[2]

Alexander Garvin describes how in 1850 a twenty-eight-year-old journalist in the United States, after visiting the recently inaugurated park in Birkenhead, wrote "all this magnificent pleasure-ground is entirely, unreservedly, and for ever the people's own. The poorest British peasant is as free to enjoy it in all its parts as the British queen."[3] The young man who wrote that was Frederick Law Olmsted, for whom the role of parks in the construction of equality became supremely important.

In 1858 Olmsted and Calvert Vaux won a competition for the design of the 341-hectare Central Park, which Mayor Ambrose Kingsland—elected in 1851 and the park's true father—had promoted. Although most of the properties where the park was to be located were rural, hundreds of people had houses there. To procure the park's terrain, New York's City Hall not only acquired land that was sold to it voluntarily but also used expropriation. In 1855, New York City had a population of 629,000,[4] less than hundreds of cities in the developing world today, and per capita income in the United States was also lower than that of many developing countries today. Sadly, not many parks have been made in the developing world's cities in the last fifty years on a scale similar to Central Park, or even to Birkenhead.

It is difficult to imagine an investment that increases a society's happiness for hundreds or thousands of years into the future as much as a park. The creation of large parks, more than a matter of funding, is a matter of political decision-making and planning. Only a small fraction of the public budget is needed to acquire properties for large parks in the expansion zones of cities, and there are mechanisms that make it possible to generate them almost free of cost.[5]

Engineers have established the optimal maximum distance between streetlights or sewer inspection pits. But only rarely do regulations establish the maximum distance of a home from a park. However, it's an important matter, perhaps to be consecrated even at the constitutional level, for a society to decide its children's proximity to parks. Studies have found that people are prepared to walk only five hundred meters or less to reach a neighborhood park.[6] So regulations could only allow homebuilding when there is a park of a certain size closer than that distance. Although it is not the same, some cities have defined minimum targets for green spaces per capita.[7]

Just as access to waterfronts is a democratic right, so too is access to nature in other urban spaces. Not everyone can have a home close to a waterfront, but if the city is well made, all citizens can live near a park.

Even a small, well-lit sports field transforms a neighborhood and improves security. What does a young man of fifteen or sixteen do on a Wednesday night in a popular neighborhood in a developing city? Probably he has nothing to do. And what does he do on Thursday, Friday, or Saturday night? It's possible that he will channel his energy, restlessness, creativity, and need for adventure into consuming alcohol or drugs, or even into some criminal activity, perhaps at least something like hurling bricks at windows. Even a small basketball court or synthetic turf micro soccer field transforms a neighborhood. When these facilities have lighting, they are always used until late at night. Criminologist John Roman writes, "The recipe for violence in any city in the world is dense clusters of young men with nothing to do."[8] Young people playing sports improves the security of the surroundings; furthermore, their presence stimulates neighbors to come out into public space, which improves it as well. If the fields have small stands for spectators so that friends, neighbors, and passersby can stop to watch, it becomes a consolidated community space.

But the parks need to have infrastructure for their enjoyment, such as hard-surfaced paths, benches, small plazas, sports fields, and lighting, and they must be well kept. Often during my 2015 mayoral campaign, people would ask me to close off their nearby park. Neighbors preferred not to have a park; they would rather have the dark, dangerous, abandoned space that in many cases had never been more than an empty lot.[9] In our four-year term, we made an investment in parks several times larger than any previous mayor.[10] We not only concentrated such investment in lower-income communities but also in those with severe crime problems. Led by the formidable executive Orlando Molano, head of parks and recreation, we illuminated thousands of parks, and in more than 1,400 we created playgrounds, gyms, and sports facilities, all of which attracted communities in droves. Especially impactful were 169 illuminated soccer fields. A study by Andes University found that in an area of 200 meters around synthetic turf pitches, there was an 88 percent reduction in robberies and a 92 percent reduction in shop burglaries.[11] Well-designed and well-maintained parks and sports facilities construct community and the sense of belonging. Neighbors come together and get to know each other in local parks. This appropriation of the territory drives away criminals and improves the perception of security.[12]

In my second term as mayor, young skateboarders were nonconformists and rebels almost by definition. Although they were often exceptional athletes, they did not adapt to traditional sports and even less so to team sports. With their tattoos, piercings, and clothes, they tended to reject the "establishment," which of course included me. In 2016, when I became mayor for a second time, Bogotá only had three small and very basic skate parks. We built ten quality ones, several of them large and according to international standards. And we located all of them in visible places, where passersby could admire the young skaters' skills. My objective was to ensure that they would feel respected and part of society. I believe that to a large extent we achieved this objective. For example, they took the initiative to help us identify drug dealers who loitered around their skate parks and asked us to expel them from the area, which of course we did. Now the city is more theirs—and they are more of the city.

The "Butterflies Path"

Even people who aren't in maximally good shape should be able to access and walk along paths in cities that have mountains. The eastern side of Bogotá is flanked by beautiful, forested mountains that have ferns, mosses, bromeliads, orchids, hummingbirds, lizards, and butterflies. Dozens of clear streams descend musically down through clefts between mountainsides. It is the nature park *par excellence* for Bogotá's residents. It would make life happier for millions to be able to walk through those mountains, but they are all but inaccessible. There are few footpaths, and some high-income citizens have found ways to close off some of those where access is through their neighborhoods, or they have managed to persuade environmental authorities to severely restrict access.

We designed a 111-kilometer path to run along the mountains for the entire length of the city. From beautiful spots on the mountains, people would be able to enjoy spectacular views of the city below. Young people from popular sectors would be able to organize nature hikes with their friends. Citizens would learn of the geography, fauna, and flora of their mountains; appreciate them more; come to love them; and have a greater sense of belonging to their city. This "Butterflies Path" (Sendero de las Mariposas), as we called it, would be one of those exceptional places in a good city—so appealing that even high-income citizens couldn't resist visiting. It would be a potent contributor to inclusion and equality and happiness. Studies have found that physical activity in natural environments reduces feelings of sadness, anger, or mental fatigue more effectively than in synthetic environments.[13]

We had the project all ready, with designs and funding, but environmental authorities were discreetly but effectively persuaded by some influential people to delay it. Some of the objectors were high-income citizens living on the edges of those mountains who did not want citizens from other sectors passing through their neighborhoods to reach mountain pathways. Others were environmentalists who, as in the case of the wetland's edges, argued that it was essential to protect these natural urban environments from human beings—except, of course, themselves. Their attitude could be called "environmental elitism." The rest of the opposition consisted of opportunistic politicians who would have opposed any project of ours. Environmental authorities invented obstacles and delays until our term came to an end.

In Colombia there are thousands of kilometers of mountainsides similar to those of Bogotá with the same climate, fauna, and vegetation. Mountains in other regions are in an even more pristine state because a significant part of the woodland in the mountains alongside Bogotá have already been felled or lost to forest fires and were replaced by imported species such as pine and eucalyptus. The eighty kilometers that frame the city can be protected and also used by the millions who live there today and the hundreds of millions who will live there in the future, so that they can enjoy lives that are physically and spiritually healthier and happier.

Had the project not been a three-meter-wide path but yet another road like many that continue to get cut through Colombia's mountains and jungles, forces such as those that obstructed the Butterflies Path in the Bogotá mountains wouldn't have stood a chance. But in the city, those interested in excluding others from public spaces that they consider their own are powerful. And citizens who would benefit from parks such as the Butterflies Path have no way of challenging state institutions that serve those who wish to exclude them. Likewise, in Colombia, tens of thousands of hectares of virgin forest are destroyed annually to plant coca or for cattle raising or illegal mining. Most of those who draw on environmental arguments to prevent the construction of infrastructure for the human enjoyment of mountains or waterfronts in the city do nothing to prevent the massive jungle deforestation. They rather prefer the visibility, political intrigue, comfort, and security of urban activism.

What is environmentally sound in the cities is not that nature should be as it was before the appearance of human beings—pristine and entirely focused on wildlife. It's not to try to return mountains, wetlands, rivers, parks, and waterfronts to their primeval state because urban areas and their surroundings have altered this environment for hundreds and even thousands of years. Rather, the goal is to make infrastructure that advances quality-of-life equality. Cities are a human habitat, and we human beings are also part of nature.

It is difficult not only to make parks but to protect them. The commonest threat is the construction of buildings and other infrastructure, putatively so meritorious as to justify their location in parkland. This includes museums, roads, universities, and public buildings. There have been hundreds of proposals for buildings in Central Park for such praiseworthy purposes that they supposedly justify their location there.

Undeveloped parkland is especially vulnerable. A mayor built housing on property that in my first term of office we had purchased for a park.[14]

When I took office, I discovered that a mayor a few years before had handed over three large properties in the Simón Bolívar Park to the city's professional soccer teams and the Colombian Soccer Federation. This amazed me since Simón Bolívar Park is Bogotá's most important one. The land was handed over for the teams to make private clubs and the Soccer Federation to set up its headquarters for its bureaucrats and allegedly for the Colombian national team for the brief periods when it comes together to train, since most players are elsewhere in the world most of the time.

Although that part of the park had not yet been developed, it was part of the most central and important park in the city. It would be unimaginable that part of New York's Central Park, or any important park in an advanced city, should be given to professional sports teams for their exclusive use. That nobody objected to such an absurdity illustrates how little citizens valued parks at the time. Luckily, when I arrived in office, they had not yet built anything on that land. Through a politically and legally difficult process, we managed to recover the properties for the city.

On one of them, we built the Virgilio Barco Library and a thirteen-hectare park around it. We didn't manage to do anything with the other two plots during these three short years of my first term, which cost our citizens dearly: a subsequent administration returned one of the plots to the Soccer Federation, which built some soccer fields, a hotel, and offices for senior bureaucrats of the soccer world. And they surrounded the area with a fence.[15] Nobody stopped to think that the federation could have built those installations on the city's outskirts and not on land of the city's main park. Nobody objected to the loss of almost five hectares of the city's main park.

Should Private Urban Golf Courses Become Public Parks?

Curiously, in Bogotá, higher-income sectors have fewer parks than many popular ones. There are a few private country clubs with golf courses, which from the air look like green islands in the middle of a dense sea of buildings. When during my first term I publicly said that the Bogotá Country Club, the most exclusive of them, should become a public park, my words sent an electric shock rippling through most powerful sectors of our unequal and backward society. They had never imagined that someone would dare to challenge their lofty redoubt: business leaders, former presidents of Colombia, chief executives of major companies, and media owners were among its 1,500 members. Of course, there were a good many rather unproductive heirs in the club as well.

Former world tennis champion Andre Agassi was once in Bogotá and was invited to the country club. When he arrived, he said, surprised, "Incredible, a golf course in the middle of the city!"[16] With two golf courses and covering more than a hundred hectares, the club is located in a densely populated area with an acute scarcity of parkland. Hundreds of local people used to jog in the early mornings in the parking lot of a nearby shopping center.

That the mayor of Bogotá in 1999 should publicly say that the land of that country club should be turned into a public park was as outlandish as the mayor of London or Paris in 1700 claiming that the Royal Gardens should be so. When I announced that we would start the expropriation of the polo field, a group of members invited me to the club to talk about it. They received me with whiskey glass in hand and an air of sufficiency and condescension, self-assured that I would not dare to do anything against their collective will. I suppose they felt reassured when a few days later I accepted a dinner invitation from a former president of Colombia. He naturally was also a member of the club and the son of another former president and wanted to persuade me that it was not worth challenging the establishment in this way. The members of the club, from which the country had largely been governed in the previous hundred years, perhaps thought my proposal was an innocuous mayoral populist gimmick.[17]

Not so. My purpose was neither to offend nor to fight, and much less to make a conflict visible; it was simply to obtain public space to improve citizens' lives. I had fought a number of difficult battles for pedestrian public space, and it didn't matter whether the usurpers were wealthy aristocrats or lower-income citizens. We removed upper-income citizens' cars parked on sidewalks. We recovered sidewalks and plazas that had been taken over for many years by street vendors. We demolished the Cartucho, the twenty-three-hectare area in the center of the city held for decades by drug traffickers, and created the Tercer Milenio Park there. Moreover, there was nothing populist about the expropriation of the club's polo fields because the vast majority of people didn't know of the existence of the club, much less of its exclusivity and symbolism. The matter only interested the highest-income sectors, who understood its implications fully. I had nothing at all against club members, either: several were my friends, and some even contributed to my political activities. I was and am simply convinced that creating a park out of dozens of hectares of that site would make Bogotá a better city and millions of people happier now and in the future. And the eight-hectare polo field was a start.

Club members were not the only opponents. Organized residents in some nearby neighborhoods also opposed the park vehemently. Although only a few of them were club members, they felt its proximity improved their status. And they felt the arrival of low-income citizens to an eventual park would cause the area to deteriorate and properties to lose value. The mere thought that low-income citizens might be walking in a street close to them made them shudder. Besides being classist, such fears are unfounded. Experience worldwide shows that large parks improve their surroundings and increase their value. And, of course, for neighbors without access to the club, the park improves their lives.

In this case, as in many others, the battles I faced to make a more egalitarian and happier city were lonely ones. Those who perceive that a project is going to affect them negatively, and those who think it might be politically profitable to oppose it, fight it: they fight it politically, legally, and in the media, appealing to lies, calumny, and whatever else they consider useful. But those who will benefit by the projects stand aside impassively; some of them are even manipulated to join the opposition.

It is elementary democracy: if the public good is to prevail over private interests, then golf courses in the middle of the urban areas where there are no parks of a similar size should become parks. Fewer than four hundred golfers can use a course in a day, even starting at dawn and ending at dusk. As a public park, the same land could accommodate up to a hundred thousand visitors on any weekend.

For one of the work meetings we had with municipal employees in Villanueva, an adjacent municipality to Guatemala City, the mayor rented the premises of the Mayan Golf Club on a Monday, when it was closed to members. On a terrace with a view, employees who had never been in a place like this before couldn't stop taking photographs, amazed at the spectacular landscape of the golf course. Normally, they had no access to this exclusive space. Why is it so difficult for cities to offer parks similar to golf courses for their citizens—spaces with paths to push a grandfather's wheelchair or the baby carriage or to jog or ride a bike?

Although the symbolism of converting exclusive spaces such as clubs into parks is attractive, that is not the rationale for doing it. It is simply a matter of generating quality public space and sports facilities to increase the happiness of citizens. Would it even be imaginable that New York's Central Park instead of being a park open to all citizens were an exclusive private golf club? That is exactly what happens in many cities, particularly in the developing world: the only large, green oases in densely populated areas are not public parks but private clubs.

Haussmann wrote in his memoir that Emperor Napoleon III told him, "Do not miss an opportunity to build in all arrondissements of Paris the greatest number of squares, in order to offer Parisians, as they have in London, places for relaxation and recreation for all the families and all the children, rich and poor."[18] In developing cities the governing or dominant classes have reserved large amounts of land for private clubs but nothing equivalent for public parks and sporting facilities. We can say that clubs were how these unequal societies reserved land for public parks. They did the most difficult part, which was to preserve and protect that land. Now, it's the turn of democratic institutions to do the simple thing, which is to turn them into public parks. Although it took the French Revolution to let all citizens into the Versailles Gardens, the former exclusive hunting grounds and gardens of kings and nobles, such as Hyde Park in London, Luxembourg Gardens in Paris, and Boboli Gardens of the Medicis in Florence, became public parks without bloodletting.

Kings' ownership of their castles and gardens was as legitimate as clubs' land ownership is to their members today, particularly in developing societies. I am not suggesting, obviously, that club members should be sent to the guillotine but simply that the state should acquire those properties for the values at which they are registered today and based on which they pay property tax.

The voluntary or forcible acquisition of clubs or other private lands to create parks is nothing new. In Panama, President Omar Torrijos expropriated the Club de Golf in 1973 and turned it into the Parque Omar, as it came to be called, some years later. Of course, that caused resentment among members who enjoyed having a golf course in the middle of the city. Jaime Alemán, who was Panama's ambassador in Washington, told me that he practically grew up in that club where his father was president for a few years. "I think that with the passage of time," he said, "we have all understood the government's decision to use that land as a park for the common good was correct, as that is the only green area of an important size in the middle of the city."[19] Today Parque Omar is enjoyed by tens of thousands of citizens and adds much value to nearby buildings. Some middle-class houses adjoining the club have been replaced by apartment blocks. The park is used by citizens of all socioeconomic levels.

In Bangkok, the golf course that belonged to the Thailand State Railways was converted into Rot Fai Park.[20] Today, people walk, jog, ride bicycles, skate, play soccer or basketball, and row on the lake there. Private and public golf courses in many other cities have been turned into parks. Unfortunately, the most frequent occurrence is for clubs, after having enjoyed tax benefits as alleged green reserves, to sell their golf course land at a huge profit to be urbanized. With the proceeds of that operation, they have acquired more land in less central places to build better premises there. And there are many clubs, naturally, that are still functioning in urban and suburban areas, most enjoying tax benefits that allow them to pay less tax per square meter than other properties in the same sector.

Two left-wing presidents of Venezuela, Hugo Chávez and Nicolás Maduro, expropriated businesses and took other statizing measures characteristic of the twentieth-century left that were disastrous for efficiency and competitiveness and useless for equality. But they didn't dare touch the Caracas Country Club, which could have been converted into a splendid public park. They could also have transformed into a park the very central La Carlota Airport, used only by private business jets—and those of senior officers of the armed forces, whose support was crucial for the presidents to remain in power. They preferred to maintain the privileges of a micro-elite to land their aircraft in the middle of the city to an increase in the collective happiness that the land as a park would have yielded. The picturesque revolutionary leaders of the Venezuelan left, with quasi-dictatorial powers, were incapable of doing what Mayor Daley did, in a democracy, with the Meigs Field Airport in the capitalist city of Chicago.

The members of the Bogotá Country Club and their counterparts in cities around the world are mostly good citizens: they and their families have worked productively for their societies for generations. The conversion of their club into a park is not a punishment, just as it's not a punishment to purchase property from other citizens to build a road or an airport through voluntary sales or expropriation when necessary. It is a quite common practice and doesn't draw anyone's attention. I remember the sad case of Jaime Zambrano, aged seventy-six, whose home was purchased to widen a road to accommodate the TransMilenio bus system. The building was his residence and his source of income because he had a bakery there where he served meals morning, noon, and night. This was a neighborhood meeting place, and Jaime, who was always friendly and enjoyed a chat, was known and loved by all. No price or indemnity could compensate him for the simultaneous demolition of his building, his business, and his social relationships, built up over a lifetime. The building was the center of his life, but it was necessary to buy it from him to widen the road.

If societies are prepared to demolish homes or even whole districts, even at such profound human costs, when it's deemed essential for the public good to build a road, then what is so surprising about the idea of converting exclusive clubs into public parks? Can it be that we are ready to acquire humble citizens' properties to build infrastructure that has the support of higher-income citizens, but much less so to acquire property belonging to high-income citizens for projects that especially benefit humbler citizens?

Country clubs almost always enjoy lower levels of property tax than other properties in the sector because they are "green reserves, not available for development," "lungs," or something of that kind. It could be said that the state has already paid for the clubs' land through its foregone taxes. In any event, the low value at which clubs are officially appraised should make it easier for the state to acquire them at a low cost. Indeed, it can do so at no cost at all if after acquiring the club land it secures a change of use, for example for 20 percent of it. The state can then sell that 20 percent of the land and use the profits to pay for the rest of the property. Or it can buy 80 percent of the land of the golf course without paying a cent, paying members with a change-of-use for the 20 percent of the property remaining in their hands so that they can erect, for example, tower blocks around the new park.

The Country Park, which is what we called the one we made from the land of the country club's former polo fields, has now been open to the public for years. However, the legal pirouettes, to euphemize, used by country club directors have prevented the city administration from completing payment to the club. Meanwhile, the city has initiated and completed thousands of processes of voluntary and forcible acquisitions of properties for roads and other public purposes. In developing societies there is one law for ordinary citizens and another for elites.

By delaying City Hall payment for the Country Park land and looking for a better price for its polo fields, the club may have been digging its own grave because the value of the rest of the club has increased, and that in turn has increased its property taxes. Those taxes will continue to increase until club members themselves are forced to create a single, large park in exchange for being able to urbanize a small percentage of that land.

Even in wealthy Los Angeles, almost all the green space one sees from the air are golf clubs, not parks. Malcolm Gladwell describes the case of the Brentwood Country Club in western Los Angeles, where there is not a single park of anything like the club's size nearby.[21] Gladwell observes that citizens jog along a narrow dirt path next to the fence around the golf course and that there are many more people jogging than playing golf. A rule in the California State Constitution, probably designed to avoid forcing elderly residents to leave their homes due to gentrification and increased taxation, prevents the valuation of properties to be adjusted absent a change of owner. Gladwell tells how influential club members have been able to get a preposterous and favorable interpretation of the norm, even though naturally membership is periodically renewed. Therefore, they only pay a fraction of the taxes that they would have to pay if the value of the club's land were periodically updated. As this example makes clear, abuse of power by the wealthy is not exclusive to developing societies. Gladwell suggests that in exchange for the tax benefits golf clubs usually enjoy, they should not be allowed to have enclosures and that everyone should be allowed to enjoy them as parks in the afternoons or a couple of days a week. He recalls how the aristocratic birthplace of golf, the Royal and Ancient Club of St. Andrews, in Scotland, is open to everyone on Sundays.

Of course, green spaces or the countryside are farther out of reach for lower-income citizens in developing cities than in Los Angeles. The park shortage is also more critical in developing cities, and the contrast between an exclusive, immaculate golf course and the rest of the city is more dramatic. In the enormous Kibera slum in Nairobi, one million people live in some of the worst overcrowding in the world, with a density above two thousand inhabitants per hectare. Anyone who looks at Kibera on Google Earth may be surprised to discover that one of the adjacent properties is a golf club, with an area roughly equal to one-fifth the size of the slum. If that basic principle of democracy were to be complied with, that public good prevails over private interest, then the golf course would be converted into a park. For a child who lives in the brutal and overcrowded mud of Kibera, access to beautifully landscaped green space might feel like entering a paradise and would improve the lives even of middle-income citizens who live in sectors devoid of parks.

Country clubs are pleasant places to meet friends and to practice sports. They also have premises for weddings, parties, and other events and social rites.

They provide valuable services to the community of their members. But their organization and regulations are anachronistic, exclusionary, and classist. By definition they exclude "undesirables" in terms of social origin, nationality, and religion. I'm also disturbed by how the children of members are served by uniformed waiters and then simply sign a chit of paper to pay for anything they consume.

Even the ostensibly less exclusive clubs are not in fact so. I joined one of these clubs, consciously choosing it because it wouldn't connote social selectivity, simply to facilitate my children's sports. When I watched my son play soccer, I sometimes treated the young boys who worked as golf caddies to a soft drink while they waited to be called up by players. One day, much to my surprise, the man in charge of the golf course coffee shop told me that he had been told by his superiors to remind me that I couldn't buy food or refreshments for the caddies, even if they consumed them outside on the grass! The club rules said that they could only consume things bought at a stand for caddies, which was some distance away and out of sight of the members.

Clubs have a plethora of rules that seem to have been inspired by the court of Louis XVI. Nannies or domestic employees who have had as much to do with children's upbringing as parents, if not more, are not authorized to enter a swimming pool with the children or even to go to the clubs' restaurants or cafeterias. Neither they nor drivers nor club employees may use the sports facilities, not even on Mondays when the club is closed to its members. Clubs do the opposite of parks and public space: they exacerbate inequality and exclusion. I find no justification for the tax exemptions or benefits clubs enjoy, which are mostly based on the argument that they preserve green spaces.

The exclusionary rules of clubs are nothing exceptional, of course. Symbols and rituals to mark class difference, however subtle, are found in every society. For example, in developing countries, where children from middle- and upper-class homes go to private schools, school uniforms become powerful symbols of status and a means of social differentiation. There are even status differences among public schools, which are also reinforced by uniforms.[22] One powerful means of inclusion would be that all children in the city should have the same uniform regardless of which school they go to and independently of whether it is public or private. This would also mean that adults would relate to any child as if they occupied their social class or as if they were their own children or grandchildren.

In Latin America people kiss each other in greeting almost from the moment they're introduced, but that social kiss of greeting is only bestowed on those who are perceived to be of a similar socioeconomic standing. The greeting kiss, or lack thereof, marks social differences and exclusion. Middle- and upper-income individuals who have only just met kiss if they consider that the person they are greeting is of a similar social status. But they rarely kiss a domestic servant, even if she has been working with them for ten years, has looked after their children, and is practically part of the family. The same often applies to their secretary.

The Conversion of Public Parks into Private Gardens

The sky was cloudless and blue, and from the windows of the mayor's office, I had a particularly sharp view of the green mountains that frame Bogotá's eastern border. I was in my third year as mayor, public opinion had turned in my favor, and I wasn't anticipating any problems. Then I received a call that began a nightmare: in the Luna Park neighborhood, two people had lost their lives during the demolition of a wall put up by some neighbors to privatize a public park. The terrible accident had been broadcast live on television.

Neighbors who opposed the demolition had crowded around the backhoe that was to demolish the wall. Some of them had climbed onto the wall. After some hours, since the neighbors didn't retreat, the city officials responsible for the operation decided to take a piece out of the wall where there were no people. But accidentally, the backhoe operator did not take just a bite out of the wall but pulled down a large section of it, and it fell, killing two people. It was a tragedy.

The Luna Park process hadn't even been initiated by the city administration. The principal of a public school in the sector, who wanted students to have access to the park, had sued to have it demolished. The courts had decided in the school's favor and ordered that the wall be taken down and public space opened to all. But in the eyes of the citizenry, and as narrated by an irresponsible press, this was akin to a murder committed by the mayor. "For the mayor, public space is more important than human life," they said, because any recovery of public space was associated with my name. The appropriation of public space by individuals in many ways, including the enclosure of public parks such as Luna, was an issue that mayors had avoided for decades. It had never been an issue, but I had made it a priority.

Among the many battles to recover privatized public space from street vendors, parked cars, and other colonizers, there was the recovery of public parks illegally appropriated by neighbors who, in many parts of the city, particularly in high-income sectors, fenced them to keep others out.[23] The most common case was that of developers who deceived home buyers in gated communities, telling them that the park within the wall belonged to the condominium, when in fact it was a public park that had been illegally enclosed. In other cases, neighbors, who lived in neighborhoods that were not enclosed developments, would fence off public parks in the sector to make them de facto private gardens. Naturally, they paid no property tax for this land they stole. Hundreds of hectares of public parks had been "privatized" in these ways, and many remain so today.

There are those who argue that fencing off parks is necessary for security reasons. The reality is that these residents want to exclude undesirables, which means lower-income people, just as much if not more than they are concerned about security. But even when a safety problem does exist, there is no justification for the theft of public space. Nobody would think of appropriating a neighbor's garden. Why should we be so tolerant of the appropriation of a public garden?

Greenwich, Connecticut, north of New York City, is an iconic residential area for the white, Anglo-Saxon, Protestant wealthy of the United States. The municipality had taken over a beautiful promontory of public land along the coast of the Long Island Sound, where they had a sort of private beach club exclusively for Greenwich residents: Greenwich Point Park, covering almost sixty hectares. In 1998 a judge ruled that the land was a public park and could not be enclosed.

The local inhabitants were forced to accede to the court order. But the powerful local community, in the best "banana republic" style, made a mockery of it. They started to demand that before nonresidents entered the park, they should have to go to the mayor's office to buy an access permit. And they set parking fees for nonresidents at absurdly high levels. The little boats and other resources of the club-park were unavailable to nonresidents. In Greenwich there are no security problems. Their residents want to privatize the park so that few people will go there, and although they probably would not admit it, to exclude Latinos, African Americans, and low-income citizens whose company they find distasteful.

Parks are for many things: walking, playing, and contact with nature. But even more than that, they are places for feeling equality and inclusion. No doubt most of the Greenwich residents who designed all of these machinations to exclude lower-income undesirables from their municipality's public park want the lot of the poor to improve. Many are liberal politically. They attend religious services in which they pray for humanity. They give alms and probably make donations to charitable causes. And in the abstract, they are even in agreement with the statement "all human beings are born free and equal in dignity and rights, and . . . shall conduct themselves fraternally with each other," taken from Article 1 of the Universal Declaration of Human Rights.[24] But having lower-income intruders in their park is just a bit too much.

During my two periods as mayor, we managed to remove illegal enclosures from dozens of parks in Bogotá, with a greater or lesser degree of conflict and always at some political cost. As in most other efforts to construct inclusion, those who benefited—those who began to enjoy the park from which they had been previously excluded—barely noticed, if at all, the difficulties of the battle. But I incurred a political cost: those who were adversely affected never forgave me. Let us suppose that in ten years an illegal park fence stops just one person from entering a park, for example, the daughter of a domestic employee who works in a house in a nearby neighborhood. A democracy cannot allow that to happen. The girl has the same right to use the park as any resident in the adjacent buildings.

In some cases, opening up parks has an immediate benefit in terms of social integration. The Casablanca Park in Bogotá was an abandoned lot— dark and dangerous, located between a high-income and a low-income neighborhood. Part of it had been illegally appropriated by the high-income neighborhood, which had enclosed it and built a tennis court and some well-kept lawns. Although the ground sloped steeply, we managed to make a beautiful park with games for children that took advantage of the tiered terrain and created well-lit sports fields. To the newly built park we added the recovered land and the tennis court, taking away the high-income neighbors' fence. Contrary to what those who opposed the fence removal had feared, security not only did not deteriorate but improved. And children from neighborhoods on both sides of the park play together.

A Successful Park Is One People Want to Visit

One day when I was walking on the mountainside of one of the poorest informal settlements in Bogotá, I came across something that surprised me: while houses were clinging precariously to the steep mountain slopes, the only small flat patch in the sector, some three hundred square meters, had been reserved for a small soccer field. It had no grass and was covered in gravel, with two wobbly goalposts. Children were playing in it. Even there, in extreme poverty, they had reserved the best space in the neighborhood for a sports field.

Is access to green spaces with trees, sports facilities, and children's playgrounds a luxury or a necessity? At the end of the nineteenth century, the Dutch philosopher Johan Huizinga wrote *Homo Ludens*, in which he said that play is inherent to humankind. It's essential for our creativity and happiness. Although one can play anywhere, appropriate spaces encourage playing and sports. A number of studies have found that access to green public spaces is good for our emotions, spirit, health, and even longevity.[25] If the pandemic has made anything clear about cities and urban life, it's that there is a need to have access to parks, green spaces, and quality public pedestrian space generally.

Urban parks are green spaces with trees and sports fields. The third indispensable ingredient to make a park is people. A rich person may acquire land and cultivate a garden there, with paths, trees, flowers, and lakes. They might also create a sports field to invite friends to play. But that doesn't make it a park. A park needs a diversity of people and access at random. Jan Gehl describes a study in Copenhagen that found that the most frequently used benches in the park were not those on the most beautiful or bucolic spots but those where most people passed by.

Households are getting smaller, and thus housing spaces are becoming smaller. Moreover, many prefer a well-located, smaller home than a larger one in a less desirable place. Homes in dense, large cities tend to be small, particularly for low-income citizens. A popular housing unit generally has an area of less than fifty square meters. Many young people now live in thirty-square-meter apartments. At all income levels and with any housing size, a nearby park makes life more egalitarian and happier. But the smaller the home, the greater the need for quality pedestrian space surrounding it, such as sidewalks, plazas, and parks.

After sidewalks, parks and plazas are the most important ingredient of a good city. Developed cities usually have abundant iconic buildings, old and new. Developing cities generally do not have as many of these. But they can have parks, which beyond making life happier build civic identity and self-esteem. There are extensive sectors in developing cities, particularly those of informal origin, with a dearth or total absence of parks. Just as buildings are acquired and demolished to build road infrastructure, we need to do the same to create parks that make urban environments more fertile for a healthy and happy life, rescue cities from urban underdevelopment, and foster the ambitions and character of an advanced society.

Keeping this in mind is particularly critical when making a new part of a city. Other elements of public infrastructure—even, for example, a critical item such as a wastewater treatment plant—can be fitted in at a later time, but if land for parks is not reserved at the beginning, it is very difficult to demolish hectares of a city to create parks afterward. Demolition to make parks may be difficult, but it's not impossible. We did it in Bogotá.

Architectural prizes do not define the best parks: rather, the "best parks" are the ones that people prefer. In some cases, people prefer parks with sports facilities and children's playgrounds; in others, just footpaths running through green spaces; and in yet others, a combination of the two.

What attracts people to parks will vary depending on place, demographics, climate, and moment in history. Preferred parks in warm Seville in Spain or tropical Valledupar in Colombia are shaded by many trees. In Bogotá, high in the Andes, or in London, the cooler climate makes citizens also want trees, but they appreciate spaces without them, where sunlight can shine through and bring warmth. A park may last thousands of years in the middle of a city, but over time it can change. Initially, it may be almost totally occupied with sports facilities and playgrounds but later only with trees and paths.

The main challenge is to get the land for parks; after that comes the task of providing necessary infrastructure. But for a park to function at its best, beyond good design such as good maintenance and even the organization of events, such as sports workshops or recreation for children. Scandinavian urban parks often have recreationists who help visitors, especially children, enjoy them more. Usually, people enjoy group activities in parks, whether chess competitions or tai chi.

Plazas: The Beating Heart of the City

Plazas are the ancestors of parks as great public spaces. Peter Hall reminds us that the agora was not simply a public space but "the living heart of the city." As democracy replaced monarchy, the agora replaced the Acropolis as the center of city life.[26]

The medieval square, such as those of Siena, Ortigia in Syracuse, or Seville, was cobbled, with no vegetation and surrounded by buildings, which expressed the triumph of humans over nature. The square was a space for people to feel at ease, protected from nature, at a time when nature, often woodlands, surrounded cities. In those squares, such as El Born in Barcelona, "the nobles' jousts and acts of faith took place, and the glass fair took place as well the first day of every year. The same plaza, however, was also the marketplace. In that way, nobles and resellers, inquisitors and witches, vegetables and decked-out horses, came one after another, day after day, in the same urban space. . . . Without these ambits, if we only were to have groups of houses, we would not be able to talk of cities. . . . All European cities have been positively marked by spaces such as these, agglutinating and symbolic."[27]

All the cities founded by Spaniards in America began with the church opposite a square. Citizens of all levels would come together as equals in both places. The city would grow three or four blocks around that square, and then a new square would be created. Unfortunately, that ratio rapidly disappeared. Cities of Spanish America would have been much better if that organic proportion between squares and blocks of buildings had been maintained.

Hard squares or plazas or large spaces without trees still are the urban heart of the political institutions of many states. Red Square in Moscow, Tiananmen Square in Beijing, the Zócalo in Mexico City, the Mall in Washington, DC, or Tahir Square in Cairo are just some of these iconic spaces. They are also the settings for expressions of popular support or rejection of leaders or policies.

Plazas host markets and community activities. One Sunday in the plaza-park of Union Square in Manhattan, I saw an assemblage of tents and crowds. It was a hand-weaving fair. Hundreds of people took part in a number of activities related to hand-weaving. I had read that the German company Singer, once the world's largest producer of sewing machines, had almost gone bankrupt because it didn't anticipate that women in wealthy societies would cease to sew and start buying all of their clothes ready-made. And I had supposed that hand-weaving, something I had seen my aunts and grandmothers do in Colombia, was another of those obsolete activities. But in that plaza, in one of the wealthiest and most advanced cities in the world, hundreds of women and men, old and young, were taking courses in different hand-weaving techniques while others were selling their products. Activities that take place in plazas and parks, such as the weavers' fair in Union Square, chess instruction and championships, dance, and sports exalt and promote behaviors and construct values and community.

Although the characteristics of public space where people meet vary, they share common elements. Although people want to see green in the parks, they spend most of their time on hard surfaces and paths. They like to sit down to read, talk, or watch the world go by, and therefore good public spaces need plenty of benches. Private developers in developing cities often locate green zones and sports facilities on the edges of their projects, and therefore they are seldom used. Children like to play and do sports where people pass by, where they can see and be seen.

Access to Green Spaces Can be a Potent Generator of Equality and Inclusion

As I said earlier, in developing cities there are not abundant large parks because national and local leaders in those societies concerned themselves only with solving the need for private green areas and sports facilities, disregarding such needs in the rest of society. As if this were not enough, when there are natural spaces in these cities, such as waterfronts, wetlands, or mountains, local leaders often privatize them or invent allegedly environmental regulations, which often simply mask class prerogatives, to impede access by the majority.

It is probable that in the near future lack of access to green might become the principal source of exclusion and inequality in quality of life because, as incomes rise, even in developing cities, lower-income citizens will have access to what a few decades before seemed unachievable: household appliances, electronic devices, motor vehicles, even airplane travel. But what they will not have is access to green zones, parks, or sports facilities unless their governments act today. If they fail to do so, the only people to have access to these facilities will be high-income citizens. To acquire and reserve large expanses of urban, suburban, and rural areas for parks is to invest in a more egalitarian and inclusive society.

A Citizen's Right: Enjoying Rural Areas

After less than an hour of cycling from my home in Bogotá with a group of friends and my son, we entered a rural area, with farmhouses and few cars on the unpaved road. We ascended mountains. As we advanced, we rode through more and more native, tree-covered mountainsides, and above three thousand meters, on this fogless morning, we enjoyed exhilarating views of the windswept mountains. Half an hour after entering Chingaza National Park, when we had been riding for about five hours, we came across a family of bears beside the road. There we were, on our bicycles, with the bears and the mountains sprinkled with *frailejón* plants, moss, rocks, and streams as far as the eye could see. Such great nature parks, a few hours from our cities, are good for body and spirit. Creating them is within the reach of the state of any developing country.

In developing cities people aspire to have a car less for their daily mobility than to be able to go to the countryside or the beach, where they can have contact with nature, discover and appreciate the beauty of their country, and come to love it more. But buying a car is not of much use because most people do not have a house in the country and can hardly afford a hotel, if one exists. For all their citizens to be able to have access to nature, democratic states acquire large expanses of land for parks in regions fairly close to cities. They also build networks of rural paths and bikeways. Both regional parks and paths and bikeways are necessary to exercise a right that could also be enshrined in constitutions: the right to enjoy one's country.

An even more basic right is that of being able to enjoy one's country's landscape, at least from the road. In Europe I marveled that there were neither walls nor hedges alongside roads—or billboards—to block enjoyment of the landscape. Indeed, when passing through villages, there were noise barriers along the road, and even these had transparent panels for the motorist to see through. By contrast, the planting of hedges—mostly shrubs, sometimes pruned—alongside large and small roads is becoming popular in some developing countries. They make it impossible to enjoy the view because one travels between two green walls. Citizens who could only enjoy their country's landscape from the windows of a car or a bus are blocked from doing so.

In the tropics the plant most frequently chosen for hedges is the *swinglea*. It could be said that swinglea is the selfishness plant, because it keeps others aside from the property owner from enjoying the view. Hedges make it impossible for children to get to know cows and sheep or potatoes, corn, and cotton plants. A minimum of democracy would be to require that enclosures of rural plots facing roads should be at least 90 percent transparent.

We adopted private property because it makes it possible to manage society's resources most productively, for the entire population's benefit. But it has its limits. Just as owners of urban properties may not build anything they wish but only what is permitted according to regulations, enclosures in rural areas should also allow us to see the landscape beyond. Billboards and hedges on rural roads are incompatible with the social function of private property. We could speak of democratic roads, those free of billboards and hedges and with paths and bikeways alongside them.

In 1950 billboards next to roads contaminated the landscape in most countries. Northern European countries were first in banning billboards along roads to protect citizens' right to a landscape free of billboards. Other advanced countries have gradually followed them in eliminating road billboards. Roads in Spain were cluttered by billboards before the modernizing impact of that country's entry into the European Union. Today, there are none left, and the beautiful Spanish countryside can be appreciated on all its roads. In the United States, progress has been made in removing billboards[28] at a pace unique to each state. Some states have found that as billboards were eliminated, tourism increased. So contamination by billboards on roads today is another characteristic of underdevelopment, in which the interests of the few prevail over the interests of the many.

In addition to national and regional parks, Europe, the United States, Australia, and Canada have hundreds of thousands of kilometers of paths and bikeways across open country, through crops and cattle, over mountains, on the edge of cliffs bordering the sea, and along the banks of rivers and canals. Thousands of kilometers of these have been constructed on former railway lines. Public and private organizations promote and care for these paths, along which there are also cafeterias and small hostels.[29] The paths also are spaces of encounter for all citizens as equals.

I promoted the conversion of two abandoned railway lines that ran from 2,600 meters high—that is, the altitude of Bogotá—almost to sea level in the Magdalena River Valley and passed through a number of climates and exuberant tropical vegetation, as well as a great diversity of butterflies and birds. Although the gradient of those railway lines is too steep for the efficient functioning of trains, it is less steep than a road. That, and the absence of the threat and noise of cars, makes those paths particularly attractive for walkers and cyclists. Colombian president Iván Duque adopted the project, and thanks to him, part of it was done, as well as similar ones in other regions that our project inspired.

To be able to use a city's bikeway network to reach the surrounding countryside releases the soul. These rural bikeways can have picnic areas, points for rest and refreshment, places to camp, even formal restaurants and some basic lodges. I worked to have a path made on the Teusacá River, across the Sopó Valley, to the northeast of the mountains bordering Bogotá. But the mayor of the Sopó municipality preferred to serve the interests of the valley's landed gentry. They didn't want a path with ordinary people passing through their properties, probably considering that the gated developments that they would eventually want to make out of their rural estates would lose value.

A good city is also one in which somehow there is access to nature, trees, butterflies, mountains, sea, and silence, and to a night far from city lights where people can see the stars.

Democratic Roads

Although millions of peasant farmers in rural areas of the developing world walk or bicycle, few governments have shown them even minimum respect by incorporating quality footpaths and bikeways alongside main roads, and even less so across fields.

When I see poor peasant families or old people or children walking Colombia's roads, sometimes with a donkey, I'm ashamed by the lack of pedestrian infrastructure. The sight of children in their school uniforms, satchels on their shoulders, trudging to school along the highway that passes through their village or rural area, with trailer trucks roaring past them, terrifies me. Paths trodden into the roadside by the passage of peasant farmers and poor citizens illustrate lack of respect for those citizens and insufficient democracy. On mountain roads we frequently find that there is not even a verge but only a sloping drainage channel, which forces pedestrians to walk on the road, at great risk.

In some road stretches in Asia, I've seen more pedestrians, cyclists, and elephants than cars, yet there is no infrastructure for them. Multilateral development banks such as the World Bank or the Asian Development Bank, which finance some of these roads, demand environmental impact studies as a prerequisite for their loans. Of course, I agree that animals of the region should be protected. But there is a huge difference between zealous requirements for environmental impact studies and costly investments to minimize the negative impact on a plant or an insect and the neglect in making these roads suitable for human beings. Would it not be desirable that, just as development banks demand environmental impact studies for public works, they should also require *human* impact studies? If this were the case, then roads would have wide footpaths and bikeways alongside them, shaded with trees, particularly when they pass through densely populated peasant-farming areas. Most schools in rural areas are located on a region's main roads. Bikeways and paths could be built at least for a few kilometers around them.

Human impact studies for infrastructure projects would also mean, for example, that paths and bikeways around hydroelectric dams would be built for the recreation and enjoyment of all citizens, so that such waterfronts would not be just for the few owners of adjacent properties.

*   *   *

Seeing a gym on almost every block in Manhattan made me think that "these people, who are among the most educated and richest in the world, enjoy going to the gym. They could do many other things, and if they like doing this, then it must be good and pleasant." In Bogotá, gyms had also started to appear in many middle- and upper-income sectors. It seemed to me that it was something we could offer all our citizens, even the poorest of them. Once we provide for certain basic needs, what makes life more or less happy is not what we have but what we do. And even in a developing city such as Bogotá, it's possible to provide citizens many things that facilitate happiness and help them realize their human potential.

Of course, gyms are just one example. During my two terms as mayor, we created hundreds of parks, sports facilities, well-lit synthetic grass soccer fields, skating rinks, skateboard parks, and children's playgrounds. We offered music lessons to tens of thousands of children. We built three large libraries and invited the Santo Domingo family to construct a fourth, which they generously donated along with a formidable theater. We built five major cultural and sports centers that we called Happiness Centers. These have competition and recreational swimming pools, gyms to rival Manhattan's best, dance rooms, music rooms, auditoriums, and more.[30]

Conclusion

Our city takes us by the hand. When we open our door and go into the city, we merge with it. But we construct the city, and we can change it.

A city reflects the values of the society that makes it. Creating our city is rather similar to making our lives. It shows how its residents wish to live. But the city also constructs values, attitudes, and ways of living. Cities were born with civilization—and the better a city is, the more civilized and happier its citizens. A city that treats them with respect and exalts the human being fosters respect for life and civilized behaviors. We do not have to resign ourselves to our habitat's shortcomings. When we move from one city to another, or sometimes just from one neighborhood to another, we begin to live differently. We can imagine a different and better city and then go about making it.

A more egalitarian society produces a better city; in turn, a good city makes a more egalitarian society. It helps to ensure that nobody feels inferior or excluded and promotes happier ways of life. Its foundation is the basic principle of democracy, the equality of citizens, and the prevalence of the public good. We are so accustomed to inequalities that we often do not see them. And once we identify them, getting the city to overcome them is not painless. Those with privileges do not easily give them up.

In one way or another I've dedicated most of my life to trying to improve my city and others. In my youth I was motivated by a vision of a more egalitarian society that needed adjustment after my disillusionment with communism. Around the same time my city was experiencing exponential growth and I became fascinated by how a good city could be a powerful means for forging potent forms of equality and promote well-being. I managed to realize many dreams for my city, and I had the joy of helping to improve the lives of many citizens. But I also had many failures.

A vision has to do with ethics and aesthetics. We progressively find it with a lens that filters what we see, the bias of our ideology. With our ideology, we look at the same things that others look at, but we see them differently. The lens of concern for equality allowed me to see what I did not like in Bogotá and what I wanted it to be. But a vision is not achieved with the wave of a magic wand. Fortunately, many who have studied the city have provided us with arguments to support and strengthen our dreams and projects. And better still, there are other cities in which we can find examples and inspiration.

New ideas are rarely born with majority support, and change is always difficult. Indeed, if the change produces greater equality, then it's even harder to achieve. Machiavelli realized this and wrote in *The Prince*, "There is nothing more difficult to take in hand, more perilous to conduct, or more uncertain in its success, than to take the lead in the introduction of a new order of things. Because the innovator has for enemies all those who have done well under the old conditions, and lukewarm defenders in those who may do well under the new. This coolness arises partly from fear of the opponents, who have the laws on their side, and partly from the incredulity of men, who do not readily believe in new things until they have had a long experience of them."

Cities face a particular difficulty: often their mayors are moved more by an interest in being elected to a higher office, such as governor of a province or president of the republic, than by solving certain problems that involve large risks. Many projects and decisions are indefinitely postponed for fear of a highly visible failure. Sometimes, what is needed is passion rather than political skills, and naturally, it's better still if a mayor has both.

Citizens, particularly those with low incomes, immersed in their daily concerns, are rarely involved in the defense of projects that benefit them, leaving the field open to the powerful who oppose them. Emotion and political polarization may even lead low-income citizens to align against their own interests. They end up being dragged into that position by an exotic and opportunist alliance of populist politicians with high-income citizens keen to block a project. Perhaps low-income citizens are too busy surviving to care about these projects, or perhaps government communication explaining the projects to its citizens is poorly executed, or a combination of the two. Whatever the case, when trying to advance projects perceived as adversely affecting powerful groups, it's not always possible even to rely on the support of the projects' beneficiaries. Those who have wealth and influence in developing cities have a great capacity to mobilize the media, state institutions, and, ironically, sometimes even parties that oppose the establishment.

As I wrote earlier, policies to improve income distribution without deteriorating entrepreneurial or individual motivation or market efficiency are always welcome. In the next few years, there will no doubt continue to be progress in the eradication of poverty, and income inequality hopefully will also diminish. However, a market economy necessarily entails inequalities, and reductions in income inequality do not put an end to feelings of exclusion and inferiority.

There are moments when we come up against seemingly insuperable obstacles because we have many citizens and institutions arrayed against us, and it seems impossible to move forward. What enables us to resist and persist is a conviction that the years of dreaming, studying, and working engenders. I failed in my efforts to implement projects that would have made Bogotá more egalitarian and happier. That is one of the reasons I wanted to write this book. Those who dream of cities that are more for children, public transport, and bicycles than for cars, more for parks and public waterfronts than for retaining the status quo, are going to face ferocious attacks not only from predictable opponents but also from unexpected fronts.

Sometimes you'll fail. But when you don't you'll feel the immense satisfaction provided by a city with better-educated children, parks full of citizens of all ages and all income levels, buses in their dedicated lanes that zip by expensive cars barely moving in heavy traffic, and swarms of cyclists on bikeways that you succeeded in creating, no matter if one of them insults you as they pass by.

A good city, guided by democratic principles, may effectively reduce the feeling of exclusion. Such a city makes it possible for citizens of all income levels to meet each other as equals. It also constructs the kinds of equality that I've described throughout this book: equality of quality of life and democratic equality, in which all decisions of the state are truly made based on the prevalence of the public good.

NOTES

Introduction

1. My father was the first manager of Instituto de Reforma Agraria, serving for seven years under three presidents. When Carlos Lleras named my father minister of agriculture, his main task was to push harder for agrarian reform.

2. With indemnities, although some owners naturally thought the valuations were not high enough.

3. My father was a junior professional at the World Bank at the time I was born; we returned to Colombia when I was three months old. When I came back to Washington fifteen years later, I didn't speak a word of English, and even today I have a Spanish accent.

4. Professor Martin Bronfenbrenner was involved in the reconstruction of Japan after World War II. I took a number of his courses on Japanese economic development.

5. Expropriation, of course, at market prices to compensate owners.

6. I began to use this image frequently in my lectures after 2000. I was very pleased to find later that Jan Gehl, who heard some of them along with some members of his team, began to do the same and even included it in his books.

7. Angel, S. (2012). *Planet of Cities*. Cambridge, MA, Lincoln Institute of Land Policy, 195.

8. Winston Churchill is said to have remarked, "We shape our buildings, thereafter they shape us," in his speech to the meeting of the House of Lords, October 28, 1943.

9. Gehl, J. (2006). *La humanización del espacio urbano: La vida social entre edificios*. Barcelona, Editorial Reverté S.A., 19.

10. Although I understand in English a city is referred to as "it," here I prefer to use "her" and "she" to align with the Spanish feminine form of the word: *la ciudad*, the city.

Chapter 1

1. Bell, D. (2010). *The Coming of Post-Industrial Society: A Venture in Social Forecasting*. New York, Basic Books.

2. Bogotá and surrounding conurbations in 2018. The city itself accounts for 80 percent of that total.

3. Quoted from Bill Maher. (2010). *But I'm Not Wrong*. Dir. John Moffitt, written by Bill Maher. HBO.

4. Loschiavo, D. (June 2019). "Big-city life (dis)satisfaction? The effect of living on subjective well-being." Bank of Italy Temi di Discussione (Working Paper) No. 1221, p. 24.

5. Putnam, R. (2000). *Bowling Alone: The Collapse and Revival of American Community*. New York, Simon & Schuster, 19.

6. Glaeser, E. (2011). *Triumph of the City*. New York, Penguin Books, 36.

7. The problem is only attenuated by intense government intervention.

8. Since mid-2021 the position of governor of the Santiago Metropolitan area is elected and thus has the electoral representation it did not have when the job was done by an "intendente" appointed by the national government. However, the president of Chile still appoints a regional authority (*delegado presidencial*) with very similar roles and responsibilities as the former intendentes. Chile is still discussing how to transition to a more decentralized governance in which the regional authority's responsibilities are fully transferred to governors. This process has proven to be complicated and slow.

9. MTA.info. (2018). New York City Subway.

10. Pagh, J. (2013). "A short story of the 'Red Lots'—the Copenhagen Land Bank—and the cooperative housing associations." Copenhagen.

11. Lorrain, D. (2016). *Governing Megacities in Emerging Countries*. CNRS, France. London, Routledge, 157–158.

12. Analyzing the process posteriori, Konrad Yakabuski wrote at the end of 2003, "The amalgamation was a triumph of common sense and global vision over the parochial interests. . . . Rich and largely anglophone suburbs on the West Island contributed nothing to the maintenance of infrastructure in the city centre where their inhabitants flocked to work and where, of course, their teenagers played on Saturday night. . . . Of course, the rich municipalities were against it." Yakabuski, K. (2003, November 28). "Montreal must stay a megacity." *Globe and Mail*.

Chapter 2

1. UN Demographic Yearbooks of 1950 and 2017: A comparison of Latin American cities in the period from 1950 to 2017: São Paulo, Rio de Janeiro; the urban agglomeration of Buenos Aires and of Mexico City, Quito, Bogotá, and Santiago.

2. Angel, S. (2012) *Planet of Cities*. Cambridge, MA, Lincoln Institute of Land Policy, 176.

3. Angel, S. (2012), 24 and 26.

4. Angel, S. (2012).

5. It is also simple to require generous cessions of land for parks in new developments. But this is not enough.

6. The peculiar feature of the Van der Hammen forest reserve is that it has no trees and is formed by private property, mostly with grazing land, crops, high-income neighborhoods, and schools. Only 20 of the 1,400 hectares of forestry reserve (Bosque Las Mercedes) have any trees. Bogotá has a formidable forest reserve of more than 15,000 hectares in the mountains that line the city to the east. Large parks can also be created, larger than the Van der Hammen reserve, harmoniously integrated into urban development, charging the entire cost of those parks to the developments implemented.

7. The construction of high embankments has since eliminated the flood risk to those areas.

8. I have heard two explanations for this: one relates to the size of the blocks of bricks used to construct houses. The other is that the measurements were generalized because they were used by the state housing authority Instituto de Crédito Territorial, or ICT.

9. ONU. (2018). Sustainable Development Goals Overview. Goal 11: Sustainable cities and communities. Statistics Division ONU.

10. Inskeep, S. (2012). *Instant City: Life and Death in Karachi*. New York, Penguin Books, 100.

11. Between 1954 and 2019, 1,634 neighborhoods were legalized in Bogotá. During seven years as mayor, we legalized 438 and left a further 94 in the process of legalization. Luis Eduardo Garzón was the second most active mayor in this process, with 117 neighborhoods legalized.

12. During my two periods as mayor, one of three years and one of four, we built almost a hundred schools to very high architectural standards. Slightly over half of them were concentrated in the poorest neighborhoods.

13. This cable car was contracted by the previous mayor, but in our term we built all of it. We had to make important adjustments to its design.

14. Shlomo Angel, citing Andrew Dolkart and *Biography of a Tenement House in New York City*. Angel, S. (2012), 35–36.

15. We created Metrovivienda and Empresa de Renovación Urbana—ERU. Metrovivienda bought large tracts of land in Bosa for the projects El Recreo and Porvenir. Subsequent populist city administrations did not sell the land but gave it away, and Metrovivienda lost most of its capital in this way. Metrovivienda was designed to buy rural land to ensure that the city would grow in the right place and in the right way, and ERU was to redevelop existing areas of the city, improving quality and in some cases density. During my second term of office, Bogotá did not have much potentially urbanizable rural land left; the surrounding municipalities were not interested in joint projects, and we merged Metrovivienda into ERU.

16. Pagh, J. (2013). "A short story of the Red Lots—the Copenhagen Land Bank—and the cooperative housing associations." Copenhagen.

17. UN-Habitat. (2014). *For a Better Urban Future: Urban Planning for City Leaders*, 40.

18. Angel, S. (2012), 40.

19. Mehta, S. (2011). "Looking for the Bird of Gold." In *Living in the Endless City—The Urban Age Project by the London School of Economics and Deutsche Bank's Alfred Herrhausen Society*, ed. Burdett, R., Sudjic, D. New York, Phaidon Press, 105–106. Recently, Gautam Adani, one of Asia's richest men and a close ally of India's prime minister Narendra Modi, won a bid to redevelop Dharavi in association with the state's government. Residents who settled there before 2000 would be rehoused in apartments within its borders. Others would be offered public rental housing within a ten-kilometer radius. Many of Dharavi's cottage industries would also be relocated within Dharavi's boundaries. Adani would pay for and profit from the remaining land. But given the scandal that wiped more than $100 billion in a week from Adani's fortune, it seems unlikely that this new project will be successful either.

20. Brenthurst Foundation. (2020). *The Future of African Cities*. Taken from https:// vimeo.com/384982631.

21. Obasanjo, O., Pinzón, J. C., Mills, G., Hartley, R., Hamukoma, N., Calburn, S., Doyle, N., Games, D., Muzenda, A., Van der Merwe, E., Kilcullen, D., Davis, D. (2020). *Where the Rubber Hits the Road: Future of African Cities Project*. Special Report, 60.

22. Inskeep, S. (2013). "It would be safer if she was not the only one." *Friday Times*, Pakistan, vol. 25, no. 7.

23. Pakistan was still 60 percent rural in 2021. During the next decades the size of its cities will multiply severalfold. The Pakistani state has a formidable opportunity to make extraordinary cities.

24. Federal Government, SEDESOL. Sara Topelson, Under-Secretary for Urban Development and Land-Use Regulation. "La expansión de las ciudades, 1980–2010." Ministry of Social Development.

25. From 2005 to 2018, 489,000 homes were built in Bogotá, and its urban area increased by 2,637 hectares. In the same period, 235,000 homes were built in the 20 peripheral municipalities, and the urban area of those municipalities increased 19,494 hectares.

26. Beatley, T. *Green Urbanism: Learning from European Cities.* Washington, DC, Island Press, 57.

27. The power of some environmentalists in Bogotá is so great that they managed to create a forestry reserve of 1,396 hectares called Van der Hammen, when there were trees on only 20 hectares. The reserve, Lagos de Torca, is next to it. The entire area is private property, except for a few hectares, which we bought during my first period as mayor for the future construction of a major road. The rest of the area is used by flower growers, nurseries, grazing land, some small settlements, schools, soccer fields, and tennis courts. The technical justification for the reserve is, to say the least, peculiar since it is bordered by straight lines and a large number of right angles. And further, when it reaches a neighboring municipality, it ends. One would suppose that nature does not work in that way. Recognizing the difficulty of converting developed sectors into natural woodland, the regulations that create the reserve stipulate that 861 of the 1,396 hectares will maintain their current use, and only 535 need to be acquired by the state to turn them into woodland, similar to primary forest area that was already there. Our project almost tripled the public area of parkland generated, also securing the acquisition by mandatory session of land for development. Our critics, who succeeded us in the city administration, did not buy a single hectare of the so-called reserve and did not implement any of the other development projects in the north of the city.

28. When we did all the work to make the project a reality, which included convincing the landowners, including the Cardinal on behalf of the Catholic Church and the highest level generals in the National Army, we called the project Lagos del Tunjuelo. However, my successor changed the project's name to Reverdecer del Sur and stalled it. It will soon be under way again.

Chapter 3

1. Secretaría Distrital de Planeación. (2016). *Patrimonio Cultural del Distrito Capital.* Bogotá, Secretaría Distrital de Planeación.

2. We purchased that sculpture. But I had proposed to Botero that he should make a major donation to mount a Botero Museum in Bogotá. As a result of the negotiations, the choice of the sculpture, and so on, I was able to insist to him on the museum project. I offered to put the museum wherever he wanted and to design it following his guidelines. I even offered to set up a fund to guarantee its future operation. Initially, he rejected that idea, but after some months of insistence, he marvelously changed his mind and accepted. When the chairman of the Central Bank, Miguel Urrutia, found out about the project, he proposed to Botero that the bank build the museum. Botero preferred that the bank rather than City Hall should do it. I was happy because Bogotá gained a marvelous Botero Museum as a result of the generosity of the artist who donated not only his own work but also a major collection of other artists he had.

3. This was the finding of a study of carbon footprints of seven hundred cities in California by Renewable and Appropriate Energy Laboratory of the University of California, Berkeley. Wiener, S., Kammen, D. (2019, March 25). "Why housing policy is climate policy." *New York Times.*

4. Wiener, S., Kammen, D. (2019).

5. Wiener, S., Kammen, D. (2019).

6. Mervosh, S. (2018, December 13). "Minneapolis, tackling housing crisis and inequity, votes to end single-family zoning." *New York Times.*

7. Bliss, L. (2019, July 2). "Oregon's single-family zoning ban was a 'long time coming.'" Bloomberg City Lab.

8. Editorial. (2005, June 24). "The limits of property rights." *New York Times.*

9. Another woman, Gilma Giménez, director of social welfare, was responsible for the social care of these people.

10. We acquired the historical buildings, the properties where we demolished buildings, and the funds to design and contract the new buildings. We signed the contract for the building of the higher-education center for creative industries.

11. Decrees for the corridors of urban renewal of the TransMilenio trunk routes.

12. If those who have are important, it is not because of what they own but because of what they know.

Chapter 4

1. Smith, P. D. (2012). *City: A Guidebook for the Urban Age.* London, Bloomsbury, 54.

2. Smith, P. D. (2012), 144.

3. "Suburbia transformed the metropolis in America: as the nineteenth century drew to a close, there was a clear separation of homes and businesses." Smith, P. D. (2012), 119.

4. Howard, E. (1898). *To-morrow: A Peaceful Path to Real Reform.* 1st ed. 2nd ed., (1902) published as *Garden Cities of Tomorrow.* London, Swan Sonnenschein & Co.

5. Smith, P. D. (2012): "The decline of downtown, or the central city, was a troubling feature of late twentieth-century urban life around the world. In the 1970s and 1980s, British cities appeared to be following the example of the United States" (121).

6. Angel, S. (2012). *Planet of Cities.* Cambridge, MA, Lincoln Institute of Land Policy, 240.

7. It grew over adjoining towns also, such as Villa Nueva.

8. Putnam, R. (2000). *Bowling Alone: The Collapse and Revival of American Community.* New York, Simon & Schuster, 211.

9. In the United States between 1990 and 2000, 64 percent of the growth in journeys to work in metropolitan areas was between suburbs, while journeys from the suburbs to the center represented only 14 percent of growth. Today, journeys from the suburbs to the center account for only 9 percent of journeys to work. Pisarski, A. (2006). *Commuting in America III.* Washington, DC: Transportation Research Board, 53.

10. US Department of Transportation. (2018). *Transportation Annual Report.* Washington, DC, Bureau of Transportation Statistics, 3–8.

11. Paumgarten, N. (2007, April 16).

12. Paumgarten, N. (2007, April 16).

13. Institute for Transportation and Development Policy. (2019, May 23). "The High Cost of Transportation in the United States."

14. Centro de Investigación del Transporte. (2005, October). Observatorio de la Movilidad Metropolitana de Madrid. "Madrid: Ministerio del Medio Ambiente," 12.

15. "Driven Away." (2023, February 18). *Economist.*

16. McGuirk, J. (2011). "Understanding the numbers." In *Living in the Endless City—The Urban Age Project by the London School of Economics and Deutsche Bank's Alfred Herrhausen Society,* ed. Burdett, R., Sudjic, D. New York, Phaidon Press, 292–308.

17. Glaeser, E. (2011). *Triumph of the City.* New York, Penguin Books, 6.

18. Cervero, R. (1998). *The Transit Metropolis.* Washington, DC, Island Press.

19. From Eran Ben-Joseph, professor of urban planning at MIT; Kimmelman, M. (2012, January 6). "Paved, but still alive." *New York Times.*

20. Kimmelman, M. (2012, January 6).

21. Meeks, S., Murphy, K. C. (2016). *The Past and Future City: How Historic Preservation Is Reviving America's Communities.* Washington, DC, Island Press.

22. Meeks, S., Murphy, K. C. (2016), 183.

23. Duany, A., Plater Zyberk, E., and Speck, J. (2000). *Suburban Nation: The Rise of Sprawl and the Decline of the American Dream.* Epub. 10th anniversary ed. North Point Press, 34.

24. Congress for the New Urbanism. (1996). *The Charter of the New Urbanism.*

25. West Don Lands. (2020). "The West Don Lands is Toronto's next great neighborhood." Waterfront, Toronto, Canada.

26. Assuming households of three, which is the usual size among buyers of new housing at those prices.

27. I described Lagos de Torca in greater detail earlier.

28. New York City Economic Development Corporation. (2018, April 5). "New Yorkers and their cars."

29. WWF Scotland. (2016). "International Case Studies for Scotland's Climate Plan: Public transport, Zurich, Switzerland."

30. Stadt Zürich. (2013). "Stadtverkehr 2025: Zürich macht vorwärts." City Zurich, Department of Civil Engineering.

Chapter 5

1. Beijing and other Chinese cities have begun to introduce measures to restrict the use of cars, which can be more useful in reducing congestion. It is also worth noting that hundreds of kilometers of metro in Beijing have not done so.

2. Texas Transportation Institute of Texas A&M University, which has made annual studies of the problems of traffic congestion in the United States since 1982, has found that, for example, in 2017, the average citizen lost thirty-four hours more in traffic jams than in 1982. It also found that the traffic problem is increasing, not only at traditional peak hours but also in off-peak ones. Schrank, D., Eisele, B., Lomax, T. (2019). *Urban Mobility Report.* Texas A&M Transportation Institute, Texas A&M University System & INRIX, Exhibit 1, 2.

3. Cervero, R. (1998). *The Transit Metropolis.* Washington, DC, Island Press.

4. In the United States miles traveled by cars increased 226 percent between 1983 and 2001, while the population increased only 22 percent. Pierce, N. (2007, December 16). "Walkability =Livability=Billions." *Washington Post.*

5. Turcotte, M. (2005). "General social survey: Commuting times (2005)." Aboriginal and Social Studies Division, Statistics Canada 2005.

6. CALTRANS. (2020). "Truck-only lanes." Caltrans, State of California.

7. In Singapore, every car needs a "certificate of entitlement," which is bought at auction for more than US$20,000 and is valid for ten years.

8. Gehl, J. (2010). *Cities for People.* Washington, DC, Island Press, 55.

9. Foster and Partners, 30 St Mary Axe Tower. The building has 41 stories and 76,400 square meters of usable floor.

10. Hernández, R. (2016, February 9). "Torre BBVA Bancomer, aportación al paisaje urbano."

11. Simultaneously, we eliminated the exemption from restriction that armored cars had previously had and that had meant that thousands of cars have been armored in order to avoid the restriction. From then onward, armored cars would also be subject to the restriction like all others, unless the owners paid not to be.

12. In 2013 the Underground was used by 3.7 million and the bus by 6.4 million. "Underground, overground." (2013, October 19). *Economist*.

13. Pedestrian Observations. (2013, June 3). Comparative Subway Construction Costs." Pedestrian Observations for Walkability and Good Transit and Against Boondoggles and Pollution. Rosenthal, B. M. (2017, December 28). "The Most Expensive Mile of Subway Track on Earth." *New York Times*.

14. This is not achieved with much comfort for passengers. With very crowded buses, some TransMilenio lines in Bogotá carry more than fifty thousand passengers per hour in each direction.

15. The average speed, for example, in a twenty-five-kilometer segment, including stopping times. BRT systems can work on raised platforms similar to those of metros. Some have several kilometers of overhead segments, such as in São Paolo, Lahore, and Islamabad. With the overtaking lanes at stations, these BRTs can achieve high speeds and therefore high capacity and low operating costs.

16. If the speed is slower because the bus has to stop and start at many traffic lights, this also increases operating expenses.

17. In ALO Sur (Autopista Longitudinal de Occidente). In several newly urbanizing areas in Chinese cities, they have done likewise.

18. Mohan, D. (2008). *Mythologies, Metros and Future Urban Transport*. Indian Institute of Technology, TRIPP Report Series.

19. Mohan, D. (2008).

20. "The future of public transport in Britain." (2022, May 19). *Economist*.

21. "Travel patterns have changed for good: Transport systems should too." (2022, May 19). *Economist*.

22. William H. Whyte was a sociologist and urbanist in the United States, a pioneer in the study of human behavior in public space. His books include *The Social Life of Small Urban Spaces* and *City: Rediscovering the Center*.

23. The creation of the bikeway was one of many battles fought by the formidable former commissioner Janette Sadik-Khan.

24. California Transit Association. (2015). "A brief history of transit in California." California Transit Association, 50 years, 127.

25. Studies done by Ian Thompson of ECLA, the United Nations' Economic Commission for Latin America, arrived at that conclusion.

26. Enrique Peñalosa, "Inquietudes Sobre el Costo del Metro," *El Espectador*, August 3, 1983.

27. Peñalosa, "Inquietudes Sobre el Costo del Metro."

28. Some owners had up to five buses, but in many cases a single bus would have several owners.

29. Paulo Custodio, Pedro Szasz, and other Brazilian engineers led this task.

30. Carlos Emilio Gómez had worked with me when I managed the Colombia office of a consultancy firm with headquarters in Boston, Arthur D. Little. He later resigned from the TransMilenio project to get an MBA at Stanford University.

31. I called it TransMilenio because my period in office ended in 2000, on the change of millennium.

32. He was the senior executive of Grupo Social, a nonprofit organization owned by the Society of Jesus in Colombia. Grupo Social today has a bank, Banco Caja Social, one of the most important in the country, an insurance company, and a construction company, among other interests. Ignacio Guzmán was at one time manager of the Organización Luis Carlos Sarmiento, then Colombia's largest business group.

33. As this book goes to press, Gustavo Petro, the populist new president, is doing everything at his disposal to pressure the city to change the contract and change the design, to turn the metro under construction into an underground one. Additional costs would be large, and it would take at least five additional years to begin operation.

34. For years, model buses were sold at traffic lights, and almost every child in Bogotá had one. But I was surprised when giving lectures and seminars in several places in China in 2004 contracted by the World Bank. One day the World Bank's representative in China told me that he was going to the market to bring me a present, and the next day he brought me a couple of toy TransMilenio red buses, complete with TransMilenio legends: they were on sale in a market in Beijing!

35. Gorz, A. (1973). "La ideología social del automóvil."

Chapter 6

1. *Clavipalpus ursinus.* The fertilized female then goes back underground and lays her eggs before she dies.

2. Schemes of monthly tickets for unlimited travel in public transport might mitigate the problem.

3. For example, the proceeds of London's congestion charge are used to improve the bus system. In Vancouver, a fuel tax subsidizes public transport.

4. The most heavily used tramlines in Portland or Denver do not even move 5,000 passengers per hour per direction. Light trains such as that of San Francisco achieve 13,000 passengers per hour per direction. In some places in other countries, the rate exceeds 20,000. The light trains operate on exclusive tracks with no obstacles. TransMilenio mobilizes up to 50,000 passengers per hour per direction on roads with traffic lights.

5. "But for all this bullishness, there is no empirical link between street-cars and development." E. B. (2014, August 6). "Why trams are a waste of money." *Economist.*

6. Hook, W., Lotshaw, S., Weinstock, A. (2013, November 13). "More development for your transit dollar: An analysis of 21 North American transit corridors." ITDP, Institute for Transportation and Development Policy. https://www.itdp.org/2013/11/13/more-development-for -your-transit-dollar-an-analysis-of-21-north-american-transit-corridors/.

7. P. D. Smith, citing *Downtown: Its Rise and Fall 1880–1950* by Robert M. Fogelson. In Smith, P. D. (2012). *City: A Guidebook for the Urban Age.* London, Bloomsbury Publishing, 118.

8. Smith, P. D. (2012), 118.

9. The General Motors investments in the story were in National City Lines and Pacific City Lines. The company also held shares in other automobile-related businesses such as Firestone Tire, Standard Oil of California, and Phillips Petroleum.

10. Kay, J. (2011, August 31). "Why trams belong in museums and not on city streets." *Financial Times.*

11. E. B. (2014, August 6).

12. Glaeser, E. (2014, March 6). "Boston needs cooler buses." *Boston Globe.*

13. Blanc, C., Scanlon, K., White, K. (2020, March). *Living in a Denser London: How Residents See Their Homes.* London, LSE London/LSE Cities, 62.

14. Roberto Moreno, Amarilo CEO, said this on several occasions, including a presentation he made to an Institute for Transportation and Development Policy team in Bogotá in 2010.

15. Rodriguez, D. A., Targa, F. (2004, September). "Value of accessibility to Bogotá's rapid transit system." *Transport Reviews* 24, no. 5, 587–610; Rodriguez, D. A., Mojica, C. H. (2009, February). "Capitalization of BRT network expansions effects into prices of non-expansion areas." *Transportation Research Part A: Policy and Practice* 43, no. 5, 560–571.

16. Tsivanidis, N. (2022). Evaluating the Impact of Urban Transit Infrastructure: Evidence from Bogota's TransMilenio. University of California Working Paper.

17. Their arguments were based on the fact that I had been the chair of the board of directors of ITDP, an NGO in New York that promotes sustainable transport, and that I had received donations from Volvo, which represented 0.37 percent of its income during the years in which I was on that board. It goes without saying that neither ITDP nor I ever received one cent for the sale of a bus, and neither report ever mentioned a bus brand in our work. There would have been no legal or ethical conflict if I had sold the buses. But I did not, nor did ITDP. Further, those buses were not bought by the city administration or TransMilenio but by the private operators of the system, who made their own decisions on which make of bus they wanted.

18. As I already mentioned, the cost per kilometer of a metro is between ten and fifteen times more than that of TransMilenio.

19. Ypousafzai, F. (2020, January 23). "Government decides to revise $2bn KCR project." *Nation Pakistan*; PND. (2020, January 22). "Meeting on revival of Karachi Circular Railway (Kcr) on 18-01-2020." Planning and Development Department, Karachi, Pakistan.

20. Withrington, P., Wellings, R. (2015, February). "Paving over the tracks: A better use for Britain's railways?" Institute of Economic Affairs.

Chapter 7

1. Peter Norton mentions many legal efforts made by civic initiative to restrict cars and protect the rights of pedestrians on the street. Norton, P. (2008). *Fighting Traffic: The Dawn of the Motor Age in the American City.* Cambridge, MA, MIT Press, 258.

2. I based this phrase on Orlando Araujo: "The moon shone like the sun, but in silence." Araujo, O. (2004). *Compañero de viaje y otros relatos: Siempre hay un rio.* Caracas, Biblioteca Básica de Autores Venezolanos/Monte Ávila Editores Latinoamérica, 5.

3. World Health Organization (WHO). (2022, 20 June). "Road traffic injuries." Global Status Report on Road Safety 2018.

4. WHO (2022, June 20).

5. Freud, E. L. (1960). *Letters of Sigmund Freud.* New York, Basic Books. Letter to his sons (1907), 262.

6. Norton, P. (2008), 23.

7. Norton, P. (2008), 70.

8. Norton, P. (2008), 21. By comparison, according to the *Washington Post*, during World War II, some 235,000 American soldiers died in battle. Bump, P. (2017, August 14). "Here's how

many Americans have already died to defeat the Nazis and the Confederacy." *Washington Post*.

9. Norton, P. (2008), 24.

10. The number of motorcyclists killed in traffic accidents has been growing enormously in the first decades of the twenty-first century.

11. In 2019, 6,205 pedestrians and 846 cyclists were run down and killed by vehicles. In 2019, 236 pedestrians and 68 cyclists,169 motorcyclists, and 29 drivers died on the roads. NHTSA, US Department of Transportation. (2020, October). "2018 preview of motor vehicle traffic fatalities in 2019," 1; SIGAT Mobility Department. (2019, April). "Database of the geo-referenced Traffic Accident Information System." Mobility Department, Bogotá. A World Bank study on 135 countries found that "a 10% reduction of road traffic deaths raises per capita real GDP per capita by 3.6% over a 24 year horizon." World Bank. (2018, October 9). "Road deaths and injuries hold back economic growth in developing countries." Washington, DC, World Bank.

12. "Roundabout" was first used in Letchworth Garden City near London in 1909. There are some forty thousand of them in the world today, half of them in France, which calls them *rond point*. "The widening gyre." (2013, October 3). *Economist*.

13. Gutiérrez, J. A., Olivar, E. A. (2000, October). "Estudios de economía y ciudad." Economics Office of the City Finance Department, Bogotá, no. 13, pp. 33 and 34.

14. There is now talk of urban aerial mobility. It began as a project to use drones to send objects but is now seen as a possibility to carry people.

15. Gorz, A. (1973, September–October). "The social ideology of the motor car." *Le Sauvage*. Gorz went on to say, "That is how in both conception and original purpose the car is a luxury good. And the essence of luxury is that it cannot be democratized."

16. In 1997, 43 percent of sixteen-year-old Americans had a driver's license; in 2020 the number had fallen to 25 percent. Between 1990 and 2017 the distance driven by teenage drivers in the United States declined by 35 percent and by those aged twenty to thirty-four by 18 percent. The trend is similar in Europe. In Britain the proportion of teenagers able to drive has gone from 41 percent to 21 percent from 2003 to 2023. In "Driven away." (2023, February 18). *Economist*.

17. Harnik, P., Welle, B. (2007, April). *Nature over Traffic*. Urban Land, Minnesota Department of Transportation, 103.

18. The intersection I refer to here is that of Calle 100 with the Autopista Norte highway. Citizens must walk along the sidewalk of the Autopista, from the north side of Calle 100, cross the exit ramp on the highway toward Calle 100 to the west, and then pass under the bridge, which runs over Calle 100, to cross the Autopista, and then back up the access ramp of Calle 100 to the east in order to be able to take the highway to the north. That intersection is still the same disastrously inhumane site today.

19. "A rage for roads: Egypt is busily building expressways." (2020, October 8). *Economist*.

20. Nogés, G. (2003). *Buenos Aires, ciudad secreta*. Ebook, Buenos Aires, Editorial Sudamericana, 155–156.

21. More than 10 percent per year. ITDP. (2012, March). "The life and death of urban highways." New York, Institute for Transportation & Development Policy, 10.

22. ITDP (2012, March), 10.

23. Twenty-six acres of land were freed for the new development. ITDP (2012, March).

24. There are studies of the possibility of demolishing other sections to make a boulevard, but the cost has prevented any implementation. Some public space was generated under the highway in 2018: "The Bentway," defined as a vital arterial road of 1.75 kilometers for pedestrians and cyclists.

25. ITDP. (2012, March). "The life and death of urban highways," 12.

26. "200m of highway demolished in only eight seconds in Brazil." (2014, April 20). *La Razón*, Brazil, 3; Ibid, 12.

27. Jacobs, J. (2011). *Muerte y vida de las grandes ciudades Americanas*. Madrid, Capitán Swing Libros, 30.

28. "Homes before roads" was initially a movement in London, but it inspired other similar movements with the same name.

29. Extracts from the televised speech of Governor Francis W. Sargent on WCVB-TV in 1970. The recording was given to me by former MIT professor Kenneth Kruckemeyer. WCBV-TV. (1970). "Special report: Highways or mass transit." Governor of the Commonwealth of Massachusetts Francis W. Sargent, WCBV Studios, Boston. With formidable clarity Governor Sargent also said that it was necessary to freeze the number of parking spaces in the center of Boston: "Further to encourage transit use and to end the strangulation of downtown Boston and auto congestion, I expect to sign an agreement with the mayor freezing the number of parking spaces in the city."

30. JICA insisted on preparing more detailed designs for one of them, a flyover, free, and we gave them the green light for the more detailed designs of what they wanted to build. The JICA studies invariably recommended the same: flyovers and metros. They even proposed that for Ulan Bator, a city of only 1.5 million inhabitants. Japan is a major producer of cars and metros, and such recommendations from a Japanese government agency were hardly surprising.

31. JICA proposed a ring road of 16.6 kilometers of flyovers crossing the city from the north to the center, starting at Ave 7, with Calle 127, then following Calle 100 to Autopista Norte and finally following the Ave Norte-Quito-Sur—NQS—through the Calle 6.

32. This 12th Avenue was a flyover in the past. It was demolished to improve the human quality of the sector.

33. Some Chinese cities banned the use of electric bicycles in 2017, but even where they were illegal, the authorities tended to be tolerant. In 2019 the government started to set rules and specifications to regulate and standardize the use of these bicycles.

Chapter 8

1. Official statistics from Denmark suggest that for every 9.6 kilometers ridden on a bicycle rather than driven in a car, there is a saving of 1.6 kilograms of CO_2 emissions and of US$0.09 in health costs.

2. Bicycle Dutch. (2011, October 9). "How the Dutch got their cycle paths." NL Cycling.

3. Bicycle Dutch (2011, October 9).

4. During the period before my first term of office, my brother Guillermo had been director of the City Recreation and Sports Institute; he extended the scheme from 17 to 81 kilometers and made notable improvements to its organization with better supervision and complementary activities such as aerobics, with music at some points. During my first period of office, we extended the scheme from 81 to 121 kilometers, and in the second, to 127 kilometers.

5. More than three hundred cities around the world have been inspired by the Bogotá Bike-Ride and have engaged in similar exercises; some examples are Guadalajara, New York City, São Paulo, and Gurgaon, India.

6. Dekoster, J., Schollaert, U. (1999). *Cycling: The Way Ahead for Towns and Cities.* Luxembourg, Office of Official Publications of the European Communities.

7. Turcotte, M. (2005). "Like commuting? Workers' perceptions of their daily commute." Statistics Canada, Catalogue No. 11–008, p. 39.

8. Jacobs, J. (1961). *The Life and Death of Great American Cities.* New York, Random House.

9. McGrane, S. (2012, July 17). "Commuters pedal to work on their very own superhighway." *New York Times.*

10. Felipe González-Pacheco and Juan Ignacio Muñoz. IDU's director of public space, Alicia Naranjo, who more than anyone made the project a reality, also came on these hikes and flights.

11. The park leaves the city along the Bogotá River and reaches the La Florida park in the municipality of Cota but is administered by the city. It should naturally have been extended through Cota and crossed through agricultural zones on the spectacular savannah that surrounds Bogotá. Curiously, the municipalities close to Bogotá did not consider the idea of bikeways seriously, although in their semirural areas, many citizens mobilize on bicycles and some have serious problems of poverty.

12. Eighteen years later, during my second period as mayor, we were able to contract for the greenway alongside the wetland, which is just a small segment of a branch of the Juan Amarillo greenway dozens of kilometers long. The mayor who came after me stopped the project, and as this book goes to press, a judge has the last word on it.

13. Designed by Claudia Mejia and Lorenzo Castro, they were the starting point of more than 120 kilometers of bike highways built during my first term as mayor of Bogotá.

14. Tolley, R. (1990). *The Greening of Urban Transport: Planning for Walking and Cycling in Western Cities.* London, Belhaven Press, 3.

Chapter 9

1. The situation has notably improved recently, since the European Union Schengen area and Britain no longer require visas for Colombians. They are still required for the United States and Canada, among other countries.

2. The principle applies especially in Sweden, Norway, Finland, and Iceland and to a lesser extent in the Baltic States and even Scotland.

3. The same principle applies in Finland, where it's called "*Jokamiehenoikeus.*"

4. "Countryside Right-of-Way Act 2000."

5. McCullough, D. (2019). *The Pioneers.* New York, Simon & Schuster, 64.

6. Glaeser, E. (2012). *Triumph of the City.* New York, Penguin Books.

7. Gehl, J. (2010). *Cities for People.* Washington DC, Island Press, 68.

8. Traditional Basque-country sweetmeats.

9. Case of Amsterdam. (2014). "The governance of land use in the Netherlands."

10. Gehl, J. (1996). *Life Between Buildings.* Copenhagen, Artkitektens Forlag, 27.

11. Whyte, W. H. (1980). *The Social Life of Small Urban Spaces.*

12. Hall, P. (1998). *Cities in Civilization.* New York, Pantheon Books, 46.

13. Hall, P. (1998), 46.

14. Do Rio, J. (2013). *A alma encantadora das ruas: Crónicas*. São Paolo, Companhia das Let.

15. Chetty, Raj and others. (2022). "Social Capital 2: Determinants of Economic Connectedness," *Nature* 608, 122.

16. If the towns within the metropolitan area are included, the figure is close to ten million in 2020.

17. NUTP, UTTIPEC. (2009). *Street Design Guidelines: For Equitable Distribution of Road Space*. Delhi Development Authority, New Delhi Guidelines, adopted November 2009, rev. 1, November 2010.

18. Jacobs, J. (2011). *Muerte y vida de las grandes ciudades Americanas*. Madrid, Capitán Swing S.L., 213.

19. City of Melbourne. (2017, January). "Open space: From grey to green." *Your City of Melbourne Magazine*.

20. Avenida El Dorado, NQS, Carrera 68, and Avenida Boyacá were all built with no sidewalks. Only the extension of Carrera 10 to the south had them (and they were well-built).

21. Stendahl. (1995). *Rome, Naples, Florence: Complete Works, Vol. 1*. Mexico, Aguilar, 474.

22. Calculation of population and households in Bogotá, 1998. Number of households in Bogotá: Datos Abiertos Colombia GOV.CO-. Households by year (1998) No. of cars in Bogotá. (1997, February 22). *El Tiempo*. Some 700,000 cars are in use in Bogotá.

23. "A dodgy promenade." (1998, December 2). *El Tiempo*.

24. Mauricio Gómez, an important journalist now dead, sent me the copies of what his father had written three decades earlier, when I was being intensely attacked for getting cars off sidewalks or where there should be sidewalks. Unfortunately I lost the copies he sent me and I do not have the exact source of the quote.

25. In 1939 there were some 6,034 cars in use. Anuario Municipal de Estadística de Bogotá 1940–1953. Prieto, L. (2005). "La aventura de una vida sin control." Bogotá Movilidad y Vida Urbana 1939–1853, Universidad Nacional de Colombia.

26. Arciniegas, G. (1936). *Diario de un Peatón*. Bogotá, Imprenta Nacional Bogotá, Colombia.

27. But, happily, I ended my brief three-year period with a positive image of 70 percent, one of the highest for any mayor of Bogotá and a negative image of 22 percent. Gallup.

28. Decree 2000/2019.

Chapter 10

1. Kunstler, J. H. (1994). *The Geography of Nowhere: The Rise and Decline of America's Man-Made Landscape*. New York, Simon & Schuster, 119.

2. Sagalyn, L. B., Frieden, B. J. (1991). *Downtown Inc*. Cambridge, MA, MIT Press, 230 (251).

3. Some shopping centers in the Philippines, built mainly for high-income sectors, such as the Greenbelt in Manila and the Terraces in Cebu, built by the Ayala conglomerate, have interesting architecture and extensive tropical gardens inside. But most of them are no more than graceless boxes that do nothing to improve the city.

4. Sagalyn and Frieden (1991), 69.

5. Sagalyn and Frieden (1991), 69.

6. Adiga, A. (2009). *The White Tiger*. New York, Random House Mondadori, 142.

7. Adiga, A. (2009), 145.

8. Furthermore, when street parking is free or too cheap, many of the people using those spaces are not the customers but the shop assistants or local residents.

9. Duany, A., Plater-Zyberk, E., Speck, J. (2000). *Suburban Nation: The Rise of Sprawl and the Decline of the American Dream*. New York, North Point Press, 63.

10. BBC. (2014, November 26). "Can a city survive with no advertising on its streets?" BBC World, Latin America.

11. US Federal Reserve chair Alan Greenspan coined the expression "exuberant irrationality" in reference to the market speculation with technology firms in the 1990s.

12. Zoning Resolution. (2011). The City of New York, Article VIII Special Purpose Districts. Chapter 1: "Special Midtown District 81–372. Special Times Square signage requirements," 223–234.

13. They include the Zona Rosa, the center of Usaquén, the furniture center of 12 de Octubre, Carrera 112 in Engativá, Acacias San Francisco in Ciudad Bolívar, and Brasil in Bosa.

14. The Éxito supermarket chain, part of the French Casino group, has implemented this program in Bogotá.

15. Putnam, R. (2000). *Bowling Alone: The Collapse and Revival of American Community*. New York, Simon & Schuster, 308–309.

16. De Leon, I., Salcedo, E. (2003). "El crimen como oficio: Una interpretación del aprendizaje del delito en Colombia."

17. Serje, M. (2011). "El revés de la nación: Territorios salvajes, fronteras y tierras de nadie." Bogotá, Universidad de los Andes, Faculty of Social Sciences, Department of Anthropology, CESO, Ediciones Uniandes, 272.

18. Serje, M. (2011), 269.

19. Escobar, G. (2012). *Social Disorganization and the Public Level of Crime Control: A Spatial Analysis of Ecological Predictors of Homicide Rates in Bogotá, Colombia*. City University of New York, CUNY Academic Works.

20. James Q. Wilson and George L. Kelling first presented the broken windows theory in the article titled "Broken Windows," in the March 1982 issue of *Atlantic Monthly*.

21. Fundación Ideas para la Paz. (2017). DATAFIP, Beta Violencia Homicida en Colombia. Homicidios por años, Fundación Ideas para la Paz, Bogotá.

22. National Police Crime Observatory. (2020). DIJIN Crime Observatory.

23. My own calculations from population figures and the number of murders in 2019 reported by the mayor of Washington and the Metropolitan Police Department (official figures have not yet been published). The final figure may be the subject of an adjustment to update information. DC.gov, Mayor's Office of Community Relations and Services. (2020, January 6). "New population, new year, new housing: Recently released census data highlights urgency to build new housing in DC and across the region." https://mocrs .dc.gov/release/new-population-new-year-new-housing; DC.gov, Metropolitan Police Department. (2020, July 2). "District crime data at a glance: 2020 year-to-date crime comparison."

24. Kaldor, M., Sassen, S., eds. (2020). *Cities at War: Global Insecurity and Urban Resistance*. New York, Columbia University Press, 184, 188.

25. Jacobs, J. (1992). *The Life and Death of Great American Cities*. New York, Random House, Vintage Books ed., 35.

26. Juste Lores, R. (2011). "The Mirage and Its Limits." In Burdett, R., Sudjic, D. (2011). *Living in the Endless City: The Urban Age Project by the London School of Economics and Deutsche Bank's Alfred Herrhausen Society.* New York, Phaidon Press, 179.

Chapter 11

1. "'Kettuvallam Palam' on the Marine Drive walkway." (2012, April 27). *New Indian Express.*

2. GCDA. (2020). "Cochin Marine Drive development scheme." Kochi, India, Greater Cochin Development Authority.

3. Quoted in Wilson, B. (2020). *Metropolis.* New York, Doubleday, 218.

4. Wilson, B. (2020), 221.

5. Jordan, D. (1995). *Transforming Paris: The Life and Labours of Baron Haussmann.* New York, Free Press, 96.

6. Jordan, D. (1995), 274.

7. Caro, R. (1975). *The Power Broker: Robert Moses and the Fall of New York.* Vintage, 503.

8. Caro, R. (1975), 506.

9. A judge did the opposite of what the judge in the Columbia Yacht Club case did in a San Rafael reservoir park case: stopped the project on the flimsy argument of the "precaution principle," which only dissimulated political criteria. In the case of the park, which is around the Tominé Reservoir, an environmental agency, influenced by high-income owners of country homes around the reservoir, procrastinated in order to sabotage the construction of the park that the wealthy homeowners did not want. For both parks we had final designs and the necessary funds. I hope they are built in the future.

10. Caro, R. (1975), ebook, 2560–2561.

11. Martinko, K. (2009, July 20). "People are flocking to British rivers and lakes to swim." *Treehugger.*

12. *Glass v. Goeckel.* (2005). 473 Mich. 667, 703 N.W.2d 58.

13. Amanda Burden and Janette Sadik-Khan, New York City transport commissioner while Michael Bloomberg was mayor, visited Bogotá at the beginning of Bloomberg's term of office to find out about TransMilenio and the network of bikeways as ideas for projects that they might implement. During my second term as mayor, they both formed part of the Bloomberg Associates team that advised our administration.

14. Gehl, J. (2010). *Cities for People.* Washington, DC, Island Press, 16–17.

15. The park was built over fifteen hectares in 1978.

16. A group of citizens from Colsubsidio wanted to prevent a connection being built from Lisboa, Santa Cecilia, and other informal-origin neighborhoods into their neighborhood. It became a political argument in which they also opposed the construction of a children's playground and sporting facilities in the park we built. Oddly, they had never mobilized to oppose the construction of the huge parking lot that had been illegally built on public land corresponding to the park that we recovered and turned into a park again. The illegal occupant who owned the parking business and made money from it was naturally one of the leading opponents of the park.

17. Superior Court of Cundinamarca magistrate Nelly Villamizar, well known for her rulings in favor of environmental causes, especially in relation to the cleaning of the Bogotá River, carefully studied the case and ruled in favor of constructing the elevated path-bikeway, as well as other paths peripherical to the Juan Amarillo and Jaboque wetlands.

18. Parque del Virrey, at Carrera 15 with Calle 87.

19. Bloch, H. (2020). "Origins and birth of the age of cathedrals." In *The Age of Cathedrals*. New Haven, CT, Yale University Press, 52.

20. Braudel, F. (1995). *The Mediterranean and the Mediterranean World in the Reign of Philip II*. Berkeley, University of California Press, 52.

21. Braudel, F. (1995), 52.

22. Braudel, F. (1995), 53.

23. Braudel, F. (1995), 47, 53.

24. Braudel, F. (1995), 63.

25. Braudel, F. (1995), 66.

26. Braudel, F. (1995), 72.

27. Braudel, F. (1995), 67.

28. "Such quantities of sand." (2015, February 26). *Economist*.

29. Angel, S. (2012). *Planet of Cities*. Cambridge, MA, Lincoln Institute of Land Policy, 269.

Chapter 12

1. Taken from a four-page letter addressed to me by the deputy attorney for environmental affairs. Official Letter 081. (2019, January 2019). Bogotá.

2. "Park history: 170 years of history." (2016). Friends of Birkenhead Park.

3. Garvin, A. (2011). *Public Parks: The Key to Livable Communities*. New York, W. W. Norton, 29.

4. In 1855, New York City had a population of 629,904, according to the census: *Preliminary Report on the Census of the State of New York, for the Year 1855*. Albany, NY.

5. One example is Birkenhead; another described here is Lagos de Torca in Bogotá.

6. ITDP. (2017). *DOT Estándar*. New York, ITDP, 70.

7. Bertram, C., Rehdanz, K. (2015). "The role of urban green space for human well-being: Citing studies of Bowler et al. (2010) and Coon et al. (2011)." *Ecological Economics* 120: 139–140.

8. John Roman, criminologist at NORC, University of Chicago, cited in "In 2020 America experienced a terrible surge in murder. Why?" (2021, March 27). *Economist*.

9. A study in 2015 that parks and public spaces near their home were unsafe (Encuesta Bienal de Culturas). Referred to in Ramirez Castillo, E., Weintraub, M., Norza, E. (2021). "Does improving parks reduce crime? Evidence from Bogotá." Universidad de los Andes, Facultad de Economía, Centro de Estudios sobre Seguridad y Drogas, Documento Temático # 13.

10. We invested nearly US $600 million in parks and recreation, mostly in infrastructure. In purchasing power parity, it amounts to twice as much.

11. Ramirez Castillo, E., Weintraub, M., Norza, E. (2021).

12. The results of the "¿Bogotá Cómo Vamos?" Survey in 2015 showed that only 36 percent of citizens felt secure in their own districts. The figure rose to 50 percent in 2019. A study by Universidad de los Andes, Bogotá, at the end of my period of office found that murder significantly decreased in neighborhoods where parks were opened and that the greater use of parks brought about by the interventions led to a reduction of theft. Office of the Mayor. (2020, January 7). "Parques y crimen, un análisis de información y estudios." Bogotá.

13. Bertram, C., Rehdanz, K. (2015), 139–140.

14. We purchased a property from broadcaster Radionet, part of the Caracol Radio group to the north of the Bellavista community center, that we had built on the western side of the Kennedy complex. Mayor Luis Eduardo Garzón used it to build housing units.

15. Mayor Samuel Moreno handed part of the Simón Bolívar Park back to the Football Federation at some point in the two years he was in office, before being jailed for a large number of acts of corruption.

16. Botero, A. (2010, August 20). "Agassi: La apuesta con Pete es el orgullo." *El Tiempo.*

17. Quite a number of members accepted the idea democratically and with respect, however. They included some who had contributed to my campaigns: they never complained and always continued to support me.

18. Wilson, B. (2020). *Metropolis.* New York, Doubleday, 248.

19. Email from Jaime Alemán. (2010, August).

20. *Rot fai* is Thai for "railway."

21. Gladwell, M. (2017, June 14). *A Good Walk Spoiled.* Revisionist History podcast, season 2, episode 1. Pushkin. https://www.pushkin.fm/podcasts/revisionist-history/a-good-walk-spoiled.

22. When, as mayor, I proposed to my education secretary that we should issue a regulation to standardize school uniforms in all Bogotá's schools, she said that would create something like a nuclear war. She also said that many public-sector schools would be among those who would protest loudest. We were engaged in many other fights at the time and were not in a position to open up any more fronts. I had to resign myself to doing nothing about the idea.

23. They often enclosed an entire sector of the neighborhood, including its streets. Obviously, too, they continued to expect the city to maintain the streets, the lighting, and so on.

24. United Nations. (1948, December 10). Universal Declaration of Human Rights, Adopted and Proclaimed by the General Assembly in Resolution 217A (III), Article 1.

25. Bertram, C., Rehdanz, K. (2015), 139–140. Other studies include City Parks Alliance. (2020). "Why city parks matter." Washington, DC, City Parks Alliance; Reuben, A. (2019, May 1). "Science's newest miracle drug is free." *Outside*; Townsend, M., Henderson-Wilson, C., Warner, E., Weiss, L. (2015). "Healthy parks healthy people: The state of the evidence 2015." Prepared for Parks Victoria, School of Health and Social Development, Deakin University, Melbourne.

26. Hall, P. (1998). *Cities in Civilization.* New York, Pantheon Books, 38.

27. Centre de Cultura Contemporània de Barcelona. (1999). "La reconquista de Europa: Espacio público urbano 1980–1999." CCCB, Institut d'Edicions de la Diputació de Barcelona.

28. Scenic America. (2020). "Billboard control is good for business: The truth about billboards." Washington, DC, Scenic America.

29. In the United States, Rails to Trails; in Spain, Vias Verdes; and in the United Kingdom, Sustrans and Railway Paths Ltd. The German government is building RS1—Radschnellweg Ruhr 1—a hundred-kilometer highway for bicycles connecting ten cities from Duisburg to Hamm, along former railway lines.

30. During my first period in office, we built community centers in the Bellavista neighborhood of Ciudad Kennedy and in the Julio César Sánchez neighborhood of Usme, but on a smaller scale.

INDEX

Milton Keynes UK
Ingram Content Group UK Ltd.
UKHW010633100524
442427UK00004B/50/J